*Certainly Allah's Deen is Isl*

# *What is Islam?*

## *(Translation of Islam Kiya Hai?)*

## *What did Allah say?*
## *The Quranic Perspective*

### Ghulam Ahmed Parwez
### 1964

> *Which was bestowed by Allah on mankind as a system of life and through which the caravan of humanity was to reach its intended destination.*

**Tolu-e-Islam Trust (Regd.)**
**25 B, Gulberg-II, LAHORE**
*Islamicdawn.com*

# ALL RIGHTS RESERVED

**Title of the book:**     What is Islam?

**Author:**     Ghulam Ahmad Parwez

**Translated and Edited:**     Ejaz Rasool (Glasgow, UK)

**Technical Assistance:**     Sheraz Akhter (Norway)

**Published By:**     Tolu-e-Islam Trust

**ISBN:**     978-1974206940

**Contact:**     Tolu-e-Islam Trust
25 B Gulberg-II
Lahore-54660 Pakistan
*www.islamicdawn.com*

Tolu-e-Islam Trust®

Copyright © 2017

# List of Other Works by the Author

1. Exposition of the Quran
2. Islam: A Challenge to Religion
3. The Book of Destiny
4. The Quranic Laws
5. Reasons for the Decline of Muslims
6. Letters to Tahira
7. *Iblees* and Adam (Devil and Man)
8. *Lughat ul Quran* (Dictionary of the Quranic Words) – Volume I and II (Available from Amazon)
9. The Quranic System of Sustenance (Available from Amazon)
10. The Life in the Hereafter: What Does the Quran Say (Available from Amazon)
11. The Status of Hadeeth in Islam (Available from Amazon)

These books are available free for download at:
http://www.islamicdawn.com/

These books are also available from:

Tolu-e-Islam Trust
25 – B Gulberg 2
Lahore – 54660, Pakistan
Email: tolueislam@gmail.com
Phone: 00 92 42 35753666

# ABOUT THE AUTHOR

## Ghulam Ahmed Parwez

Ghulam Ahmad Parwez was born in Batala, Punjab, in British India on 9th July 1903 into a profoundly religious family. His grandfather, who was deeply religious and belonged to the Hanafi school of thought, was a renowned religious scholar who intended to make the author inherit his knowledge and religious understanding. As a consequence, his education and training was carried out under the direction of his grandfather. While he studied the traditional religious teachings, he also had the desire and inkling to question its content using his intellect and reasoning. This led to his inner conflict with the external religious environment and he continued to question the prevalent religious concepts and practices. He noticed that whatever was being taught as part of the religion was being referred to some Imam or religious scholar for authority. It was also noted in the religious literature that whatever the forefathers had followed should be obeyed without any question, and this was considered to be a requirement of Islam.

For Parwez this did not satisfy his desire to seek reason and logic in every claim and statement made within the religious literature. However, he could not express these doubts and reservations initially due to his respect for his grandfather, and the constraints of the religious environment which prevailed at the time in his town. Later, due to his employment, he moved to Lahore (now part of Pakistan), and found a degree of freedom to question some of these religious concepts and beliefs. After the death of his grandfather, he found complete freedom to pursue his line of enquiry and research into the prevalent Islamic beliefs, doctrines, ideologies and religious practices.

This led to his discovering that most of these have been acquired from others. He tried to study the Quran using the traditional religious approach but was unable to find the answers to all his doubts, which required satisfaction from a logical point of view. He also studied the life of the last messenger and the establishment of the Islamic State in the seventh century in his quest to determine the cause which contributed to this greatest revolution based on the Quran. He especially paid attention to the statement from the last messenger, 'The Quran is not a product of my thinking or that of any other human being' and that this is the message from Allah. He soon learnt the procedure to understand the Quran.

Through his contact with the famous philosopher and poet, Allama Iqbal, who had a deep interest in the Quran, Parwez concluded that to understand the Quran one has to understand three fundamentally important points:

(1) The Quran calls itself Light (*Nur*) and a light does not need any external source or aid to make itself visible. It makes itself evident and also exposes the reality of those things which are within its domain.

(2) The Quran is revealed in the Arabic language and, to understand it correctly, one needs to understand the Arabic context which was prevalent at the time of its revelation.

(3) The Quran has guided us by saying that through *Tasreef-ul-Ayat* (through cross reference within the verses of the Quran) it makes its guidance clear e.g. see (6:106).

In order to meet the second requirement regarding the precise meaning of the Arabic words in the Quran, he researched and compiled a *Lughat-ul-Quran* (now translated into English), which is a dictionary of all the words and terms used in the Quran and which includes the meanings which were prevalent among the Arabs at the time of the Quranic Revelation. For the third requirement of *Tasreef-ul-Ayat*, the Quran is different from books written by human beings, where the latter are usually divided based on various subjects - the Quran is based on mentioning a reality in one verse or verses and then its further explanation is noted in another place or places. For example in Surah *Al An'am* the Quran states:

*And thus do We explain the signs by various verses, so that they acknowledge 'You have explained them', and We make the Quran clear for a people who know. (6:106)*

In order to meet this requirement, Parwez felt the need to compile all the verses under one subject as referred in various verses of the Quran and he compiled a book in Urdu titled *Tabweeb-ul-Quran* i.e. Classification of the Quran. This made it easy to refer to various subjects and look at all the verses mentioned in the Quran relating to a subject.

Along with writing and producing literature on the Quran, Parwez also held a regular weekly meeting in Lahore to deliver a *Dars* (lecture explaining the Quran) in Urdu, and these are also available as audio and video recordings. He dedicated most of his life to researching the Quran and its significance in relation to presenting an alternative solution to human problems, and answering questions relating to human creation, its purpose and the question of death and the next life.

He also participated in the struggle for Independence during the period 1938-1947 and the creation of Pakistan, which was based on the ideology of the Quran, with a view to establishing an Islamic State for the Muslims of the sub-continent. He worked very closely with the founder of Pakistan, Muhammad Ali Jinnah (*Quaid-e-Azam* or Great Leader) and had regular discussions with him on various aspects of the message of the Quran. In order to support the movement for a separate State for the Muslims of India and to counter the arguments put forward by some of the religious lobby who opposed the creation of Pakistan, he published a monthly journal called *Tolu-e-Islam* (Dawn of Islam), commencing in 1938.

Parwez joined the Indian Civil Service in the Home Department in 1927, and after the creation of Pakistan he migrated to Karachi, and continued to serve in the same department till 1955, when he took early retirement and devoted the rest of his life fully to his work on the Quran. He moved to Lahore from Karachi and settled there.

He left this life on 24th February 1985 in Lahore and his body was laid to rest in Lahore.

# FOREWORD

It was a while ago that I considered a written structure in order to present Islam in its true colours. And it was this - to first of all explain in a completely unbiased way what human intellect alone has achieved to date in finding solutions for the important problems of life (without the help of Divine Revelation), and whether it has been successful in its aim? If it has found satisfactory solutions to these problems of life then the need for another source of knowledge does not even arise (beyond human intellect). But if it has not been successful in its aim then we need to look at the source of knowledge which is beyond the reach of human intellect, (i.e. Divine Revelation) and which is now preserved in its true form within the Quran, and what solutions it presents to these problems. Accordingly, under this scheme, the first book in this connection titled 'What Did Man Think'[1] was published in 1955, in which, starting from the time of the Greek philosophers to the modern times, research was presented from philosophers, historians and scientists and it was shown, how despite all this exertion and struggle they accept the fact that it is not possible for the human intellect alone to find the solutions to the important problems of life.

After this, in this connection, there was to be another book, the title of which was proposed as 'What Did Allah Say'. During this period, many colleagues suggested that there was a requirement for a self-sufficient book in which it was detailed what Islam is, because nothing is available in this exact form. And (leaving aside non-Muslims) even Muslims themselves do not have a clear concept of Deen[2] in front of them. I too was strongly aware of the need for this kind of a book and I thought that once I am free from the writing of the book 'What Did Allah Say', then I will turn my attention to this issue. But when I started drafting the book 'What Did Allah Say', I felt that if a small change was made to it, then it can become that very same book which has been referred to earlier. Hence, I started to re-examine the arrangement of this book and started to write it in such a way that on the one hand it becomes the second part of 'What Did Man Think', and on the other hand it becomes a self-contained book which can be presented so that it will be known as 'What is Islam'[3]. Therefore, this book is now presented to you. In this book at some places it was felt necessary to quote Western thinkers who are referred to in the book 'What Did Man Think'. At these places, rather than being directed to refer to those parts of the book, these have been fully quoted so that the subject under discussion is complete.

---

[1] *Insaan Nein Kiya Socha – What Did Man Think* is a book written in Urdu by the author.
[2] Deen – this is Islam as a system which is presented in the Quran. (Ed)
[3] *Islam: A Challenge to Religion* by the author contains details of references from the book titled, *What Did Man Think*. (Ed)

It is our claim (and this claim is based on our Eimaan[4]) that Islam is bestowed from Allah as the final and complete Deen which deals with all the difficulties of mankind i.e. it holds within it the solution to all the fundamental problems of life. But when we wish to determine what Islam is, then in response, different voices emerge from different quarters. And when these voices are combined, their outcome is nothing more than the issues related to Namaz (prayers), Roza (fasting), Hajj (pilgrimage), Zakat, etc. Now it is obvious that the Islam whose concept relates only to this cannot present solutions to the problems of even Muslims themselves (never mind the problems of the whole of mankind).

Islam is a system of life whose foundations are based on a few solid and immutable concepts. As long as these fundamental concepts do not appear in clear, unambiguous and precisely defined forms, it cannot be understood what that system of life is which is proclaimed as Islam, and which contains the solution for the important problems of life. In this book, I have presented these concepts.

Here this question may arise, as to what is the authority for these concepts which are presented as the foundation of Islam? The answer to this question is easy. The Quran is the code of the Laws of Islam. Deen has been completed and secured within it. Therefore, Islamic concepts are those whose authentic validity is available from the Quran. I have drawn these concepts from the Quran according to my own vision and understanding, and presented these with the Quranic authority. It is possible that my interpretation may have erred in understanding some meaning of the Quran (because in any case this is a human effort in which there is a possibility of error and mistake) but it can never happen that I would deliberately present a non-Quranic concept as Quranic. In my opinion doing this is *Shirk*[5] and there is no greater crime in the court of Allah than this.

As I have been continuously saying for a while, Islam is Deen and not *Madhab* (religion) and I have explained the fundamental difference between Deen and religion in detail on various occasions.[6] At this juncture it will be sufficient to understand this much that the messengers of Allah used to present Deen in its original form through *Wahi* (revelation). Afterwards, their followers used to alter this Deen – usually deliberately, in order to serve their vested interests, but sometimes unwittingly as well – this altered form of Deen is called religion (*Madhab*). Like the Deen presented by the previous messengers of Allah, the same thing also happened to Islam, and its followers too gradually brought it down from the higher status of Deen to the level of religion. After becoming a religion, Islam,

---

[4] Eimaan – this is conviction in the Quran by accepting the concept of Allah, His messengers, His revelation, His angels (forces) and conviction in the Hereafter. See verse (2:177). (Ed)
[5] *Shirk* – this term is used in the Quran when the Divine Laws are mixed with man-made laws and consequently Deen cannot be established. (Ed)
[6] This is covered in the book titled, *Islam: A Challenge to Religion* by the author. (Ed)

a lively, fully awake and dynamic system of life, instead of leading the caravan of mankind to its intended destination, was reduced only to a collection of some lifeless beliefs and soul-less rituals. The consequence of this was not just that the worshipping nation of this religion became deprived of all the prosperities of life, but that the caravan of humanity was not itself able to tread on the right path (when the beacon of Deen was not even in front of it, how could it tread on the right path!). This is the reason that today all nations of the world are caught in the hell of fear and discord from which they do not see any way out.

Although the followers of Islam have (deliberately or unwittingly) turned it into a religion, there is a fundamental difference between it and other worldly religions – and this is that difference which can serve as a hope for the caravan of mankind to find the right path, indeed it is a surety – and that is that the code of Laws of the Deen of Islam i.e. the Quran, is available to man in its original and unaltered form. Therefore, whenever they wish, they can turn this religion back into Deen.

My humble effort has always been this (in which I have been continuously immersed for the last 25 to 30 years), and that is to distil non-Quranic elements from Divine Deen in order that I can present it again in its true and pristine form to the world, so that the Muslim Ummah can itself find its lost status once again and the caravan of mankind can march on the right path of life. This book is part of my ongoing effort in this connection. I understand that if this book is given in the hands of our young educated class (religion-influenced), then they can be attracted to Islam with the full satisfaction of their hearts and minds based on their own observed and acquired evidence. Similarly, if this is passed on to non-Muslims then their misconceptions about Islam can be removed. As far as our educated youth are concerned, on the one hand we teach them the Theory of Relativity by Einstein, the philosophy of history by Hegel, the knowledge of the self by Freud, and the philosophy by Whitehead, while on the other hand in *Islamia'at* we provide education in the same tales of the past based on superstitions, aimless rituals and soulless beliefs, and assume that we have convinced them about the truth of 'Deen' and that they will become true Muslims. As a consequence of this, far from becoming 'true Muslims', instead their doubts and scepticism about Islam are definitely reinforced. The need is for Islam to be presented in the light of the latest modern knowledge and to inform them that having reached that place at which human intellect comes to a dead-end, how Deen takes them forward from this point onwards.

As far as non-Muslims are concerned, their knowledge about Islam is taken from those ancient books of ours in which are found all types of invented narrations and tales, and nonsensical accounts far removed from knowledge and intellect. Since we have given these books the status of piety and sanctification, they have therefore become an authority on Islam[7]. The Islam gleaned from these books will be such from which every truth seeker will run afar. Present Islam as revealed through the Quran to these people, and then see how they become convinced to bow their heads before this. I have experienced this myself.

I am hopeful that this effort of mine will be successful in fulfilling this purpose. Finally, I would like to reiterate these words which I have written at the end of 'What did man think' – *'if through these efforts of mine even a few such individuals are born in whose hearts the conviction of the guidance of the Quran emerges based on their own perceptive evidence, I will then acknowledge that I have received the reward of my unremitting visionary exertions and my heartfelt endeavours'.*

G. A. Parwez
25 B
Gulberg 2, Lahore
Pakistan
September 1964

---

[7] This is further explored in the book written by the author titled, *The Status of Hadeeth in Islam*, available free at Islamicdawn.com. (Ed)

# EDITOR'S NOTE

This book is an English translation of the Urdu book titled '*Islam Kya Hai*' (What is Islam?) written by G. A. Parwez in 1964. This book covers the salient aspects of Islam as revealed in the Quran. Parvez later wrote a book in English titled 'Islam: A challenge to Religion' which is a more detailed version published in 1969 and which is available free at Islamicdawn.com.

This translation covers all of the aspects which are discussed in the original Urdu version, however the Arabic text of the verses from the Quran has not been included and readers are directed to the Quran for these details. The English translations used for the Arabic verses of the Quran are mainly taken from the translation of the Quran by Abdullah Yusuf Ali, with some amendments made using the 'Exposition of the Quran' (published by Tolu-e-Islam) to elaborate meanings where required. The verses of the Quran are given in the format (2:177) in which 2 refers to the chapter (Surah) of the Quran and 177 is the number of the verse itself.

As is the case with all translations, it is difficult to translate everything literally, as this can affect the flow and meaning of the original text. In order to clarify some of the words and terms, additional explanations have been provided as footnotes at the bottom of the page and (Ed) is written against these additions indicating this as being from the editor. Footnotes without (Ed) written against them are to be considered as being from the author himself.

This book is divided into 17 chapters which cover various topics including: Deen as a System, the Human Self, Intellect and Deen, the Law of Requital, The Life in the Hereafter, The Islamic System of Sustenance, Deen as a Political System, The Rise and Fall of Nations, The Permanent Values and Woman.

The term 'Allah' has been used throughout the book when referring to the Quran and the term 'God' is only used when the text does not refer to any specific parts of the Quran. 'Allah' as used in the Quran is a very comprehensive designation which encompasses all of His Divine attributes and refers to His complete sovereignty in the universe.

As noted by the author, the Quran is not a book of 'religion' (*Madhab*)- it is a revelation from Allah for mankind for all times and provides details of a system called Deen. Deen is not a religion but a system just like capitalism or communism and covers all aspects of human life. The following points about the Quran should be noted:

- Historically, the Quran was revealed over a period of twenty three years as a guidance to all of mankind. The last messenger of Allah, Muhammad (PBUH[8]), disseminated this message among the people which resulted in the establishment of an Islamic State based on Quranic Values in the Arabian Peninsula in the 7th century AD.

- The Quran states that the purpose of the creation of the universe and the earth is to hold every individual accountable for his or her deeds so that no-one is dealt with unjustly, and it explains how this process of accountability functions and its impact on our life which includes the life of the hereafter.[9] It declares:

> 'Allah created the heavens and the earth as Truth; so that every self finds the recompense of what it has earned and none is dealt with unjustly' (45:22).

- Everything in the universe is provided with inbuilt guidance from Allah except man, who by virtue of possessing free will, has no inner guidance. However, man is given guidance as an external criterion in the light of which he can choose to exercise this free will. This guidance is provided in the form of revelation from Allah through His messengers who were chosen by Him from among men. These messengers were the recipients of the revelation which they then passed on to their fellow human beings. The Quran is the complete and final revelation from Allah which was revealed through the last messenger Muhammad and has been preserved and protected since then in its original form. Since then this process of revelation has stopped for ever as far as this world is concerned.

- The Quran describes the state of the world or of a society when the guidance given in the Quran is not followed and also the result when it does follow this. It addresses itself to an individual first, and by appealing to the intellect and reasoning, invites the individual to consider the guidance given within it. It then addresses those who accept its guidance (the Momineen[10]) and directs them to establish a collective system for the good of the whole of mankind. The Quran calls this system Deen.

---

[8] PBUH – peace be upon him.
[9] The life in the hereafter is discussed in detail in the book by the author titled, *The Life in the Hereafter; What Does the Quran Say*. (Ed)
[10] Momineen is the plural of Momin – the term is used for those who, through their own volition, accept Eimaan and then live their life within the confines of the Permanent Values of the Quran. (Ed)

- The Quran contains non-human thinking and this is the reason no human being can produce anything like it. However, the values given and illustrated in the Quran can be understood through the use of human intellect and reasoning and Deen as a system can be established in the light of these values.

- The concept of Allah given in the Quran is unique and is not available anywhere else. Human beings possess a self which needs a model for its development and the concept of Allah based on the Divine attributes serves as a model for the human self to acquire these attributes within the constraints of being human.

- The Quran is a complete book and does not require any other source for its interpretation and explanation. It is non-emotive and provides reality as it is, then it leaves it to us to understand it in the light of the developments and circumstances of the time in which we live.

I wish to give thanks to and acknowledge the support provided by Hussain Kaisrani of Tolu-e-Islam Trust, Lahore, Asif Jalil, Karachi, and Sheraz Akhter, Norway. I am profoundly grateful to my wife for her help and encouragement in the translation work and revision.

Finally, this work is a translation and as such any ambiguity in the text in the English version which is not present in the Urdu version is my responsibility as a translator and editor and not of the original author. If readers have any questions or comments after reading this book, they are welcome to contact the Tolu-e-Islam Trust.

Ejaz Rasool
Glasgow, UK
August 2017

# TABLE OF CONTENTS

# 1 THE BASIS OF DEEN

If you traverse any period of human history, and cast an eye on any part of the world, you will find that there is one thing every place, every nation and every era has in common, and that is that people will have devised some sort of being (either a tangible or abstract thing or an intangible perceptive power) in front of which they bow down, which they worship and of whose anger or displeasure they are fearful and whose pleasure they consider to be a reason for blessings and approval for themselves. Leaving aside the civilized and developed nations, if you go to such an island where no outsider has previously stepped (according to history), then no matter how different the population residing there may be in other matters, in this common issue their practice too will be equivalent.

## 1.1 Universality of Religion (*Madhab*[11])

Plutarch, who flourished in the first century of the Christian era, with extensive knowledge of the world of his time affirms:

*'In wandering over the earth, you can find cities without walls, without science, without rulers, without palaces, without treasures, without money, without gymnasium or theatre, but a city without temples to gods, without prayer, oaths and prophecy - such a city no mortal has yet seen and will never see'.*[12]

This mentality or way of man in which he has given a certain thing (or power) the status of an object of worship, is commonly known as religion. But despite the universality of this religious fervour or belief, the reality that it has not been possible up until even the present time for it to be established as to what it is that is known as religion, is not in the least surprising. Common people aside, the world's greatest thinkers, historians and writers have expended great efforts to try and fix a definition for religion, but none among their definitions either matched with another's, nor could any such comprehensive definition be devised which could fully cover all the different concepts of religion.

## 1.2 The Definition of Religion

According to Kant, for example, 'religion is (subjectively regarded) the recognition of all duties as Divine command'. According to Friedrich Schleiermacher, 'religion

---

[11] *Madhab* – literally means way or course. This word does not occur in the Quran. The English word religion is usually translated as *Madhab*. (Ed)

[12] W. M. Urban, *Humanity and Deity*, p. 15

is to take everything individual as a part of the whole, everything limited as a representation of the infinite'. According to Hoffding, 'that which expresses the innermost tendency of all religions is the axiom of the conservation of values.' William James holds religion to be 'the feelings, acts and experiences of individual men in their solitude, so far as they apprehend themselves to stand in relation to whatever they may consider the divine'. Calverton takes a different view of religion. 'Magic and religion,' he affirms, 'evolved as (a) means whereby (man) believed he was able to acquire power (over his environment) and make the universe bend to his wishes.' Professor Whitehead speaks of religion as 'what the individual does with his own solitariness', and in another place, defines it as a 'force of belief cleansing the inward parts'. Whitehead's considered opinion on the nature of religion is stated more fully and clearly in the following passage which occurs in his book, 'Science and the Modern World':

*'Religion is the vision of something which stands beyond, behind, and within, the passing influx of immediate things; something which is real, and yet waiting to be realised; something which is a remote possibility, and yet the greatest of present facts; something that gives meaning to all that passes, and yet eludes apprehension; something whose possession is the final good, and yet is beyond all reach; something which is the ultimate ideal and the hopeless quest'.[13]*

Commenting on various definitions of religion, in his book, 'The Philosophy of Religion', Professor G. Galloway says, 'When we keep in mind the psychological factors of the religious consciousness and the way in which they work, some definitions of religion strike us by their inadequacy and one-sidedness. We find, perhaps, that they are applicable to certain stages of religion but not to others, or that they leave out what is important'. However, undeterred by the lack of success which had attended the efforts of so many great scholars, Galloway has advanced his own definition. He defines religion as, 'Man's faith in a power beyond himself whereby he seeks to satisfy emotional needs and gain stability of life, and which he expresses in acts of worship and service'.[14]

From these various examples, you will have seen that not only do the various definitions regarding religion differ from each other, but not even one of these definitions is comprehensive enough in this regard to encompass all these concepts, nor is it so clear that it makes the matter comprehensible. This is the reason that the famous thinker P. D. Ouspensky quotes his mentor, the Russian mystic G. Gurdjiefe, as saying:

---

[13] A. N. Whitehead, *Science and the Modern World*, p. 222
[14] G. Galloway, *The Philosophy of Religion*, pp. 181, 184.

*'Religion is a human concept. Whatever the level of understanding of a man, his religion will be of the same type. Therefore, it can be possible that the religion of one man may not be completely suitable for another man'.*[15]

## 1.3 Common Value

If we combine the various concepts surrounding religion, then such a concept will emerge from its sum total which can be deemed to be a common value, i.e. the concept of a supernatural being or power (which is commonly called 'God'), though there are religions which are not convinced of a god. But a far greater difficulty than that which is encountered in defining religion, is faced in relation to the definition of God. In this regard too, the concept of any one philosopher does not accord with another's. For example, Kant speaks of God as 'the moral law-giver'. William James declares God 'the Higher part of the universe'. Matthew Arnold believes God to be 'the power that makes for righteousness'. For Sir James Jeans, He is 'the greatest of mathematicians'. Bergson, in one of his earlier works, identified Him with creative energy. Later on, when his thought had taken a mystical turn, he spoke of God as 'Love and the Beloved'.[16]

This fact will have become apparent from these few examples, that (like religion) these philosophers have also not arrived at any one conclusion regarding the true concept of 'God'. Each among them has a dissimilar concept, and a differing definition. This is because, when these people talk about God, this discourse is not of God, but is regarding that concept which they hold in their own minds regarding God. And since the invented concept in the mind of every individual is different, this is why the concept of one cannot concur with that of another.

In the words of Sheen, 'the only God attained by a purely affective approach is a subjective God born of one's own feelings'.[17]

## 1.4 Concept of God

As far as this question is concerned, as to what gave rise to the idea of God (i.e. some supernatural being or power) in the mind of man, Western scholars of sociology thought that when early man (while his consciousness was still developing) saw that some events occur, the cause and effect of which he could not determine, (e.g. lightening, thunder, storms, earthquakes, tornados, epidemics etc.), the thought arose in his heart that it is possible that there are great powers operating behind these events which are not visible. From this, the concept of

---

[15] P. D. Ouspensky, *In Search of the Miraculous*, p. 299
[16] Henry Bergson, *The Two Sources of Religion and Morality*, pp. 245-6
[17] Fulton J. Sheen, *Philosophy of Religion*, p. 238

God (goddesses, gods) was born in his mind. This concept was different in different nations depending upon their circumstances, and was different within the environment of different tribes.

## 1.5    Evolving Concept of God

After this, as time passed and progressed and the human mind matured, there was improvement and refinement in this concept also. Gradually, in this way that concept of 'God' came into existence which is presented by the more developed religions of the world. This doctrine is called 'the evolved concept of God'. Details are available (for example) in Grant Allen's book, 'The Evolution of the Idea of God', or Sir James George Frazer's book, 'Golden Bough'.

At this point it will not be inappropriate to make it clear that subsequent researchers have contradicted this doctrine, and said that the concept of God which is found in developed religions has not been reached here by an evolutionary process, it was like this from the beginning.[18] Dr Arnold Toynbee, the famous historian of modern times, therefore writes in this regard:

*'Professor Schmidt's research shows that the concept of the worship of god presented by developed religions is not a new concept which they have invented. The oldest religion of mankind was also this, which has been renewed by developed religions'.[19]*

The book by Professor Schmidt from which the above is quoted by Dr Toynbee, is considered as an authentic discourse on this subject. In it, he has described in clear terms that the concept of a higher deity which existed in earlier human civilizations is the same concept which is presented by those religions that profess the oneness of God. Therefore, it can be stated with authority regarding most of the oldest tribes of mankind, that this was their concept about god. Hence, the concept of evolutionary religion is now liquidated from the field of sociology.

However, this is a digression from the main subject. We were saying that (according to the scholars of sociology) the idea of 'god' was born in the human mind as a result of those events and occurrences whose cause or effect they were unable to comprehend. The man of this era had, more often than not, to face the destruction resulting from these events and occurrences (because he had not yet acquired the knowledge about how to harness natural forces), and therefore he felt weak and helpless in the face of these disasters. In order to save himself from these

---

[18] As we will later explain, the concept of God which was presented by revelation was the same from the beginning to the end. When human ideas became intermixed with the revelation, the concept of God also underwent change. Now the correct concept of God can only be obtained from where there is no contamination of the revelation by human ideas i.e. from the Quran.

[19] Arnold Toynbee, *An Historian's Approach to Religion*.

losses, he could not think of anything other than that he should bow before them, prostrate himself and humbly implore, and in this way, try to alter their annoyance into favour. This is what is called 'worship'.

## 1.6    The Ages of Worship and Magic

Therefore, this first era (according to these scholars) was the Age of Worship. After this, when some 'wiser' individuals were born (from whom the Institution of Priest-craft emerged), they said that the method by which to gain protection from the fury of these wild forces was not to prostrate in front of them, or to implore before them – we will tell you of such a 'procedure' due to which these forces will become subservient, and will start to function according to your desires. Consequently, the counting of beads and the uttering of magical words and chants came into existence, which is known as magic. These scholars call this era the Age of Magic.[20]

## 1.7    The Age of *Malukiyat* (Dictatorship)

Proceeding further, human civilization invented the institution of kingship, through which one man acquired so much power (or was considered to be in control of such forces) that every command of his was considered immutable and every decision absolute. If he became enraged, he would destroy habitation upon habitation. If he was pleased, he would bestow hamlets upon hamlets as a gift. There was neither any law[21] or principle defined for his pleasure, nor was there any reason or cause for his rage. To please him and to keep him contented, praises were sung in his glory, prostrations were performed in his presence and donations were presented. Obviously, every person could not have access to such a powerful and mighty being, so on the path to access him, there were hundreds of courtiers and guards. Therefore, in order to present their requests to him, the public would search for means of access and hunt for intercessors. For this, sometimes they had to beseech the courtiers and sometimes they had to bribe his close connections, so that at some opportune moment, (when his royal highness was in a good mood), their petition could be laid before him. In view of these unlimited powers of a king, some people would of their own accord accept him as their 'god', while others stated that God, with similar qualities and attributes, is sitting up in the heavens and that the king is his shadow on earth. In this way, the concept of God in the human mind was established as a tyrant and dictator (rajah, sultan or emperor).

---

[20] See *Magic and Religion*, which is part of the book, *Golden Bough*, by Frazer.
[21] In this era, man was not yet familiar with the concept of law, nor had he the knowledge of the laws of the universe nor could the concept of law come into his mind.

## 1.8    The Doctrine of Marx[22]

Marx and others consider that this belief in God became established in the minds of the people automatically. In fact, with the help of priesthood, that group which took control of both wealth and the reins of power into their own hands, expressly indoctrinated the minds of the public so that their vested interests could acquire the veneer of Divine Authority. And in this way, the working class was not able to escape from their clutches. In any case, whatever the reality is, it remains a fact that, from that time to the present time, regarding the concept of God, the human mind is lost in such mazes from where he does not see a way out.

Be aware that whatever we have discussed up until now regarding god worship is about that concept which is the product of the human mind. It is possible that it could be stated at this point that even in the great religions of the world, (which claim that their teaching is not the product of the human mind but is based on revelation), we see that a similar concept of God exists. But in different religions of the world human ideas, concepts, doctrines and beliefs have been incorporated into the teaching of revelation to such an extent that no difference remains between the original and the invented. Nor do they have in front of them any such criterion according to which they can separate the pure teaching of revelation from human concepts. This is a truth which the scholars and priests of these religions themselves openly accept. Therefore, none among them claims today (nor can) that the book which they call the Divine Revelation, is word for word the same which the messenger of God had received.[23] This is the reason that whatever concept of God is presented in these books, it is very similar to the concept which the human mind had invented.

## 1.9    The Concept of God (Allah) in Islam

After this introduction, we come to Islam. Be aware that when we discuss Islam, the authority for this will be the Quran. And regarding the Quran, this fact is well known both to Muslims and non-Muslims alike, that it is word for word the same as that which Rasul-ullah[24] (after receiving the revelation from Allah) gave to the Ummah.

Before talking about Allah, the Quran talks about man. It says that there are two concepts of human life. One is that which is called the materialistic concept of life.

---

[22] Karl Marx – the German philosopher in the 19th century. (Ed)

[23] The details of this are available in my book, *The Divine Books of the Religions of the World.*

[24] Rasul-ullah – this term means messenger of Allah and is usually taken to refer to Muhammad, the final messenger of Allah. (Ed)

## 1.9.1 The Materialistic Concept of Life

According to this concept, it is accepted that man is defined by his physical body which comes into existence according to physical laws; it remains functioning according to these laws, and ultimately it comes to an end according to these same laws. In this way, with the disintegration of the human body, human life comes to an end. Obviously, according to this doctrine of life, man has neither the need to believe in God nor the need for any external guidance. At an individual level, growth of the body takes place according to physical laws and whichever person obeys these laws will have his health and vitality remaining good. Whoever goes against these, will become sick and weak. The treatment of these diseases can also be dispensed through physical laws. When his limbs become weak (or some accident befalls him), then death comes to him and the matter is concluded. As far as the collective life is concerned, certain rules and regulations can be formulated in the light of intellect and experience, according to which a nation (comprising of different kinds of people), continues to develop – its interests are preserved, its strengths are not only maintained but continue to increase (so that it can face those causes and events which are out to cause its disintegration). In the formulation and implementation of such laws, there is only one criterion before them, and that is that through these laws their collective strength and balance is maintained, and that there is a continual increase in their domination and supremacy. In the formulation of man-made laws, national interest will be the fundamental motive and any change and modification in these will be implemented according to this aim. For this, there is neither a need for God, nor a requirement for any guidance from Him. The Quran declares this life to be an animal life, and states:

> ...but those who disbelieve[25](Kafir) enjoy themselves and eat as grazing livestock eat...(47:12)

At another place, the Quran states that the outlook and purpose of life of such people is only to follow the emotions of their self-interest. Instead of using their intellect and reasoning in doing right, they are enslaved to their emotions, and these become the instruments for fulfilling their selfish desires. The Quran states:

> Have you seen the one who takes as his god his own desire? Then would you be responsible for him? Or do you think that most of them hear or reason? They are only like cattle; Nay, they are worse astray in path. (25:43-44)

Even if such people recognise this fact that the great creation of the outer universe is functioning according to the Laws of Allah, even then the Quran does not recognise this as Eimaan in Allah. It says about these very same people:

---

[25] The Quran uses the term *Kafir* for unbelievers. The term *Kufr* means to deny the truth, to prevent, to defy the laws of Allah. (Ed)

*If you asked them, 'Who created the heavens and earth and subjected the sun and the moon to laws?' They would surely say, 'Allah'. Then how are they deluded? (29:61)*

These are those people who:

*And they say, 'What is there but our life in this world? We shall die and we live, and nothing but time destroys us'. But of that they have no knowledge: they merely conjecture. (45:24)*

This is one concept of life regarding which the Quran says that it is based only on conjecture and presumption, and not on knowledge and truth.

### 1.9.2 The Quranic Concept of Life

The second concept of life is one according to which man is not only defined by the physical body, but apart from the body there is another thing which is called the human personality, the self or 'I' (in the Quran the term used for this is *Nafs* and it has been termed as Divine Energy). Regarding the creation of man, the Quran has stated:

*He Who has made everything which He has created most good: He began the creation of man with clay. And made his progeny from a quintessence of the nature of a liquid (reproduction process): And He fashioned him in due proportion and breathed into him from His Divine Energy. And He gave you[26] the faculties of hearing and sight and heart (and understanding): Little thanks[27] do you give! (32:7-9)*

Allah began the process of the creation of man from lifeless matter. Then, passing him through various stages of evolution, he brought him to that point beyond which his progeny was to continue through the process of sexual reproduction. Up until this point there was no difference between man and animal. Then, from this He tailored him precisely and created in him special balance and proportion, and put in him a spark of His Divine Energy and (in this way) having endowed you with hearing, seeing and intellect, he brought you to that point of capability where you could gain different types of knowledge. But there are very few among you who make use of these abilities and potentials in a proper way.

---

[26] In this verse the Quran is firstly explaining man's creation in the third person, then after stating, '...breathed into him from His Divine Energy', changes to the first person i.e. 'you', thus making man responsible due to the possession of a self and thereby the freedom to choose. (Ed)

[27] The word used here is *Shukr* which is translated as giving thanks, whereas its deeper meaning is to use these faculties appropriately in order to achieve optimum results as explained in the next paragraph. (Ed)

At this place the Quran has informed us that, in the chain of organic evolution, man was also at the level of other animals. When man progressed forward, a unique attribute emerged in him, as a result of which he became a separate kind of creation. This unique attribute is that which the Quran has declared as Divine Energy.[28]

It should be made clear that the term *Ruh* in the Quran is not included in those meanings which are used as an antonym of matter i.e. it does not mean spirit or soul. This is that Divine Energy which is called the human self (or *Nafs*[29]). The senses (hearing and seeing) and mind are those means which provide information to the human self and help it to differentiate and distinguish. This self, in the light of this knowledge, using its own intentions and freedom to choose, makes decisions about matters of life using its own resources i.e. we can say it uses the body and its powers to bring its decisions to fruition.

### 1.9.3 Divine Energy

It is also important to understand that the verse '...*breathed into him from His energy (Ruh)*...' (32:9) does not mean that Allah gave a part of His Self to man. The self (personality) is an indivisible whole and cannot be divided into parts.[30] Therefore this belief is wrong that the human self is a part of the Self of Allah which, having separated from its origin, is trapped in materialistic comforts, and the aim of its efforts and endeavours is for this part to return and merge with the whole like a drop of water merges with a river. This concept is against the Quran. The Self of Allah is a complete entity in itself, and the human self (even though bestowed by Allah), retains its own permanent status. This concept of human life (that 'man' is not just the name for a physical body but contains something within it apart from the body which is called the self) is that foundation on which the whole edifice of Deen is raised. If this is accepted, then the matter of Deen progresses forward. If this is not accepted, then the question of Deen does not even arise.

### 1.9.4 Allah and the Human Self

Having accepted this premise, some of the important points which then arise are:

---

[28] The Quran uses the term *Ruh* which means energy. This is discussed in more detail in Chapter 2. (Ed)

[29] The term *Nafs* is used in the Quran to denote the self. For further details regarding this term refer to *Lughat ul Quran*, Volume 2, (Islamicdawn.com), p 615. (Ed)

[30] Allah has an infinitely developed Self and man cannot have a part of this as man can only attain a self which he himself has developed through his own efforts using his free will. If this self was a part of the Self of Allah, then it would already have fully developed attributes. The Quran has clarified this point in many verses e.g. (5:48). (Ed)

(1) Wherever there is a self it will have the same basic characteristics.

(2) Man does not receive a self in a fully developed form. He receives it in a latent or potent or dormant shape, or in a form with realisable possibilities in life. The purpose of human life is to actualise or to manifest it which is called the development of the human self.

(3) For an undeveloped self or personality, it is necessary that some developed personality should be in front of him to remain as an external objective standard. If man does not have this type of external objective standard before him, then he can never say with surety whether his self is becoming developed, and if it is developing, then to what extent it is doing so.

(4) In this universe, either a self is Allah's, or below Him, man's. The Self of Allah is the most comprehensive, most eminent and fully developed – that is why only this Self can serve as an external objective standard for the human self. (It should be made clear that the Self of Allah, unlike the human self, did not develop gradually stage by stage to reach a complete or developed form. It was in itself complete and developed, and remains so).

(5) We cannot know anything about the form, state, composition, or nature of the Self of Allah (leaving aside the Self of Allah, we cannot even say anything about the form and nature of our own self). A self is recognized by its attributes. These are the attributes which we have interpreted above as basic characteristics. These attributes and characteristics are, in reality, the various facets of a self.

(6) As we noted above, wherever there is a self its basic characteristics (or attributes) will be the same. Therefore, apart from those attributes which are specific to the Self of Allah e.g. the First, the Last, the Infinite etc. the characteristics of the human self and the Self of Allah are the same. Then because the Self of Allah is the most complete, most eminent and infinite, its attributes are therefore also the most complete, most eminent and without limits. In contrast with the human self however, these attributes are constrained within human limits. This difference between the human self and the Self of Allah should always be borne in mind.

(7) The Quran has explained these Divine attributes in such detail with such elucidations and such exquisiteness, that there can remain no kind of doubt, suspicion or confusion whatsoever for these not becoming a criterion for man.

(8) The Quran has also given that code which, if a life is lived according to it, will then result in the latent and hidden potentials of the human self to progressively manifest, or in other words, for the human self to continue to develop. He (man) becomes coloured in the 'colours' of Allah or it can be said that he attains 'closeness to Allah'. This system or code is called *Al Deen*.

(9) According to this system or code, the development of the human self takes place by living within a society, not in monasteries and hermitages.

Therefore, in the society in which *Al Deen* takes practical shape, the self of every individual keeps developing, and all the citizens of this society live a life of success, eminence, achievement and prosperity.

(10) Every deed of man, indeed every desire, intention and all thoughts passing through his heart, have an impact on his self. This is called the Law of Requital.[31] Every deed which helps and assists in the development of his self is called a righteous act. Contrary to this, the deed which results in weakness and causes decline in his self is called an evil act. In other words, in the same way that there are laws fixed for the growth and weakness and death of the human body, there are laws established for the development and destruction and ruin of the human self. If development of the human self continues to take place, then events affecting the human body including even death will have no effect on it i.e. a developed self achieves an immortal life and this is called the life in the hereafter.

From the above discussion, this truth has become apparent that, according to the Quran:

(a) Allah is the name of the most complete, most eminent and fully developed Self Whose attributes serve as an external objective standard for the development of the human self. Keeping these Divine attributes (*Asma'a ul Husna*) as an objective standard in front, and manifesting these outwardly (within the constraints as a human being), and making these the aim of life, is called Eimaan in Allah.

(b) Deen is the name of that practical code of life or system of life, within which, when society is shaped according to it, human self-development takes place. The collective laws for this system are the Quran. Note that the term *Madhab*[32] translated as religion does not appear anywhere in the Quran. It only talks about Deen i.e. about a practical system of life. In short, you can understand Deen as teaching man to rise up from an animal level to live life at a human level, as a result of which an individual will live a life of success and prosperity both in this life and will also, in the life to come (the hereafter), keep progressing through further evolutionary stages.

---

[31] This is covered in detail in the book titled, *The Life in the Hereafter: What Does the Quran Say*, by the author.

[32] Because there was no separate word for Deen in the English language, Islam was therefore also declared to be a religion like the other religions, even though none of the types of definition given to the term religion previously, or the common concept which it has, is applicable to Islam. Islam is Deen and not religion, and the meaning of Deen is that system of life, that form of a collection of people, which is shaped in line with the Permanent Values bestowed by Allah. From this the fundamental difference between religion and Deen becomes clear. The essence of religion or its ultimate aim is stated as being the internal personal experience which is completely an individual matter, whereas Deen is the name of a system of life which is wholly collective.

## 1.9.5  Difference Between the Quranic Concept and Mysticism

At this point, the question arises that if the purpose of Deen is to develop the self of individuals, then this is that same concept of individuality which is presented by monasticism, *Vedant*[33] and mysticism in their own way. What is the difference between these two, and what effect does it have on the world or on collective human life? This is an important question and it is imperative to examine it carefully.

## 1.9.6  Creation and *Rabubiyat* (Sustenance)

The creative action of Allah and His system of sustenance[34] in everything within the universe is functioning according to His laws. Before proceeding further, it is also essential that we should consider what is meant by creation and the system of sustenance.

The Quran informs us that one system is that according to which the initial form of different things of the universe came into existence from non-existence. How this happens, we cannot comprehend at all. The Quran has called it *Amr*[35] i.e. that aspect in which the intention and decision of Allah manifests into a practical from:

*Verily, when He intends a thing, His Command is, 'be', and it is! (36:82)*

After the advent of this first form, within these different elements, new creative forms keep appearing through ever new combinations – this is called creation. The term *Khalq* (creation) means creating with correct balance and proportion. In this manner, creative additions continue to manifest in the universe:

*…He adds to Creation as He pleases (as per His laws): for Allah has power over all things. (35:1)*

This is the process of creation by Allah. After this, His system of sustenance commences. *Rabubiyat* means to take a thing from its starting point and slowly and gradually pass it through stages to its point of completion. As has been noted above, this creative process and *Rabubiyat* of Allah is ongoing in every part of the universe. But (as per our time scales), its pace is very slow. The schemes of nature, in order to reach their completion, pass through such stages whose every single

---

[33] *Vedant* – Hindu philosophy of reincarnation. (Ed)
[34] For more details see the book titled, *The Quranic System of Sustenance*, by the author. (Ed)
[35] *Amr* - this is the universe in which Allah 'plans' and makes His decisions. We do not know how this process works. (Ed)

period comprises of thousands and thousands of years. In Surah *Al Sajdah* the Quran states:

*He rules all affairs from the heavens to the earth: in the end will (all affairs) go up to Him, on a Day, the space whereof will be as a thousand years of your reckoning.*
*(32:5)*

In another verse, the Quran declares these evolutionary stages to be of the duration of even fifty thousands of years (70:4). If you wish to know anything about the lengthy periods of these stages, then ask the experts in the Theory of Organic Evolution. They will tell us how, for a small change to take place in a species, a period of hundreds of thousands of years is required.[36]

## 1.9.7 The Companionship of Man

In the universe, when Allah's scheme (alone) is functioning, then different things progress through their evolutionary stages at a slow pace. But if man becomes a companion of Allah in this creative programme, then not only will this very long duration shrink to days and months, there are ever new increases in creations.[37] These are the men who become companions in the creative programme of Allah, and whom the Quran describes using the term 'creator', with the difference that Allah is the Best of the Creators (23:14) i.e. the One in Whose creation beauty and balance have reached their highest pinnacle.

## 1.9.8 Companionship in the Human World

In the creative programme of Allah, human companionship is no less important, but its true importance becomes apparent at that point when he becomes a companion in His Law of Requital. Just as in the outer universe Allah's Law of Requital gives rise to an effect from every cause, in the same way in the human world too, every deed produces its own effect – and will ensure it is produced. If, according to His law, the result of a certain deed is prosperity and contentment, then it is not possible that that deed will not manifest prosperity and contentment in life, and the deed whose consequence is ruin and disaster, that nations will not then be ruined and destroyed by it likewise. But, as with the system of the universe, in this aspect the working of Allah's Law of Requital is also very slow – the same as that where one day is equal to thousands and thousands of years (22:47). The slow operation of the Divine laws in the outer universe does not affect man much,

---

[36] Leaving aside changes in 'species', experts estimate that in a time period of 50,000 years, day and night (24 hours), one second is added to time, because the speed of the earth is slowing down.
[37] For example, new knowledge and new inventions by mankind leading to further creative activity in the world. (Ed)

but in human society this slow pace produces doubts and suspicions piercing the hearts, and the suffocation of anguish and torment. For example, His law is:

*...But verily the wrong-doers never shall prosper. (6:21)*

This is an immutable law of Allah, that the harvest of unjust people can never prosper. But, instead, we observe that unjust people prosper and victims are exploited, the consequence of which is that those who do not accept the Law of Requital derisively taunt that, if the Law of Requital had any truth in it, then why do the harvests of unjust people keep multiplying? From this, it is plain that the way of the world is that 'might is right' (the one who holds a stick owns the buffalo). As long as a despot is wielding power, there is none to hold him accountable. This is that very truth which is referred to in the following declaration by the Quran:

*They ask you to hasten on the Punishment! But Allah will not fail in His Promise. Verily a Day in the sight of your Sustainer is like a thousand years of your reckoning. (22:47)*

The truth is that Allah's law is an absolute reality, but each day of Allah's is as a thousand years in human reckoning. But the one who is oppressed cannot gain satisfaction from this, that a tyrant will be destroyed after five hundred or a thousand years. When it is said to him that the promises of Allah are absolutely true, he says, I know that too, but 'if it is not in my lifetime, then what is the point of all that'. In reply, the Quran states that if you wish the Law of Requital to bear results according to your calculations of time and scale, then become His companion in His programme. Hence, this is that point where it was said to the last messenger of Allah:

*Say: 'O my people! Do whatever you can: I will do my part: soon will you know who it is whose end will be (best) in the Hereafter: certain it is that the wrong-doers will not prosper.' (6:135)*

In the outer universe, every nation can participate in the creative programme of Allah (this is the very purpose of the physical sciences). But to make the Divine law productive in human society, only that *Jamaat*[38] can become a companion of Allah, which maintains complete conviction in the immutability of this law, and the selfs of those individuals of whom this *Jamaat* comprises should manifest the Divine attributes. These are those individuals who, whatever takes place through their hands (in relation to companionship with Allah), Allah relates this back to Himself. Consequently, when this *Jamaat* (to demonstrate to the unjust that their harvest cannot be reaped) selflessly and courageously reached the battlefield of

---

[38] *Jamaat* - a group, team or collection of people with one objective and aim.

*Badr[39]* during the time of Rasul-ullah, and, having killed and subjugated the opponents returned victorious and successful, then (in this connection) Allah declared:

> *It is not you who slew them; it was Allah: when you threw (arrows), it was not your act, but Allah's: in order that He might test the Believers by a gracious trial from Himself: for Allah is He Who hears and knows. (8:17)*

This section was about the role of human companionship within the Law of Requital of Allah.

## 1.10 The System of Sustenance

Proceeding from here, then comes the System of Sustenance of Allah. For the present, we are not concerned with the functioning of this system in the outer universe. Regarding the human world, the Quran states:

> *There is no moving creature on earth but its sustenance depends on Allah...(11:6)*

But we see that there are millions of such people in the world who do not get two square meals in a day. Therefore, those who raise objections say, what kind of responsibility of Allah's is this, in which human beings die of hunger? This thought arises in the hearts of those who believe that Allah fulfils such responsibilities directly. The Quran states that this responsibility is fulfilled through the hands of those individuals in whose selfs the Divine attribute of *Rabubiyat* for mankind manifests itself. These people establish such a system in which *Rizq* (resources of sustenance) does not remain confined piled up, but is freely available for the nourishment of mankind. Hence, in Surah *Yasin* it is stated:

> *And when they are told, 'Spend you of (the bounties) with which Allah has provided you,' the Unbelievers say to those who believe: 'Shall we then feed those whom, if Allah had so willed, He would have fed, (Himself)? You are in nothing but manifest error.' (36:47)*

Say to them, what kind of evident misconception are you suffering from regarding the Divine system of sustenance. This system of sustenance (in which no-one is deprived of the means for nourishment) will take shape after thousands of years according to the pace of the Divine law of the universe, but if man becomes a companion of Allah, then this same system can be established in days (as happened

---

[39] Historically this was the first battle in 624 A.D. between the Muslims (led by the last messenger) and the Quraish of Makkah. The battle ended in a defeat for the Quraish and a decisive victory for the Muslims. (Ed)

in the initial days of Islam). This was the same system (Islamic Society) which demonstrated practically the fulfillment of the following proclamation of Allah:

*...We provide sustenance for you and your progeny...(6:152)*

From these explanations, you will have seen that the purpose and aim of human life which the Quran has stated (i.e. development of the self of individuals) is not an individual act - it encompasses the collective character of the whole body of mankind (in fact the whole outer world). And every part of collective life is affected by it. The development of the human self can neither take place individually, nor can the light of the developed self remain confined within the breast of this individual. By this, every aspect of the human collective character is enlightened, and the path of human society is shaped along the correct lines. This is the reason that the life of monasticism (and mysticism), and the Quranic Doctrine and its system of life are so different.[40]

## 1.11  The Concept of Worship

From this, you may also have comprehended that, according to the concept of Allah which has been presented by the Quran, and the definition of the relationship of man with Allah, neither the meaning of 'worship' remains, in which man, being fearful of some very powerful being, bows beseechingly before him, or sings His praises to please Him, or presents donations and sacrifices to Him in order to avoid his wrath, nor is obedience of the laws of Allah equivalent to the submission to the blind orders of a despot.

According to this concept, the attributes of Allah are those external objective standards according to which man develops his self. And the Divine laws and injunctions are those practical techniques through which man's self can develop. The example of these injunctions and laws is similar to the instructions given by a doctor, according to which he instructs a patient to follow certain actions, and advises him to refrain from some other things. It is obvious that, by following these directions from a doctor, the benefit is only the patient's own welfare. The anger or pleasure of the doctor has no bearing on this. The Quran states:

*If you did well, you did well for your own selves; if you did evil, (you did it) against your own selves...(17:7)*

*...Allah stands not in need of any of His creatures. (3:97)*

---

[40] To find out about mysticism and its history refer to the book titled, *Tasawwaf kee Haqiqat (The Truth About Mysticism)* by the author.

## 1.12  Freedom to Choose and Intention

Since only those deeds can affect the human self which he does willingly using his own free will and intention, no person can therefore be forced to adopt the way of life which is proposed by Allah for the development of the human self. Freedom to choose, and intention, is the fundamental attribute of a personality. Therefore, by taking this away from man and compelling him to accept something, is to take him from the human level to the animal level. How can a practice (i.e. forcible acceptance) which causes the human self to lose its fundamental characteristic, help to develop the human self? This is why the Quran proclaims:

*There is no compulsion in Deen...(2:256)*

No-one can be forced to accept or reject Deen. The paths of right and wrong have been made clear through Divine Revelation (2:256). He who wishes, can adopt the right path, and he who wishes, can reject this. The Quran states:

*Say, 'The truth is from your Sustainer': Let him who will, accept Eimaan, and let him who will, reject (it)...(18:29)*

## 1.13  Accepting Restrictions Willingly

But when, with the full satisfaction of your heart, you willingly accept the path advocated by Deen, then it will become imperative on you to obey all these laws and injunctions which have been worked out for the development of the human self and for maintaining discipline in the society, within which the self can be nourished and manifested. The growth of the self is not possible without defining limits. Although these limits will not be imposed from outside, these are those limits which man accepts willingly for the development of his own self.

Islam is the name for the way of life which man accepts with wholehearted willingness for the development of his self. Through this, not only is his own self developed, but the beauty of the universe is continually enhanced, and every aspect of the collective human consciousness becomes bright and enlightened. This is only possible within a system in which the means of sustenance reaches all members of humanity without misery and suffering, and in which there are full arrangements in place for the development of their latent potentials.

Deen (i.e. the Quranic system of life) is a reality,[41] and reality is always beyond the constraints and confines of time and space. But sometimes, due to the demands

---

[41] The word used is *Haqeeqat* (root *Haqq*) which means something based on evidence and established beyond doubt which manifests itself as a truth and reality. (Ed)

of the era, it happens that some aspects attain special significance in a particular way, and come to the fore more conspicuously. In our times, two aspects of this reality have gained very prominent status. One is this, that, due to the spread of communication and transportation, the whole world has shrunk to become one village, and the human population appears to be becoming like one unit. From this viewpoint, the universality of the Quranic system of life is coming glaringly into view. The Quran had indeed addressed *A(l)'naas*[42] (mankind) itself, so in order now for the manifestation of its system, the conditions are becoming conducive in themselves.

The second is that our current era calls itself the age of economics. In this, the economic requirements have attained great significance, but till now the world has not discovered that kind of economic system in which the individual freedom and respect of man can remain intact, while at the same time his basic needs can also continue to be met with dignity. It has been an age since the discovery of the bankruptcy of the capitalist system. Communism had challenged the world in the form of a new experiment but hardly had it taken a few steps before it stumbled badly and collapsed, and there appears to be no hope of its being able to restore itself. This is because its downfall was concealed within its foundation.[43] The world is again standing muddled at a crossroads from where only the Quranic system of life can take it in the right direction.

But this does not mean that the remaining aspects of the collective human character have less importance. Human life is one indivisible unit and its every aspect holds equal importance. Islam views man as a whole single entity, and with this status in mind, proposes a system of life. The edifice of this system rises on the recognition and acceptance of the human self. In the coming chapters, you will find details of these aspects.

To conclude, we have said above that the development of the human self can take place within the collective system of Deen. This does not mean that if the collective system of Deen is not established then there is no possibility for the development of the human self. In such circumstances, an individual can follow those values on which it is possible to act at an individual level e.g. protecting one's chastity, not deceiving anyone, helping the needy, keeping in view the respect of humanity etc. etc. By following these values, the development of the human self can take place on an individual level as well.[44] The thing which is important is to

---

[42] See verses (114:1-3). (Ed)

[43] This book was written in 1964 and the author died in 1985. Since then communism as a system has disappeared and opposition to the capitalist system is also gradually increasing. (Ed)

[44] The important point to remember here is that when Deen is not yet established within a society, the responsibility of those individuals who accept the Quranic guidance and thus acquire Eimaan is to develop their selfs by doing righteous deeds to such an extent that the promise of Allah to establish them in this life can manifest (24:55). (Ed)

see how you use your free will and intention. In whatever part of life and to whatever extent it will be possible for you to use your free will and intention, you will be judged within that scope as to how you make use of your choice.

# 2 HUMAN PERSONALITY

In the previous chapter it has been noted that:

(1) Man is not defined by his physical body alone; other than the body there is another 'thing' within him which is called the human self.
(2) We can determine nothing about the nature and reality of the self (regardless of whether it is the Self of Allah or the self of man). We can assess it through its attributes and actions.

In this chapter, the traits, attributes and deeds of the human self will be discussed. The experts of human biology tell us that the human body is composed of countless cells, but these cells are not such that, once they have somehow or other come into existence, they will remain and continue to exist in the same shape and form as long as man is alive. They state that in every moment there is change and alteration occurring in these cells (this is termed metabolism). Innumerable cells are wasted (this is termed catabolism), and in their place innumerable new cells are formed (this productive process is termed anabolism).

## 2.1 Change in the Human Body Every Moment

The consequence of this continuous metabolism is that, after some time, the human body (which is composed of these cells) transforms into a new body, and nothing remains in this (new body) from the previous one. According to earlier research, the previous body converted into the new body in seven years. Now, it is professed that this transformation occurs in three years. In any case, whether this change happens in three years or seven years, there is no contradiction in their research that, after a period of some time, the previous body of man changes into a new body.

Now consider that, if man is defined by his physical body alone, then after three or seven years the previous individual will come to an end, and a new individual will take his place. What effect this will have in the practical world can be illustrated through an example. Ten years ago, Zaid borrowed some money from you and gave you a written receipt. Now he refuses to return the loan. You present his receipt in the court. In his defence, he presents evidence from a doctor that the Zaid who had written this receipt ten years previously, does not have a single cell remaining in his body of that Zaid. That Zaid disappeared a long time ago, now in his place a new Zaid has appeared. If the money is recovered from this (present) Zaid, then it means that a loan is taken by one person while it is paid by another. And if, due to non-recovery of this loan, he is given some punishment, then it will mean that a crime is committed by one, and punishment is handed out to another. This will be a gross injustice. Now contemplate that, if this doctrine that man is only defined by his body is accepted as being true, then what will be the consequences in the practical world? No pact or agreement will endure, or commitment or word, nor can anyone be forced to follow the law and regulation, or be held accountable or responsible. Nor will it be possible to mete out punishment to anyone for a crime or hold him responsible for a crime. So much so that, if after ten years a wife says to her husband that the woman with whom you entered into a marriage contract is finished, and I am not bound by that contract, then (according to the above stated doctrine) she will have a right to declare this. In light of this reality, Brightman[45] says:

*'If a person is not a true identical unity through all the changes in his experience, then spiritual development is impossible. Moral growth, for example, rests on the postulate that I am responsible to myself for the past purposes and contracts; yet if I am not the one who entertained those purposes and made those contracts, I experience neither responsibility nor continuous growth'.*

Irrespective of these external examples, look at your own self and you will understand this matter. If your present age is forty years, then (according to the above doctrine) you will have changed at least five or six times and have become a brand new 'individual'. But contrary to this, the truth is that, even today, the memory of the event which affected you at the age of ten years, produces the same happy or sad state of feelings which you had felt at that time. Regarding the feelings which you experienced at that point, you cannot imagine even for a moment that the individual who felt those emotions at that time was not me, but another person.

## 2.2 Continuation of the Self

Who among us will say that those indulgences and gratifications, those frustrations and regrets, whose memory often visits us in the quiet of night shortly before sleep, intermixed with feelings of sorrow and pleasure which produce a spectrum of the rainbow on the horizon of the heart, the tearful splashes of colour they continually create, that those were not mine but belong to someone else, because having transformed due to the disappearance of the cells of my body, and due to metabolism, I have ceased to exist a long while back. Our own experiences, our own feelings are living evidence to this fact that 'I' is not the name of this body which becomes renewed every three or seven years. 'I' is the name of that established reality which always remains changeless despite the metabolism of the body. In the turbulent ocean of change, this radiant luminous pearl which is unfamiliar to change, is called the human self. Berdyaev[46] has rightly observed that, 'Personality is changelessness in change'. This 'I' (or human self) is that which is

---

[45] E.S. Brightman, A Philosophy of Religion, p.196
[46] Nicolas Berdyaev, *Slavery and Freedom*, p. 8

responsible for all the deeds of an individual and is affected by their results and outcomes.

## 2.3 The Self and Memory

It can be said that the matters which we have discussed above are the magic of human memory, and it has nothing to do with the self. If an individual loses his memory, then he neither remembers any events of his previous life nor does the mention of any event have any effect on him. When memory is restored, then the events of the past start having an effect in the same way. Therefore, this is all a game of memory.

But this idea is the outcome of superficial thinking, and is not based on truth. To carry out its decisions, the human self uses the parts of the body as its tools. You decide to grasp something. Your hand moves forward and holds this thing. If (Allah forbid), your hand is paralyzed, then it will not move forward to grasp this thing. Due to the inability of your hand to move, will you reach this conclusion that there is nothing inside you which can make an intent? This was all based on the hand! When the hand became unable to function, then the whole matter ended? You will never say this. That thing which makes a decision or intent still resides inside you. The difference is only that now its intent cannot manifest itself in a visible form in front of you because the hand which was to demonstrate that intent has become devoid of feeling and movement. Now let us move forward from this example.

All of man's deeds (whether these are desires of his heart or tangible actions) leave imprints on his self. The human self manifests these imprints through its brain. This is called memory. If the brain becomes damaged due to some disease or accident, then it loses the ability to manifest these imprints on the human self. When it recovers, then the same characteristics are restored in it.

This can also be understood through an illustration. On a radio station some singer, from the fire of his soul, is spreading the flame of his voice and creating a melodious effect through the turbulent ocean of the air. Your radio set is receiving these radio waves and in this way the same voice is reproduced. You are in the throes of enjoyment of this music when suddenly the fuse of the radio blows. That voice disappears. The singer is still singing at the radio station, radio waves are still present in your room, but you are not aware of them because the instrument which was the medium for converting these waves into sound has stopped working. The sound of the voice is still there but its means to manifest itself is no longer there. The brain is the radio set and the human self is the singer broadcasting from the radio station. The failure of the radio set does not mean that there is no longer a singer at the radio station - he is still present. The means to listen to his voice has malfunctioned. Or, for example, you see your reflection in a mirror. The mirror falls and is shattered into pieces, and now you do not see your reflection on the wall. This does not mean you no longer exist, you are still there, but the means through which your reflection was displayed does not exist anymore.

The brain is therefore not the actual self, it is that screen on which the self manifests its imprints. Bergson has written an excellent book on this subject which is called 'Matter and Memory'. After discussing this point that memory is not the product of solid matter, rather it is the manifestation of the actions of a human self, he writes:

*'We understand then why a remembrance cannot be the result of a state of the brain. The state of the brain continues the remembrance, it gives it a hold on the present by the materiality which it confers on it but pure memory is a spiritual manifestation. With memory we are in very truth in the domain of spirit'.*[47]

Dr Galloway, while discussing immortality in his book, has also debated this point, 'Is memory a function of the brain?' As his view has a direct bearing on the question we are considering, it is quoted in full:

*'It may, however, be objected that memory has its basis in neural traces and so cannot survive dissolution of the body. Certainly we are not entitled to say that memory is purely an affair of the mind, for many mental habits appear to be rooted in the structure of the nervous system. And the failure of memory under pathological conditions, or when in old age degeneration of tissue reaches the association areas of the cortex, is positive evidence of some dependence of memory on cerebral traces or processes. The problem turns on the character and degree of this dependence. Now, neural traces are not the sole, nor even the most important condition of remembering; for if so, memory would depend directly on repetition. But this is plainly not the case. The truth is that memory depends far more on the presence of meaning in the things remembered,*[48] *and meaning must be referred for its maintenance in the mind to psychical not to cerebral dispositions. It is, therefore, possible that the soul, which includes within it the psychical dispositions formed during this life, may carry with it the means of preserving a continuity between the present order and a higher order of existence. If a world of meanings can be maintained by the soul despite the physiological changes of the body in a lifetime, it is conceivable it might be maintained through a more radical transformation. At all events a group of memories might remain, sufficient to give the sense of personal continuity'.*[49]

---

[47] Henri Bergson, *Matter and Memory*, p. 320
[48] This is our daily observation that if a meaningful sentence is seen once, it is remembered. But if its words are jumbled up then, in order to memorise this meaningless collection of words, we will need to repeat them many times over.
[49] George Galloway, *The Philosophy of Religion*, pp. 565-6

Mental habits are things at an animal level of life. That which is repeated many times becomes a well-established 'habit', which subsequently is performed mechanically. In fact, this is the exact technique used to train animals by making them repeat an act over and over. This is related to the mechanical action of the brain and not to the mind. Memory is related to that consciousness which is a trait at the level of human life. Therefore, its basis is the human self, not the human body.

## 2.4 The Human Self Can Never Be Destroyed

Professor Schrodinger has written a short, but very good book titled, 'What is Life'. He ends it with these words, what is this 'I'?:

*'Yet each of us has the undisputable impression that the sum total of his own experience and memory forms a unity, quite distinct from that of any other person. He refers to it as 'I'. What is this 'I'?*

*If you analyse it closely you will, I think, find that it is just a little bit more than a collection of single data (experiences and memories) namely the canvas upon which they are collected. And you will, on close introspection, find that what you really mean by 'I' is that ground stuff upon which they are collected. You may come to a distant country, lose sight of all your friends, may all but forget them; you acquire new friends, you share life with them as intensely as you ever did with your old ones. Less and less important will become the fact that, while living your new life, you still recollect the old one. 'The youth that was I,' you may come to speak to him in the third person, indeed the protagonist of the novel you are reading is probably nearer to your heart, certainly more intensely alive and better known to you. Yet there has been no intermediate break, no death. And even if a skilled hypnotist succeeded in blotting out entirely all your earlier reminiscences, you would not find that he had killed you. In no case is there a loss of personal existence to deplore. Nor will there ever be'.* [50]

This is that 'I' (human self) on which the changes occurring in the human body do not leave any impact. We have seen that when the human hand becomes paralysed, even then the human self exists, even when the leg becomes paralysed, or the liver becomes deranged, or the brain becomes damaged i.e. however many parts of the human body become damaged or are finished, the human self does not end. Therefore, even if the whole human body disintegrates, even then nothing can destroy the human self, i.e. even if physical death occurs, his self still remains

---

[50] Erwin Schrodinger, *What is Life*, p. 91-92.

intact. The shock of death does not cause any change to the human self; it lives even after this, and this is called life after death.

As has already been noted in Chapter 1, the purpose of life is the development of the human self, and this is the very responsibility of the Islamic society. If the human self is developed properly, then it becomes worthy of progressive journeying through further evolutionary stages after the demise of the physical human body. (Details of this will be covered in later chapters).

Ouspensky has cited Gurdjieff in support of his view:

*'If a man is changing every minute, if there is nothing in him that can withstand external influences, it means that there is nothing in him that can withstand death. But if he becomes independent of external influences, if there appears in him something that can live by itself; this something may not die. In ordinary circumstances we die every moment.*
*External influences change and we change with them, i.e. many of our 'Is' die. If a man develops in himself a permanent 'I' that can survive a change in external conditions, it can survive the death of the physical body'.*[51]

In the words of the philosopher, Iqbal:

*Life is like unto a shell and the self is the pearl drop (concretion) therein;*
*What is the shell worth if it cannot transform the pearl drop into a pearl.*
*Through self-knowledge, self-control and self-development,*
*The self can even conquer death'.*[52]

As has been noted in Chapter 1, the Divine Self is the most accomplished self about which the Quran states:

*Every moment there is a change in everything in the universe, but it is only the Divine Self which is free from any change and is possessor of great Majesty and Honour.*[53]
*(55:26-27)*

As the development of the human self keeps taking place, the Divine attributes proceed to manifest themselves in it (within the constraints of human limits). Remaining unaffected from external changes is among the fundamental attributes of Allah, so such a human being will also remain unaffected from external incidents.

---

[51] P. D. Ouspensky, *In Search of the Miraculous*, p. 101.
[52] M. Iqbal, *Darb -e-Kaleem*, p. 29
[53] This is not a translation but is the meaning of the verse as explained by the author. (Ed)

## 2.5 Life Out of Death

In ordinary circumstances, our condition is such that (for example), before going to sleep at night, I decided that I will rise at five o'clock in the morning. The alarm rang at five o'clock and I woke up, but because of the cold outside and the warmth and comfort of my bed, I made the decision that I will forgo it today, but will definitely get up early tomorrow morning and go for a walk. The question is that, is the 'I' who made the decision at night prior to going to sleep and the 'I' who went against this decision the next morning, one and the same? Or, for example, I have promised you that I will support you in a certain matter, but right at the last moment, I withdraw my support. The question is, whether the 'I' which made the promise and the 'I' which deserted you, was it the same one? The meaning of these changes in 'I' in this way means that my self is very weak, and has not been developed. The first sign of a developed self is that it does not change its decisions by becoming influenced by external events. Regarding those individuals in whom development of the self begins (i.e. the *Jamaat* of Momineen), the Quran states:

> *In the case of those who say, 'Our Sustainer is Allah', and, further, stand straight and steadfast...(41:30)*

Those who once acquire Eimaan in this reality, that Allah is our Sustainer, and then stand steadfast in this conviction, throngs of opposition cannot then create the slightest tremor in their resolute stance - on the contrary, this further reinforces their Eimaan (3:173). This is the first indication of the development of the human self. Even the cognizance of death cannot produce any kind of transformation in it. The birth of a new 'I' in every moment in an individual (i.e. his constantly changing) is *Shirk*[54] with his own self, and *Shirk* is the cause of humiliation as a human being. The Oneness[55] of Allah also means that His Self is changeless:

> *Say: He is Allah, the One and Only. (112:1)*

## 2.6 The Quran is About Man

As noted previously, the Quran has explained the Divine attributes in detail. Leaving aside those attributes which are specifically for the Divine Self (e.g. He is the First), the remainder are those whose manifestation can be within the human self. Looking at it from this angle, the explanation of these attributes is the

---

[54] *Shirk* – the term is used for the association of any other law with the laws of the Quran. The Quran has declared this to be an 'unpardonable' crime as it does not produce the results which are obtained by following the Permanent Values. For more details see the *Lughat ul Quran*, Volume 1, page 746-748. (Ed)
[55] See verse (112:1).

explanation of the essentials and characteristics of the human self itself. This is why it is stated in the Quran:

*We have revealed for you (O men!) a Book in which is a Message for your eminence*[56]*: will you not use your intellect? (21:10)*

We have revealed to you such a Book that, if you employ your intellect and reasoning, you will see that it is all about your own eminence. These attributes are numerous, but some of these are such that they hold a fundamental status in one respect – these attributes are explained very comprehensively in Surah *Al Ikhlas* (though it consists of only four short verses, if we expand these verses in meaning, then all four aspects of the universe of the human self converge together before us). The first verse is:

*Say: He is Allah, the One and Only; (112:1)*

In other words, the first attribute of a self is its oneness. Oneness is a very comprehensive term which cannot be translated in one word. This contains all the connotations of uniqueness, one-ness and wholeness. The self, first and last – evident and immanent - is only a self (57:3). There is nothing in it of even an iota of adulteration by any other thing.

We have seen earlier that the state of the under-developed self is such that it is one thing at the time of going to sleep and another when waking up next morning, one thing when making a commitment and another when breaking it, one thing in the state of anger and another in the state of stress – this is not a sign of the unity of the self (*Tauheed*), it is a sign of *Shirk*. *Tauheed* (one-ness) means that the self does not keep changing by being influenced by external events or internal sentiments – it should always remain steadfast in its traits and characteristics (this attribute of the self is called immutable principles or immutable laws). The Quran terms it *Sunnat Ullah*:

*...No change will you find in the practice of Allah (Sunnat Ullah). (33:62)*

This attribute of the human self is called 'character'. In the words of Berdyaev, the manifestation of the self is through character.[57] Professor Whitehead remarks:

---

[56] The word used here is *Zikr* which is also translated as eminence. Its wider meaning is that if the Quran is followed, then all those results of righteousness will be achieved which are noted in the Quran with respect to a *Momin*, and it will lead to a balanced life in this life and there will also be opportunities for further development in the hereafter. (Ed)
[57] Nicolas Berdyaevm, *Slavery and Freedom*, p. 8

*Truth is the conformation of appearance to reality.*[58]

The expression of unity in both the outer and inner states of the human self is a sign of its living proof and manifested evidence.

## 2.7 The Law of Requital[59]

The natural consequence of the human self is that I myself am responsible for all my intentions, decisions, deeds and actions. Therefore, the effects and consequences of these will have to be borne by me alone, no-one else can become a partner in this. The foundation of the whole structure of the Law of Requital of the Quran rests on this basic principle:

> *...no bearer of burdens can bear the burden of another...(6:164)*

In this respect, no intercession can benefit anyone nor compensation, nor can anyone be the source of atonement or reparation for someone else or provide help or support to another:

> *Then protect yourselves against a day when one self shall not avail another nor shall intercession be accepted for him, nor shall compensation be taken from him, nor shall anyone be helped (from outside). (2:48)*

This is the proclamation concerning the Law of Requital and (as mentioned above) this is the natural consequence of the individuality of the human self. When my headache cannot be removed by the intercession, atonement or compensation of another, then how can these things remove the effects of my deeds? My *Jannat* (paradise) and *Jahannum* (hell) will be shaped according to these, and no other person can interfere in this (details will be covered in later chapters).

The second verse of Surah *Al Ikhlas* states:

> *Allah, the Eternally enduring, Absolutely free. (112:2)*

*Samde'at* is the second trait of the self. This is also a comprehensive expression which means to be free from dependency on external support, being master of your own intentions and self-sufficient in your own decisions. The Quran states about the Divine Self:

> *...for Allah carries out all that He wills. (22:18)*

---

[58] A. N. Whitehead, *Adventures of Ideas*, p. 309
[59] The Law of Requital and the hereafter is covered in detail in the book titled, *The Life in the Hereafter: What Does the Quran Say?* by the author. (Ed)

*...for Allah does command according to His will and plan. (5:1)*

Such verses as these are mirrors of this attribute. It is on the basis of this very trait of the self that man has been made an individual possessing responsibility and intent and given the right to choose from many different possibilities. The Quran states:

*...Do whatever you wish...(41:40)*

And then in another verse:

*Say, 'The truth is from your Sustainer': Let him who will, believe, and let him who will, reject (it)...(18:29)*

None else in the universe has been given the freedom to choose and make decisions. Since intent and choice are the fundamental traits of the human self, growth and development can thus only take place via those deeds which man carries out willingly using his ability of free choice and intent. Neither good under compulsion is actual good, nor is evil under duress, evil. The Quran has made it clear:

*There is no compulsion in Deen...(2:256)*

This is what is meant by this declaration. Man's freedom of choice and intent are respected to such an extent that, never mind anyone else, even Allah (despite His infinite powers) does not interfere in this freedom. This is His own decision on which He remains firm. In the words of the philosopher, Iqbal:

*God Himself cannot feel, judge and choose for me when more than one course of action are open to me.* [60]

The humanity of a man is connected to his choice and intent. This is a requirement of the attribute of *Samde'at* of the self. It should be made clear that to put restrictions on oneself through one's own choice is not against its own freedom. (A constraint on freedom is that which another imposes externally on a self against its will). Allah Himself has imposed these types of constraints on Himself. For example, the Quran states:

*...your Sustainer has inscribed for Himself (the rule of) Rehmat and Rabubiyat ...(6:54)*

---

[60] M. Iqbal, *The Reconstruction of Religious Thought in Islam*, Chapter 4, *His Freedom and Immortality* p. 100.

Whatever restrictions man puts willingly on his self for its development, these are not against the essence of being human. A Quranic society is a model of this fundamental concept of freedom and constraint in which the self of an individual keeps on developing and continuing to progress forward.

The third verse of Surah *Al Ikhlas* states:

*He begetteth not, nor is He begotten. (112:3)*

The common translation of this is, 'He has neither given birth to anyone through procreation nor was He born by procreation through anyone'. This is also a fundamental trait of the self. The human body is born through procreation. This 'birth' is at an animal level. In this manner, an individual becomes the offspring of his father and his own children are born in this same way. But the human self is not the consequence of this process of birth. In the process of birth through reproduction and procreation, a part of the father separates and becomes part of the body of his child. But the self is an indivisible entity, it cannot be divided into parts. If a part of the self separates from it, then the self remains incomplete, and the self becoming incomplete is against its fundamental trait. Procreation (i.e. producing children through reproduction) is necessary for the continuation of the human race, but the requirement of the self is not procreation but creation. As has been noted in Chapter 1, it is a trait of a human being that he participates in the creative programme of the Creator of the universe (because no other thing in the universe has been endowed with a self) and this is the reason for human eminence. The fourth verse of Surah *Al Ikhlas* states:

*And there is none like unto Him. (112:4)*

There is none like Him or His equivalent. Compared to that nation in which its people are developing their selfs, no other nation in the world will be equivalent to it.

When the Quran said about the *Jamaat-e*-Momineen, 'You will overcome all…'(3:139), that same truth was being referred to. As has been previously stated, the Quran has presented the Divine attributes with great emphasis and detail, and these are referred to at various places in its verses, dispersed like sparkling pearls. The reflection of these attributes in the human self is a sign of the development of the self. In the following chapter, the technique to develop the human self, or how man receives instructions for this self-development, will be elucidated.

As has been clarified in Chapter 1, the edifice of Deen is raised on the foundation of acceptance of the concept of the human self. From this aspect, the degree to which this concept or belief is significant in the system of Deen is very evident. In the coming chapters, you will come across references to the human self frequently in many places, and details of its various attributes and features will appear before you. But in view of the significance of this concept, we wish at this juncture to briefly summarise various aspects of the human self again, so that wherever it is referred to in the following pages, these facts are kept in view in order that no wrong idea is formed about it at any point. Please attend to these carefully:

(1) In relation to living things, the Quran has, in numerous places, referred to the process of creation and its various stages. During this process that point is reached where the creative act takes place through procreation and reproduction i.e. the creation of animals, in which the embryo grows in the womb for a specified duration. In this connection, the Quran has first mentioned all the stages which all animal and human embryos go through in the womb e.g. the fertilized egg transforming into an embryo; the embryo taking shape as a piece of flesh; then the formation of bones within it; then the casing of these bones by a covering of flesh – these are those stages through which both animal and human offspring pass in a similar fashion. After this, the Quran states about the human embryo:

*… then we created out of it another creature…(23:14)*

This means that, having reached this stage, man then became a completely different creature from other animals. At another place, it is proclaimed about this clearly differentiating change:

*…and breathed into him something of His Ruh (Divine Energy)…(32:9)*

This is that trait due to which man becomes divergent from other animals, and because of which the universal forces (angels) bow before him. In Surah *Saad*, it is stated:

*Behold, your Sustainer said to the angels (universal forces): 'I am about to create man (beginning creation) from clay (inanimate matter): When I have fashioned him (in due proportion) and breathed into him of My Ruh (Divine Energy), fall you down in obeisance unto him. (38:71-72)*

This thing which Allah has called 'His Own Energy' has been bestowed on man alone, and none other. In this regard (that man is a totally different creation from animals), an expert on evolution of our time, Simpson, has written:

*To say that man is nothing but an animal is to deny, by implication, that he has essential attributes other than those of animals… It is important to realise that the essence of his unique nature lies precisely in those characteristics that are not shared with any other animal. His place in nature and its supreme significance to man are not defined by his animality but his humanity. Man has certain basic diagnostic features which set him off most sharply from any other animal and which have involved other developments not only increasing this sharp distinction but also making it an absolute difference in kind and not only a relative difference of degree.*[61]

(2) This thing is not intellect either. Since there is detailed discussion in Chapter 4 about intellect and Deen, there is no need at this point to expand further on this aspect as details will be covered later.

(3) Neither is it that entity which psychologists term as the psyche, or which is referred to as the sub-conscious mind according to psychoanalysis. (Nor is it that thing which was called the spirit in ancient philosophy and which was considered to be the opposite of physical matter). The reality is that, according to research in the modern era, the original concept itself of matter which was generally prevalent previously in human philosophical thinking no longer remains. Matter is now no longer something which possesses a solid state. Sir James Jeans terms it as bottled up waves. Russell calls it interrelated events. Einstein gives it the name of considered thoughts. Ouspensky views it as merely a condition. If we look at it purely from the physical point of view, then a material object consists of smaller particles which are called molecules. If these are further analysed, they are found to consist of even smaller elements which are called atoms. Proceeding further, these convert into electrons and protons which are called particles of electricity on which the definition of matter does not even fit. In this way, matter (according to ancient belief) becomes non-matter itself. Therefore, the duality of spirit and matter which had confused philosophers of previous generations so much, has now practically disappeared. The Quran does not even mention matter as the opposite of spirit, so much so that there is no mention of the spirit as the soul in the Quran. Having referred to the beginning of the creation of the material universe in Allah's *Alam-e-Amr* (universe of *Amr*), the Quran moves forward because the human mind enclosed in the physical world cannot envisage the truth and reality of the metaphysical world (*Alam-e-Amr*).

Therefore, the thing which made man eminently different from other creations is not even *Ruh*, meaning it is neither spirit nor soul.

---

[61] G.G. Simpson, *'The Meaning of Evolution'*, pp 281-4.

## 2.8   This *Al-Nafs* is the Human Self

(4) The Quran has declared this 'entity' as different from intellect, consciousness, mind, psyche, spirit or soul and stated it using the term *Nafs*. In Surah *Al Shams*, the Quran declares:

> *By the Nafs (self), and the proportion and order given to it; And its enlightenment as to its wrong and its right; Truly he succeeds who purifies it, And he fails who corrupts it! (91:7-10)*

*Nafs*, and all those means and elements which set it right and help it to achieve completion, are a witness to this truth that Allah has kept within it as possibilities both the potential of disintegration and the ability to remain protected from this disintegration. He who developed it, became successful, and he who suppressed it (did not allow it to flourish and blossom), failed and remained unsuccessful. You will have seen how the Quran declares the human *Nafs* to be a unique, specific and permanent entity. This is what is called human personality. The latent potentials of both development and disintegration have been kept within it.

For scholars and philosophers this fact is not unfamiliar that, when we use the term 'I' in philosophical usage, its meaning is one thing, but when we use this word 'I' in our general daily speech, it means something different. The Quran has also used this word *Nafs* with different meanings. In our daily conversations, the word *Nafs* has also been used for those that we classify as 'that person' or 'I myself' etc, and this word is also used for the specific meaning of the human self. For the student of the Quran, it is important to always keep this difference in mind.

## 2.9   The Human Self is Not Part of the Self of Allah

(5) The human *Nafs* is granted by Allah and it is not part of the Self of Allah. Allah has called it *Min-Ruh-hee* (i.e. Divine energy from Me) or *Min-Ruh-hena* (i.e. Divine energy from Us), but He (Allah) has never called Himself as *Ruh* i.e. if it was written in the Quran that Allah is *Ruh* and that He has given a part of it (*Ruh*) to man, then it could be said that the human self is part of the Self of Allah[62]. But the Quran has not said such a thing anywhere, therefore this is not part of the Self of Allah. A self cannot be sub-divided into parts. The human self is the expression of Allah's *Ruh* (Divine Energy) i.e. from it can emerge the Divine attributes, though these

---

[62] The human self is bestowed on man in an undeveloped form, while Allah's Self is (and always was) fully developed with all the attributes detailed in the Quran. (Ed)

will only be within the constraints of human limitations and will not be limitless and infinite like Allah.

## 2.10  Life in the Hereafter

(6)  We have seen that Allah has called the human self a 'new or unique creation'. Hence, this is neither the product of physical evolution nor is it governed by the physical laws under which the human body remains alive and functions. This is the reason why, with physical death, the human self does not come to an end, and remains even after this physical death. This is called the life in the hereafter, or life after death. In Surah *Bani Israel*, it is stated:

> *They say: 'What! when we are reduced to bones and dust, should we really be raised up to be a new creation?' (17:49)*

The objection (and question) of those who believe in the materialistic concept of life is that, when death occurs with the disintegration of the physical body, will it be possible to get a new life after this? How can it be obtained? In reply to this it is stated:

> *Say: '(Nay!) be you stones or iron, Or created matter which, in your minds, is hardest (to be raised up) - (Yet shall you be raised up)!' then will they say: 'Who will cause us to return?' Say: 'He who created you first!' Then will they wag their heads towards you, and say, 'When will that be?' Say, 'Maybe it will be quite soon!' (17:50-51)*

Say to them, yes, you will certainly get life after death, even if, with the passage of time, your material constituents convert into stones or turn into iron or any other creation about which you consider that life cannot emerge from it. At this they will retort, who will bring us back to life. Say to them, that same Allah Who brought you into life from nothing the first time. That same Allah Who can create existence from non-existence, can make life continue even after the death of the body. At this time, the vehicle of life will be the human *Nafs* (self). In this way, the stream of life will flow forward after the physical life. If the human *Nafs* was under the control of physical laws like the human body, then with the death of the body, this too would have ended. But, because this is not dependent on the support of the body for its existence, it therefore does not die with the demise of the body.

## 2.11 The Immortal Life

(7) One is survival after death, and the other is immortality. Survival after death is for every conscious human being, but immortality can only belong to that self which has been developed accordingly (this is called *Tazkia Nafs*[63]). It should be made clear that completion of the development of the human self does not happen in this world alone. For this it will have to pass through further stages in the life of paradise in the hereafter. In this world, the development process commences and if this reaches a certain level (which the Quran has called tilting the balance with righteous deeds), then it becomes enabled to progress through the next stages (101:6-7). If this does not happen, then its development halts (this is called the life of hell).

(8) Regarding the life of paradise of the human self in the hereafter, we have stated that it will achieve 'immortal life'. This means that after physical death in the worldly life it will not endure another death. The Quran states:

*Nor will they there taste Death, except the first death...(44:56)*

In this, apart from the first death (the flavour of which they have already tasted), these people will not taste death. They will journey through further evolutionary stages of life but this immortal life is not like the *Abde'at*[64] of Allah. None can get that kind of *Azle'at* (beginning) or *Abde'at* (immortality) like Him. Regarding these people it has been stated in numerous places in the Quran, 'They will stay in paradise forever', but regarding this *Abde'at* it is stated in another verse:

*They will dwell therein for all the time that the heavens and the earth endure, except as your Sustainer wills: a gift without break. (11:108)*

They will stay in it during the time that the heavens and the earth remain except as is in the Will of Allah. (The last part is taken to mean that the Will of Allah is that it should be like this. That is, the existence of the inhabitants of paradise will be till such a time that the heavens and earth remain in place according to the Will of Allah). At the present level of our consciousness, we cannot comprehend how long the duration of this state will be. However, this is clear that this *Abde'at* (of the developed human self) is definitely not like the *Abde'at* of Allah. This is our meaning of immortal life.

(9) The purpose of human life is to develop the human self. The Quran has given that code according to which development of the human self takes

---

[63] *Tazkia Nafs* - literally means purification of the self. (Ed)
[64] *Abde'at* – this means forever i.e. no beginning and no end. (Ed)

place. Therefore, according to the Quran, the purpose of 'ethics' is not only that a society can be established so that a life of prosperity and peace is lived – from this the purpose is that by living life according to these values, development of the human self takes place. Hence, a righteous deed is that due to which the human self develops and an evil deed is that due to which development of the human self halts.

This is that very standard for righteousness and evil (right and wrong) of a nation or society. In the nation or society in which the self of individuals develops, that is in accordance with *Haqq* (the Quranic Values), in the one in which the development of the human self stops, that is *Batil* (evil). This is what is called freedom and slavery. Those individuals whose self is developed, are free. Those whose development has halted, are enslaved and subjugated, even if they have their own government.

From this you will have seen how the structure of both the political system and the society is also based on the concept of the human self, and how the system of ethics revolves around this very focus.

## 2.12  The Human Self Develops by Giving

(10) Just as there are laws established for the growth of the human body, similarly there are laws defined for the development of the human self. These laws are called the Permanent Values, details of which will be covered in a separate chapter. At this stage, it will be enough to make a reference to a central point. The human body grows as a result of those things which a person himself eats or utilises. Contrary to this, the human self develops with all those things which this person gives for the development of others. In other words, the body grows by 'taking' whereas the self grows by 'giving':

*Those who spend their wealth for increase in self-purification…(92:18)*

That individual who gives away everything in his possession (which is beyond his needs, see verse 2:219) to fulfil the needs of others so that his self can develop, and whose self becomes developed, achieves the purpose of life (details will be given in the next chapter):

*But those will prosper who purify themselves (87:14)*

## 2.13  Basis of the Islamic Economic System

The Quranic system of sustenance is established on this same basis. If you reflect on the history of mankind then this truth will become apparent, that the question which has kept man in a disturbed and perturbed state is:

(a) Different people have differing abilities to work and earn.
(b) The result of this is that the one who earns more gains wealth beyond his needs.
(c) The one who has a lesser ability to earn does not earn enough to meet his needs.
(d) In order to maintain a balance within society, and to provide sustenance to the people, it is essential that those who have surplus money spend their wealth on those whose needs are unmet.
(e) The question is, why should those who have surplus money give their wealth to others?

The solution presented by ethics is that the sentiments of the wealthy should be appealed to on the basis of compassion for humanity, so that they give their wealth in charity.[65] But experience tells us that these appeals are very rarely successful, therefore even this cannot be a satisfactory solution to this question. In addition, the self of human beings who are nourished through charity is harmed and they develop an inferiority complex. From this point of view also, this proposal cannot be viewed as correct. The governments of the world impose taxes for this, and in this way acquire spare wealth from the rich. The wealthy regard this as forcible acquisition and so utilise such techniques through which they can escape the government's grip. As a consequence, the malady of dishonesty becomes commonplace in society. If they fail in these efforts of theirs, then they will just stop trying to earn more. They say, why should we work so hard day and night to produce such wealth which we cannot keep. Why should we not earn only that much which can remain with us. This affects the productivity of society very badly. This is the difficulty in which today's communist system[66] is badly ensnared i.e. there is no incentive within it due to which people work to their fullest ability to increase the wealth of the nation, and then retain only that which meets their needs, and hand over the rest to the government.

---

[65] We see how both those who are wealthy and the general public respond to emotive appeals when there is, for example, some natural disaster. However after a short while it is soon forgotten and human problems continue to multiply in the world. The interesting part of this process is that these people have this spare money which they do not donate when there is no specific disaster even though fellow human beings continue to be badly in need of it for their daily subsistence. (Ed)
[66] The communist system collapsed in the former Soviet Union in 1990 for the same reason which the author has noted here. (Ed)

## 2.14 The Solution to This Problem

This incentive can only be found from the Quran, which says that the self of that individual who earns to whatever great an extent he can, and then donates his surplus wealth for the nourishment of others, will develop proportionally. According to this doctrine, every individual works to his fullest capability but does not keep surplus wealth. From this, on the one hand, the root of the capitalist system is severed (since the very foundation of this system is based on 'surplus capital'), and on the other hand, a satisfactory solution becomes available for this difficult issue due to which the communist system has to use the whip of force and is now failing badly (details of these are given later).

From the above discussion, the fundamental traits of the human self have been presented before you, and it has also become evident how the structures of the Islamic economic, social, ethical and political system are raised on such a foundation. In the following chapters the details of these will appear before you.

# 3  THE ROOT OF GUIDANCE

As has been noted in Chapter 1, none of the things in the universe is created in its final form from the very first day itself. Its beginning commences from the first point of creation and after this its journey of evolution begins. At every stage in this journey it becomes refined through a process of trimming and pruning, shaping and improving, and progresses forward till it reaches the final destination which has been defined for it (according to the Divine programme). It traverses all these stages through the guidance which it gets from the Creator of the universe. This is that great truth about the process of creation and evolution which the Quran has summed up in a few words[67]:

> *Who has created, and further, given order and proportion; Who has ordained laws. And granted guidance; (87:2-3)*

Allah is He Who initiates the creation of everything, then shapes and hones it to produce balance in it. Then He fixes a scale for it, as to what extent it has to go forward and what it is to become, and He provides guidance on the journey through all of these stages. The subject under consideration deals with the last part of this verse (*Fa-hada*) i.e. granting guidance. From this the following reality becomes evident, that in order for the things of the universe to traverse their evolutionary stages, guidance is also received from Allah. This is that reality to which everything in the universe is a witness, therefore there is no need for proof or ideological argument for this. This 'direction' (guidance) has been embedded within each thing - the Quran has labelled this with the term *Wahi* (revelation).[68] The meaning of *Wahi* is a fine but sharp signal. For example, about the great heavenly bodies swimming in the universe, the Quran states:

> *…and inspired (Wahi) in each heaven its command…(41:12)*

About the earth it says:

> *Because your Sustainer will have inspired (Wahi) it. (99:5)*

Similarly, for the honey bee:

> *And your Sustainer inspired (Wahi) the bee…(16:68)*

---

[67] The Arabic words used in the Quran are *Khalaqa* (created), *Sawwa* (balanced it), *Qaddara* (fixed scales) and *Hada* (guided). (Ed)

[68] Professor Galloway has written, 'In the widest sense of the word, the order of nature is a revelation, for it unfolds a meaning which has its ultimate source in God'. Galloway G., *The Philosophy of Religion*, p. 582

In Surah *Al Nur* this aspect is condensed into a few words:

> *Do you not see that it is Allah Whose laws all beings in the heavens and on earth follow and the birds with wings outspread? Each one knows its own Salat[69] (guidance) and its task. And Allah knows well all that they do. (24:41)*

Have you not paid attention to this, that whatever is in the heavens and the earth, including the birds which fly with their wings widespread, all remain actively engaged in fulfilling the established and defined programme of Allah. Every single one among these also knows of that path which they have to traverse in obedience to the Divine law (they have not been left without a purpose). They remain under the constant surveillance of the Divine law which monitors how they carry out their duties. (In this verse, the words *Salat* and *Tasbih*[70] are worth attention).

This reality is explained in Surah *Al An'am* as follows:

> *There is not an animal (that lives) on the earth, nor a being that flies on its wings, but forms part of communities like you. Nothing (of the guidance) have We omitted from the Book (of the universe), and they (all) are gathered around the law of their Sustainer. (6:38)*

This is that guidance which is commonly called instinct, or in the words of Iqbal,[71] the 'trackless way' of a bird i.e. such a path along which there are no signposts. See how migratory birds after travelling thousands of miles crossing the vastness of the oceans, jungles and deserts, reach their place of destination as if someone has brought them there by holding their hands. This is the first characteristic of the things of the universe i.e. the guidance for their duties of life and their functioning is provided by nature, and this guidance is put into everything (and every individual of a species) and kept within it. By every individual of a species is meant, for example, that chickens are one species. Every chick gets this guidance from nature. This is the reason (for example) that if some hen eggs and some duck eggs are left under a hen for hatching, and they all hatch at the same time, the ducklings will head for water whereas the chicks will remain on dry land, and from among them each brood will do the same, regardless of whether they are in the desert of Africa or in the city of New York.

---

[69] *Salat* – this term is used frequently in the Quran and it means to follow the Divine laws. In traditional translations, this is translated as prayer. The Quran directs the *Momineen* to establish *Salat* which points to the establishment of the Islamic system called Deen. (Ed)
[70] *Tasbih* means to pursue a goal persistently, each and every time. (Ed)
[71] Iqbal M., *The Reconstruction of Religious Thought in Islam*, Chapter I, Knowledge and Religious Experience, p.1

## 3.1 Constraints on the Things of the Universe

The second characteristic of the things of the universe is that they are born with the constraint to obey whatever guidance has been provided to them by nature. These do not have the choice that, if they wish they can follow this guidance, or if they wish they can select an opposing path:

> *And to Allah do obeisance all that is in the heavens and on earth, whether moving (living) creatures or the universal forces: for none are arrogant (before their Sustainer). (16:49)*

Whatever is in the highs and lows of the universe, and whatever kind of living creatures are on earth, even all the universal forces, all have been made subservient to the guidance of Allah and these never rebel against this. This is called the nature of these things. From the above discussion, it is evident that:

(i) Everything in the universe obtains its guidance from Allah according to which, by traversing its evolutionary stages, it reaches the intended destination.

(ii) Everything is obliged to follow the path of this guidance. This is called the nature of this thing, which it cannot change.

Now let us proceed. Man is also included within the Divine creation. Therefore, providing him with guidance is also the responsibility of Allah. But, in this regard, man's position is different from the other things of the universe. We have seen above that (for example) among animals, every species and every individual in each species gets guidance automatically from birth, according to which it has to pass its life. The physical life of man is like that of other animals. Therefore, the child of man, just like the offspring of animals, brings guidance for its physical requirements at the time of its birth. It also, on entering this world, is drawn to the fountains of milk, and learns the technique to suck milk through its instincts. But as it gradually grows up, a difference arises between him and the offspring of animals e.g. if a chick avoided water from the beginning, it will continue to remain distant from water till the end. But the state of a human child is such that, he will sometimes put his hand into fire, sometimes will fall into a tub of water and gasp to remain afloat, sometimes will touch his eyes with chillies, and sometimes will put a coal into his mouth. From this it is obvious that, in these matters, he does not get any guidance from nature.

This is also obvious that the demands of human life are not just physical but are also human requirements. In other words, his life is not merely that of an animal, but is also a life of a human being. The sense of responsibility, regret for a mistake, an eye on the future - these are all expressions of human life. To understand it fundamentally, a human being is not only defined by his body but (as explained in previous chapters) he also possesses some other thing besides his body, which is called the human personality.

## 3.2 Development of the Human Self

Just as the nourishment of the body is a requirement of his animal life, similarly, the development of his self is the requirement of his human life. For this, man does not get any guidance from nature. In other words, there is no ability inbuilt in man to differentiate between right and wrong. This is the reason that man invites evil as repeatedly as good. He happens to be very hasty:

> The prayer that man should make for good, he makes for evil; for man is given to hasty (deeds). (17:11)

He leaps towards immediate gains, even if, in the long run, these prove to be harmful for him. There is a common view prevalent among Muslims for generations that the ability to distinguish between right and wrong is embedded within man by nature. In support of this belief, they even quote a verse of the Quran:

> By the Self, and the proportion and order given to it. And its enlightenment as to its wrong and its right. (91:7-8)

They translate this verse as meaning that Allah has inspired the human self about right and wrong. But not only is this translation of this verse incorrect, this concept as a whole is against Quranic teaching.

## 3.3 Ability to Distinguish Between Right and Wrong is Not Inbuilt in Man

Firstly because, if the ability to differentiate between right and wrong has been placed within each individual, then the whole process of providing guidance through the messengers of Allah becomes meaningless. This type of differentiation has been put in other things of the universe (e.g. animals), therefore there was no need to send a *Nabi* to them. Furthermore, this is also against our experience and observation. A human child picks up ideas and beliefs from whatever type of environment he is brought up in and educated in. Eating meat is an extremely hateful thing for a Hindu child, but a Muslim child eats meat with great gusto. Therefore, this concept is wrong that the differentiation between good and bad, and between virtue and evil, has been placed within man. The meaning of the verses quoted above from Surah *Al Shams* is that the human self has been endowed with realisable potentials and possibilities, so that if he wishes he can guard himself, or if he wishes he can ruin himself. The individual who develops these will be successful, whereas the one who suppresses these will be ruined and destroyed.

In fact, in these verses this point has been clarified that the human self is not provided in a developed and evolved form - it is only a collection of realisable potentials. If man develops these potentials correctly, then the human self becomes developed. If he does not do so, then it gets destroyed. There are potentials present within it for both growth and destruction.

## 3.4 Meaning of *Fitrat Ullah* (Nature of Man)

In this regard, another wrong belief is prevalent among Muslims, and that is that Allah has created man in His own nature i.e. whatever the nature of Allah is, this is the same nature possessed by man, and Islam is the Deen of nature i.e. that this Deen is based on the nature of man which is based on the nature of Allah. In support of this erroneous belief, the following verse from Surah *Al Rum* is presented:

*So set your face steadily and truly to the Faith: (establish) Allah's handiwork according to the pattern on which He has made mankind: no change (let there be) in the work (wrought) by Allah: that is the standard Deen: but most among mankind understand not. (30:30)*

Even though in this verse and in fact in the Arabic language of the era of the revelation of the Quran, the word *Fitrat* was not used for those meanings for which it is now used. It is now taken to mean nature. In the Arabic language, and in the Quran, *Fatara* means to create something for the first time (e.g. *Say: 'He who created you first! 17:51*). Therefore, *Fitrat* means Allah's Law of Creation. From this view, the meaning of the verse of Surah *Al Rum* is: *Allah has created man according to His same Law of Creation according to which He has created other things of the universe.*

If we accept this view, that Allah has created man in His Own nature, then the form of the *Fitrat* of Allah which emerges can never be befitting to that of Allah. For example, the Quran states about man:

*...For man was created weak. (4:28)*

*Man is a creature of haste...(21:37)*

*...for man is given to hasty (deeds). (17:11)*

*...for man is (ever) niggardly! (17:100)*

*Truly man was created very impatient…(70:19)*

*…But man is, in most things, contentious. (18:54)*

*…He was indeed unjust and foolish…(33:72)*

These are those conspicuous traits of *'Fitrat'* of man which Allah has mentioned in the Quran. If we accept that Allah has created man in His *Fitrat*, then we will have to accept (Allah forbid) that Allah's own *Fitrat* is also like this. Therefore, this belief is also wrong that man's *Fitrat* is the same as that of Allah. Man has no *Fitrat*.

## 3.5 Man Has No *Fitrat* (Nature)

'Man has no *Fitrat*' is a great revolutionary proclamation which goes completely against this idea which is widely accepted in the world as an established fact. 'Human *Fitrat'* is such an expression which has been sounded into human ears for centuries, and in this way, it has adopted the status of an established truth. But the reality is that man has no *Fitrat*. We call the nature of something as those fundamental characteristics which are present in a thing from the time of its birth, and according to which it is obliged to live its life. The nature of water is to flow downhill. The nature of fire is to provide heat. The nature of sheep is to eat grass. The nature of a lion is to eat meat and to not even glance at the grass. All these things of the universe and animals are obligated to live their life according to their own individual nature. They cannot change their nature. *Fitrat* is meant to be immutable.

As far as the animal life of humans is concerned (i.e. the physical life), the laws of nature are applicable to it in the same way as for animals. But there is nothing in his life as a human being which can be called his *Fitrat*. This was the mistaken belief regarding human *Fitrat* - that a group of people declared that evil is inherently present in the nature of man. The doctrine that 'every human child is born sinful' is the product of this same wrong concept. On the other hand, there is an optimistic group of people whose doctrine is that man happens to be noble by nature. Both these beliefs are *Batil* (wrong). Man is neither naturally good nor bad. Certain potentials have been kept in him and those too in an undeveloped form. It has been left to his choice: (1) whether he develops these potentials or leaves them unrealised and (2) when he develops these he can then use these however he likes. If he uses these for constructive purposes for mankind it will be called righteousness; if he uses these for destructive purposes it will be called evil.

The guidance of *Wahi* informs us of the method by which to develop these potentials and their correct application. That which has been quoted above from some of the verses of the Quran, that man is such and such, is only to show that if man does not live according to the light of *Wahi*, and declares the fulfilment of his physical needs alone as being his purpose in life, then he becomes just like this. But if he uses his potentials in the light of *Wahi*, then his attributes will be those which the Quran declares as 'the life of a Momin' i.e. such a life which is at peace from inner conflicts, and due to which the whole of mankind remains at peace also.

It should be again reiterated that '*Fitrat*' and 'choice and intent' are two opposing things. *Fitrat* belongs to the 'helpless', not to the one who possesses choice and intent, and since man has been given choice and the ability to decide, he has therefore no *Fitrat* - neither good nor evil. He becomes good or evil by the choice of his actions.

## 3.6 The Voice of Conscience

Just as this belief is incorrect that the ability to differentiate between good and evil is contained in the *Fitrat* of man, similarly this idea is also incorrect that there is another thing contained in man which is called his conscience[72] and which differentiates between good and bad and between virtue and evil. This concept is also wrong. The voice of conscience is formed from man's early upbringing, training and his social environment. In reality, this is internalised society (as the following of forefathers is called society divinised).[73] From these brief explanations, it becomes evident that the techniques used for the guidance of other things in the universe by Allah have not been used in the case of man.

## 3.7 Guidance for Man

The technique adopted in the case of man was to select an individual from among men themselves, and through him guidance was provided via *Wahi*, by travelling in the light of which the caravan of humanity could reach its destination. The selected person (who was called *Nabi* and *Rasul*[74]) would pass this guidance on to other human beings. In Surah *Al A'raf* it is stated:

*O you Children of Adam! Whenever there come to you messengers from amongst you, rehearsing My signs unto you, those who are righteous and mend (their lives), on them shall be no fear nor shall they grieve. (7:35)*

---

[72] This is why it is said that man should follow the voice of his conscience.
[73] This aspect has been discussed in other books and articles of mine so further details are not given here e.g. see *Islam: A Challenge to Religion.*
[74] *Nabi* (pl. *Anbiya*) is the status of a messenger as a recipient of revelation from Allah and *Rasul* refers to the status of passing on the revelation to mankind. (Ed)

O mankind! When from amongst you, My messengers come to you and present My commands to you, whoever from amongst you follows these laws and mends his ways, then on such people there will be no fear and no grief.

We have seen (in previous pages) that when any of a species gets guidance directly from Allah (e.g. animals), that entity is then obliged to spend life according to this guidance. But man is given choice and the ability to make decisions, therefore in his case the technique selected for guidance is such that his ability to choose and make decisions is not curbed. This is the reason that, in explaining this form of guidance, Allah has stated clearly that in this respect every individual is free: he who wishes can live life according to it, he who wishes can go against it:

> Say, 'The truth is from your Sustainer': Let him who will believe, and let him who will, reject (it)…(18:29)

Whatever path he selects, the consequences will be according to this selection.

## 3.8 *Wahi* Is Not Based on Human Effort

In the same way that the revelation given to things of the universe is not a product of these things themselves (they receive it directly from Allah), similarly, the revelation sent from Allah to the messengers is not a product of their own intellect and thinking. In other words, the possessor of revelation does not discover the truth through his own effort and striving. The truth reveals itself on him. The receipt of revelation in this way from an external source (objectivity) is described by the Quran using the word *Nazul* (descends). This means that instead of these truths emerging outwards from within man, they are received by man from the outside. It is stated in the Quran:

> Verily it is We Who have revealed the Book to you in Truth…(39:2)

The descent of revelation means that man does not obtain it through his own skill and ability, effort and exertion, instead the individual selected by Allah gets it without any work or effort:

> …But Allah chooses for His special Mercy whom He will…(2:105)

> Nor does he say (aught) of (his own) Desire. It is no less than inspiration sent down to him…(53:3-4)

The one who is receiving this revelation does not have even an iota of his own ideas contained within it. He says nothing of his own thoughts, inclinations and preferences. This is revelation which is made to descend on him. Since we cannot

71

comprehend the nature of revelation, it is not only difficult for us to understand it but is in fact impossible. So, in one area, he (like other human beings) makes such conversation which is the outcome of his own thinking and choices, and in another domain he explains such realities which are neither the product of his own intellect and reasoning, nor has he read or learnt this or heard it from someone else. But the life of a *Nabi* used to be divided into this kind of two domains. This was the reason why, when the opponents used to ask Rasul-ullah to make slight modifications to these laws which were presented before them, so that some form of compromise could be made, it was said to them in reply:

> *...(They) say: 'Bring us a reading other than this, or change this,' Say: 'It is not for me, of my own accord, to change it: I follow naught but what is revealed unto me'...(10:15)*

It is not possible for me to make any alterations to it of my own accord. I only follow that which is sent to me through the process of revelation.

## 3.9 A *Nabi* Has No Prior Knowledge of it Whatsoever

Since *Wahi* was not the outcome of the hard work and effort of the individual, he (before becoming a *Nabi*) would not have even the slightest inkling or knowledge that he will receive this revelation. In Surah *Al Shura* it is stated:

> *And thus have We, by Our Command, sent inspiration to you: you knew not (before) what was Revelation, and what was Eimaan...(42:52)*

So much so, that he had not the slightest expectation of it:

> *And you had not expected that the Book would be sent to you. This is sent as a Mercy from your Sustainer... (28:86)*

You could not have had any anticipation of this, that this Book will be descended in your direction. This is purely the outcome of the mercy of Allah that you have become the possessor of *Wahi*.

But this does not mean that the crown of *Wahi* would be placed on the head of any individual found roaming about in the streets – not in the slightest. The training of whichever righteous self it was decided would be the ultimate intended recipient of *Wahi* would be under the direct scrutiny of Allah right from the start.

## 3.10  Training of a *Nabi*

Hence, in the narration in the Quran of the event regarding Moses, when the revelation was bestowed on him on the summits of Mount Tur, he expressed his feelings of gratitude to Allah and said that this is a great favour from You. In reply to this, Allah said this is not Our first favour on you for which you are being grateful. The course of these favours had started a long time before this from the day you were born and we told your mother to put you in a chest and float you down the river. Then, your upbringing took place in the palaces of Pharaoh, so that, despite being a member of an oppressed people, you become familiar with the machinations of politics (because you were ultimately going to stand in opposition to them). Then, from there you were taken to the valleys of Madian, so that you could pass some days of your life in the open natural environment. You were ultimately going to train the Bani Israel in these very valleys. When you (O Moses) were put through all these stages:

*...Then did you come here as ordained, O Moses! and I have prepared you for Myself (for service)...(20:40-41)*

And We selected you for our mission – it is not that you come for fire and receive messenger-hood. The supervision of the righteous self which was to house the revelation was carried out by Allah Himself from the start. This statement, that his supervision was undertaken by the Divine Self, does not mean that the life of the *Nabi* was like a machine controlled by Allah, and that he did not do anything of his own accord. The *Nabi*, just like other human beings, had the freedom to make choices in all his deeds and whatever he did was according to his choice and intent. He was therefore declared responsible for all of his actions.

From this account it is clear that the *Wahi* received by a *Nabi* is completely different from that thing which is called 'religious experience' or 'revelations of a mystic'. These acts and manifestations are the outcome of his own human exertion and skill, these are not the consequences of *Wahi*. This is just the manifestation of the hidden potentials of man which takes place through a particular technique and practice. For this there is no need for a certain belief or religion.[75] Since messenger-hood ended on Rasul-ullah, the issue of continuation of *Wahi* has consequently stopped. Thus, in Islam the 'hidden experience' of anyone has no authenticity or status. Nor is there any possibility now of anyone having conversation with Allah. The only means to converse with Allah was through *Wahi* which ended on the person of Rasul-Ullah. Apart from *Wahi*, there is no mention in the Quran of any method of acquiring knowledge directly from Allah. Terms like *Kashaf, Ilhaam*[76] etc

---

[75] For further details on this see my book, *Tasawaf ki Haqeeqat (The Truth of Mysticism)*.
[76] *Kashaf, Ilhaam* – these terms are used to mean making contact with the Divine to obtain messages. (Ed)

are later terms which have nothing to do with the Quran. This is also a fundamental characteristic on the basis of which 'Deen' (Islam) becomes separate from *Madhab* (religion). The greatest ability of man in *Madhab* is said to be that he talks with Allah directly. Deen (Islam) states that the proclamation of Allah is preserved in His last Book and the task of man is to live his life in accordance with this *Wahi*. The consequence of following it will lead to prosperity in this life and successes in the life after death. Its outcome is not to gain any kind of 'hidden knowledge'. Hiddenness and Deen are two opposite things.

## 3.11 Responsibilities of Messenger-hood

Now let us proceed from here. The claimants of 'hidden practices' (mystics) say that the state of the person who sees some glimpse of reality becomes such that he is lost in this euphoric and ecstatic state. Therefore, never mind passing on the details of these feelings to others, they have no cognisance of themselves either. But when a *Nabi* becomes exposed to the reality (i.e. he receives *Wahi*), he is given great responsibilities. He has to communicate his *Wahi* to other human beings. And not only to pass it on, but according to this, he has to establish in practical terms a new society in place of the former (wrong) society. These are the great responsibilities referred to when Rasul-ullah is told:

*And removed from you is your burden, the which did gall your back. 94:2-3)*

Iqbal states this truth in a very striking manner. He writes:

*'Muhammad of Arabia ascended the highest Heaven and returned. I swear by God that if I had reached that point, I should never have returned.'*
*These are the words of a great Muslim saint, Abdul Quddus of Gangob. In the whole range of sufi literature, it will be, probably, difficult to find words which, in a single sentence, disclose such acute perception of the psychological difference between the prophetic and mystic types of consciousness. The mystic does not wish to return from the repose of 'unitary experience'; and when he does return, as he must, his return does not mean much for mankind at large. The prophet's return is creative. He returns to insert himself into the sweep of time with a view to control the forces of history, and thereby to create a fresh world of ideals. For the mystic, the repose of 'unitary experience' is something final; for the prophet it is awakening, within him, of world-shaking psychological forces, calculated to completely transform the human world. The desire to see his religious experience transformed into a living world-force, is supreme in the prophet. Thus his return amounts to a kind of pragmatic test of the value of his religious experience. In its creative act the prophet's will judges both itself and the world of concrete fact in which it endeavours to objectify itself. In penetrating the impervious material before him, the prophet discovers himself for himself, and unveils himself to the eye of history. Another way of judging the value of the prophet's religious*

*experience, therefore, would be to examine the type of manhood that he has created, and the cultural world that has sprung out of the spirit of his message.*[77]

This trait of a *Nabi*, (that he receives *Wahi* from Allah), is commonly called *Nabuwat*, and it is this responsibility that he has to pass on this *Wahi* to others and establish a new world according to it which is known as *Risalat*. To carry out this responsibility of *Risalat*, he has to gather those people around him who have determined to live their life under the guidance of *Wahi*. This is that group which becomes the companion of Allah in order to disclose the beauty of the universe, and to bring out the results in human society as per the Law of Requital of Allah according to human calculation and counting. This is called the *Jamaat-e-Momineen*.

From the above discussion, the following reality will have become apparent:

(1) Everything in the universe receives guidance from Allah to live life so that it can reach its intended destination.

(2) This guidance is kept inside everything from the beginning, it does not come from outside. The things of the universe are constrained to live their life according to this internal guidance – this is called their *Fitrat* (nature), which is immutable.

(3) Since man has been created with the ability to choose and be responsible, that technique of giving guidance has not therefore been adopted in his case, according to which he would have been forced to live. Hence, this guidance has not been kept inside him.

(4) For him, this technique has been adopted - that from among men one individual is to be selected and *Wahi* is to be sent to him. He will then pass on this revelation to other people and those who accept the truth of this *Wahi*, i.e. have Eimaan in it, will come together and shape such a society in which the human self can keep developing.

(5) The guidance which a *Nabi* received (*Wahi*) from Allah was free from any effect of his own intellect, thoughts, ideas and desires. This is because the guidance of *Wahi* is not the product of the human intellect.

## 3.12 Process of Revelation

The Quran tells us that when man started living his social life and there was a clash in their mutual interests as a consequence (which it metaphorically calls 'the story of Adam'), then the process of *Wahi* started for his guidance. Its declaration is that

---

[77] M. Iqbal, *The Reconstruction of Religious Thought in Islam*, Chapter V, The Spirit of Muslim Culture, pp. 124-125.

*Anbiya* were sent to every tribe and nation for this purpose from Allah. Principally, they all had the same message and invitation:

*We have sent you inspiration, as We sent it to Noah and the Messengers after him...(4:163)*

Since the initial addressees of the Quran were Arabs, therefore those messengers have been mentioned by name with whom these Arabs were well versed e.g. Noah, Abraham, Ishmael, Isaac, Joseph, Moses, Aaron, David, Solomon, Jesus etc. and details of the rest are not given:

*Of some messengers We have already told you the story; of others We have not...(4:164)*

But whether a messenger has been mentioned or not, an individual cannot become a Muslim unless he has Eimaan on this fact that messengers kept coming to every nation of the world and they received the true teaching from Allah. If someone differentiates in their being messengers, then he cannot be a Muslim (2:285).

## 3.13  End of Messenger-hood

In the very beginning, the human mind was immature and his knowledge was very faulty, therefore he was provided with details through *Wahi* for even minor matters. This process continued in this way till that period was reached in human history following which human knowledge was to expand on a daily basis - metaphorically we can understand it by saying that man had grown beyond childhood and reached adulthood. There was a need now to provide him with those Permanent Values in their complete form which were required for the development of humanity. And after this he was free to exercise his choices, while remaining within the four walls of these values, according to the needs of his era, using his intellect and vision to define his own paths in life. Hence these values were given in the Quran for the last time through the last messenger, Mohammad. The responsibility for maintaining the integrity[78] of the Quran was taken by Allah Himself:

*We have, without doubt, sent down the Message; and We will assuredly protect it. (15:9)*

---

[78] This fact is proved through historical evidence that the Quran is the same, word for word, which was revealed to the last messenger of Allah. Contrary to this, no other people claim or prove that the book revealed to the founders of their religions remains with them in its original form.

And after this the practice of messenger-hood was ended. The ending of 'messenger-hood' is in reality the greatest revolution in human history. Following this, except for those defined limits which have been stated in the Quran, man gained complete freedom in the business of his life. The purpose of these limits is that there should be no mutual conflict and thus the caravan of humanity should, through mutual cooperation and support, take life to higher summits. Now there are only two sources of guidance for man – the Quranic teaching, and human knowledge and vision. This teaching of the Quran is for the whole of mankind, and by having Eimaan in it, man is declared a Muslim.

Now this question arises, as to how to have Eimaan in these laws (*Wahi*) i.e. how do those people who accept these as being the truth, reach this conclusion that these laws are true. The discussion concerning this will be covered in the next chapter, in which the relationship between *Wahi* and human intellect will be clarified.

## 3.14  What Does it Mean to Have Eimaan in Allah

Before we turn the page over to the next chapter, it is imperative to understand one important fact. We have seen that for human guidance there is a need for *Wahi*, and that *Wahi* is not the product of human intellect – it is received from Allah. Therefore, the practical meaning of Eimaan in Allah means to have Eimaan in the revelation bestowed by Him.

One status of Allah is that He is the Creator of the universe. The system of the universe is functioning under the laws established by Him. He is the one who possesses control of these laws. There is a group of thinkers and scientists in the West who have Eimaan in this particular status of Allah, but as far as human guidance is concerned, they consider human intellect to be sufficient for this and do not accept the concept of revelation from Allah. The title of the book by Julian Huxley, 'Religion Without Revelation,' reflects this line of thinking. According to the Quran, this type of Eimaan in Allah is not in reality termed as Eimaan. The Quran states about such followers of God:

*Say: 'To whom belong the earth and all beings therein? If you know!' (23:84)*

Regarding the earth and whatever is in it, ask them Whose programme is it that all these things are engaged in accomplishing and Who is their Owner and Sovereign. And, along with this, say that they should give a reply based not on ignorance and prejudice but given in the light of knowledge and vision. They will truly say in reply that all this is for the completion of the programme of Allah and He is indeed the Master of it all, because from the wellspring of knowledge, no other reply apart from this can be obtained. After this, the Quran says that when your knowledge and vision take you to this conclusion, then why do you not bring forth the real truth in front of you (23:85). The Quran then says to them:

*Say: 'Who is the Sustainer of the seven heavens, and the Sustainer of the Throne (of Glory) Supreme?' (23:85)*

Ask them, Who has control over the galaxies floating in the heavens? Indeed, ask them, Who has the central authority and sovereignty over the whole of the universe. In reply to this, too, they will say it is in Allah's Hand. After this, the Quran says, ask them, when this is the truth then why do you not pay attention to it? Then the Quran says, question them:

*Say: 'Who is it in whose hands is the governance of all things - Who protects (all), but is not protected (of any)? If you know.' (23:88)*

Who has control and sovereignty over the universe? Who is He towards Whom everything looks for its refuge and protection. And whoever goes against His law will not find refuge anywhere. Say, what answer does your knowledge and vision have for this? In reply to this, too, their answer will be that all this is happening according to the laws of Allah.

After acceptance by these people of the functioning of the Divine laws in the outer universe, the Quran states, ask them that, when their knowledge and vision brings them to this conclusion that all things are working according to the Divine laws, then why are they deceived in this, that the Divine laws are not required in the human world – and that here man can live life according to his own manmade laws (23:89). For human life also, permanent and immutable laws can only be obtained from Allah (23:90). But if they do not accept this truth and consider Eimaan in Allah to mean only having Eimaan in the God who is controlling the external universe, then they are liars in their claim. The Quran states:

*We have sent them the Truth: but they indeed practice falsehood! (23:90)*

The claim of having Eimaan in Allah belongs only to the one who, along with acceptance of the sovereignty of Allah in the outer universe, also has Eimaan in this reality that guidance to man is also only received from Allah. This is called *Wahi* (revelation). In other words, without Eimaan in *Wahi*, there remains no truth in having Eimaan in Allah. In the words of Ouspensky:

*If there is no idea of revelation, there is no religion. And in religion there is always something unknowable by the ordinary mind and ordinary thinking. For this reason, no attempts to create an artificial synthetic religion by intellectual methods have ever led, or can ever lead anywhere.*[79]

Therefore, in order to have Eimaan in Allah it is necessary to have Eimaan in *Wahi*. This Eimaan is called Eimaan in the messengers and in the Books of Allah. Because the Quran from Allah is descended *Wahi* in its final, complete and explained code, and mankind has received this through Mohammad, Rasul-ullah (who is the last in the chain of *Anbiya* and messengers), Eimaan in the Quran and Mohammad Rasul-ullah is therefore an essential part of Eimaan in Allah.

---

[79] P. D. Ouspensky, *A New Model of the Universe*, p. 34

# 4 INTELLECT AND DEEN

In the previous chapter, the fact that the development of the human self occurs through those laws which are received through *Wahi* and that *Wahi* is not a product of the human intellect, was presented. Its source is not the human mind. This does not mean that the facts and the system of life which revelation puts forward cannot be understood through human intellect either. This point will be clarified later.

## 4.1    Limits of Human Intellect

At this point, this much should be understood, that intellect also strives to discover the truth, but just as an eye (without binoculars) can only see up to a certain extent and not beyond it, similarly the scope of the intellect has certain limits. It is not able to do any research and investigation about matters which are outside this scope.[80] Secondly, whatever research is done through the use of human intellect, we can never truly say at any point that this is the final word on this subject - i.e. that there is nothing beyond this. In this regard, a professor of physics, Professor James Arnold Crowther of Reading University, writes:

*'The system of nature is so enthralling in its profound basic simplicity that in the world of science the final word on any subject has to be left to the last man'. (Translated from Urdu).*

This limitation and scope of the intellect is with regard to the external universe. As far as the human world is concerned, in this its mode of research is different. In this connection, its technique is empirical.

## 4.2    Empirical Technique

Human intellect takes a single issue, ponders on a solution for it, and then begins to experiment on this solution. After experimenting for centuries, it is found that the experiment has failed and that particular solution was wrong. Then it considers another solution, and starts to experiment on this and in this way after many failed experiments it achieves success. During this period, the degree of loss which humanity suffers can be judged from the pages of history. For example, when man started living a social life, his intellect wished to decide what sort of system should be devised for the solution of his collective matters and the mutual conflicts between individuals, tribes, and nations. He started this experiment with autocratic rule. The experience of centuries showed that this method is very damaging for the development of humanity. He then came up with another solution. When this

---

[80] For example, Dr Atex, ex-Director of California Observatory, states, 'We do not know anything about the beginning and end of the universe'. From his book, *The Great Design*.

one failed as well, another solution was put forward. In this way, gradually and slowly, it (intellect) has reached the stage of democracy. Now, consider how many centuries it took for the human intellect to reach democracy from the initial form of government, and during this period how many rivers of blood mankind had to swim through, and how many ditches of fire had to be negotiated. And even this democracy does not provide a guarantee of peace and tranquility. With this one illustration, we can imagine and evaluate other issues of life.

## 4.3    Religion and Intellect

We have seen above that the scope of action of the intellect is limited and its modus operandi is empirical. But its limitation does not mean that man should chase it with a stick and throw it out of the human world. If the eye can only see to a certain limit and cannot go beyond this, it does not mean that a sane individual should burst his eye due to this limitation. But the self-created religion of people (whose basis in reality is of that mysticism which originates from an erroneous view of Plutonic thought) did this very thing to human intellect. All the religious literature of the world (whether belonging to *Shariat* or *Tariqat*[81]) is filled not only with repudiation and criticism of the intellect, but is full of condemnation and denunciation. So much so, that even our prevalent religion (i.e. that of Muslims), which is a derivative of this same mysticism or is a collection of beliefs influenced by it, in the pursuit of this, declares the same about the human intellect. Hence, from every podium and platform of ours this voice is raised that the intellect and Eimaan are two contradictory elements which can never co-exist in one place. Eimaan is the name of shutting your eyes and blindly accepting something - Eimaan cannot be attained through intellect, reasoning, wisdom, sense, knowledge, vision, logic and evidence. And then to support such a doctrine, such invented narrations are presented in which (for example) it is stated the place of foolish people is paradise. This is the state of the followers of *Shariat*. The followers of *Tariqat* are a hundred steps ahead even of them. It appears that the whole mission of their life is only to condemn intellect and reasoning so severely that no sane person should wish to come anywhere near this 'evil'. Amongst them, knowledge is declared to be *Hijab-e-Akbar* (the great veil).

## 4.4    Intellect and the Quran

After looking at these self-created beliefs of people, let us see what the Quran says on this issue. If we wish to sum up the Quranic teachings in just a few words, then

---

[81]*Shariat* – laws based on historical sectarian understanding as per the books of *Ahadeeth* (sayings attributed to the last messenger Mohammad) and the Quran. Every sect of prevalent Islam has its own *Shariat*. *Tariqat* – this is an order or way related to the practices of sufism or mysticism. For more details see Wikipedia. (Ed)

we can declare unhesitatingly that the Quran is *Zarbe Kaleemi*[82] (strike by Moses) against 'Pharaonic trickeries' and *Taisha-e-Ibraheemi* (axe of Abraham) against stone idols. It uprooted all these destructive beliefs of life which were lying as a great obstacle in the path of humanity, from their roots. As far as the subject under discussion is concerned, it has bestowed a very high status to human intellect. First of all, we see that in an animal it accords the status of special differentiation to the trait of human intellect. It says that in the early stages of creation both man and animals had one path:

*...He began the creation of man with clay. (32:7)*

The beginning of human life was (like animals) also from inorganic matter. Then, after going through various evolutionary stages, it reached that point where the process of reproduction takes place through birth:

*And made his progeny from a quintessence of the nature of an insignificant fluid. (32:8)*

Up till this point there was no difference between man and other animals:

*But He fashioned him in due proportion...(32:9)*

Then, according to the law of evolution, after refining and perfecting him, a special balance and proportion was created in him. From here, that destination was reached from which he became different from other animals, so different that the Quran called it a 'new creation':

*...then we created out of it another creature...(23:14)*

At this stage Allah bestowed on him something of His energy:

*...and breathed into him something of His energy. And He gave you (the faculties of) hearing and sight and thinking (and understanding)...(32:9)*

You were given senses through which you process information about your external environment, and with these, given a mind from which you draw conclusions using your intellect and reasoning. After this, the Quran states that there are very few among you who use these correctly (32:9).

---

[82] *Zarbe Kaleemi* – this term is used regarding Moses and his strike against Pharaoh to topple his tyranny.

## 4.5    The Worst of Creation

The first stage of human knowledge is perceptual knowledge. After this, the second stage is conceptual knowledge. All this is a result of intellect and reasoning which is an exclusively human trait. No other creation of the universe shares this trait. The Quran explains in clear words that those who do not use this exclusive differentiating trait (i.e. intellect) are the worst of creation:

*For the worst of beasts in the sight of Allah are the deaf and the dumb - those who do not use intellect and reasoning. (8:22)*

In the world of religion, the ultimate aim of human life is declared to be to save oneself from the torment of hell. The Quran says, come and We will tell you which people will go to *Jahannum*[83]:

*Many are the Jinns[84] and men We have made for Hell (due to their deeds): They have hearts wherewith they understand not, eyes wherewith they see not, and ears wherewith they hear not. They are like cattle – nay, more misguided: for they are heedless (of warning). (7:179)*

About them in Surah *Al Furqan* it is also stated:

*Or do you think that most of them listen or understand? They are only like cattle - nay, they are worse astray from the Path. (25:44)*

Do you think that there is a majority among them who hear and make use of their intellect and reasoning? By no means. They are merely cattle, in fact even more astray than them. Cattle at least make use of whatever direction they receive from nature.

## 4.6    Who are the Inhabitants of *Jahannum* (Hell)

Regarding the inhabitants of hell, in another verse it is stated:

*They will further say: 'Had we but listened or used our intelligence, we should not (now) be among the companions of the Blazing Fire!' (67:10)*

In Surah *Yasin* it is stated that at the time of the manifestation of results, mankind will be reminded that you were told, do not follow 'Satan'[85], he is your open enemy.

---

[83] *Jahannum* – normally translated as hell.
[84] *Jinn* - here this refers to those people living in rural areas or who were nomads. (Ed)
[85] Human desires and emotions are referred to as 'Satan'. (Ed)

Only follow and obey Allah, as this is that very path which will take you to the intended destination of life:

*But he did lead astray a great multitude of you. Did you not then understand? (36:62)*

He misguided many parties among you. Did you not use your intellect and reasoning, that you became deceived by him? Now:

*This is the Hell of which you were warned! (36:63)*

This is that hell about which you were informed that, if you do not make use of your intellect and reasoning and if you follow your desires, your abode will be in it. From these explanations, it is clear that, according to the Quran:

(i) The differentiating trait between man and animals is the ability of intellect and reasoning.
(ii) Those people who do not use this ability live their life at the level of animals - indeed lower than them and are the worst of creation.
(iii) They are those people who 'Satan' traps in his web of deception and the ones whose abode is hell.

## 4.7    Reasoning and Insight

The invitation of the Quran is entirely an invitation based on knowledge and vision. At every step, it directs us to use our thinking and reasoning and places emphasis on the use of intellect and consciousness. It asks about those people who refuse this invitation:

*Do they not reflect in the Quran?...(4:82)*

These are the same people about whom in another place it is stated:

*Such are the men whom Allah has cursed for He has made them deaf and blinded their sight. Do they not then earnestly seek to understand the Quran, or are their hearts locked up by them? (47:23-24)*

These are those people who become deprived of the ability to think and reflect due to not using their intellect and reasoning. Despite having ears, they are deaf and despite having eyes, they are blind. It is astonishing that these people do not think and reflect on the Quran. What, do they have locks on their hearts? After explaining its commands and values, the Quran states:

*...Thus does Allah make clear to you His Signs: In order that you*

*may consider - (their bearings) on this life and the hereafter...(2:219-220)*

Allah makes His commands clear for you in an unambiguous fashion so that you are able to reflect and reason on their immediate benefits and on the consequences yet to become manifest in the future. Pay particular attention to the fact that in this verse emphasis is placed on thinking and reflecting on both 'this life and the life of the hereafter'.

## 4.8    Use of Intellect and Reason in War

In a situation when armies are facing each other in a battlefield, it is commonly said and understood that the army whose soldiers have emotions and sentiments of greater intensity will fight with greater courage and valour. Thus, they will be victorious. Intellect and reasoning has no place in war. If soldiers start to think in this situation, then none will be willing to lay down his life. Only blind emotions can be of use there. But even in this kind of place, the Quran emphasises making use of intellect and reasoning. It addresses the *Jamaat* of Momineen, saying that if among you there are one hundred soldiers who are those who will use courage and perseverance, then they will be able to overcome one thousand (or at least two hundred) of the enemy's men. This is because:

*...if a hundred, they will vanquish a thousand of the Unbelievers: for these are a people without understanding. (8:65)*

The opposing party does not make use of intellect and reasoning, whereas you never let the faculties of thinking and reasoning slip from your grasp, even during such a trying time.

From the above it is clear how much importance the Quran assigns to intellect and reasoning. In this regard, there is a verse in Surah *Saba* which is so comprehensive that in it the Quran has condensed all these details in just a few words and if it were said that on this subject this is the last word, then it would not be an exaggeration. Now reflect that Rasul-ullah remained busy throughout his life in inviting and preaching and presenting the Quranic teaching to the people in various ways. Day and night, he remained engaged in announcing and disseminating his message. It is obvious that Quranic teaching has many aspects and facets. It embraces every aspect of human life. The vastness of its teaching does not recognize any limits and is boundless. But ponder on this, that for this kind of vast and boundless knowledge, its messenger addresses his listeners, saying, 'I do not wish to say a great deal – I only wish to say one thing, just one thing':

*Say: 'I do admonish you on one point: that you do stand up before Allah – (it may be) in pairs, or (it may be) singly...(34:46)*

Just imagine how important will this one matter be? It will be such a description into which the whole teaching of Islam can be condensed and which is the hallmark of this Divine guidance. Every person will be eager to listen to such a description, if not to accept it, then even simply out of curiosity as to what it is.

After this, the messenger says to them that this is not such a fact which can be listened to while just sauntering along – it needs to be heard by halting and standing stock still. If you all do not wish to stop, then it is fine, you can stop singly, or in pairs, and stop for Allah's sake. Reflect how, in this manner, what psychological refinements are implied. When, in this way, he had drawn all attention towards him, he said, so listen to what that one thing is which I wish to relate to you, and within which all other matters are encompassed. That one thing is:

*...and reflect within yourself...(34:46)*

## 4.9    Reflect

Pay attention and reflect, think, endeavour to understand, use your intellect – once you start to use intellect and reasoning then you will adopt the right path; this is because the invitation that we extend to the right path is an invitation based on evidence and reason. Our appeal only occurs through knowledge, vision, reasoning and wisdom:

*Say you: This is my way: I do invite unto Allah - on evidence clear as the seeing with one's eyes - I and whoever follows me...(12:108)*

If you have a disagreement with this invitation, then present your argument and evidence in support of your assertion:

*...Say: Produce your evidence if you are truthful. (2:111)*

## 4.10    Present your Reasoning

To keep on wrangling like this without knowledge and vision, and facts and evidence, can never be called the right approach:

*...but why do you dispute in matters of which you have no knowledge?...(3:66)*

Leaving aside disputing with others, you yourself should not argue about something regarding which you have no knowledge:

*And pursue not that of which you have no knowledge...(17:36)*

And then the knowledge should not be guesswork, and sceptical. It should be such certain knowledge the evidence for which is provided by your hearing, your seeing and your mind. The Quran states:

*...for every act of hearing, or of seeing or of (feeling in) the heart will be enquired into. (17:36)*

As has already been stated, the beginning of knowledge is with perceptual knowledge. Hearing and seeing relates to this knowledge, and our mind relates to conceptual knowledge. Therefore, only that knowledge is capable of being called knowledge in which the evidence of the senses and support of the mind is present. Presumption and conjecture can never be called knowledge.

## 4.11    Presumption and Conjecture is not Knowledge

Therefore, regarding those who oppose the truth, the Quran states:

*But they have no knowledge therein. They follow nothing but conjecture; and conjecture avails nothing against Truth. (53:28)*

Leaving aside presumption and conjecture, in this regard the Quran goes so far as to state that merely casting a cursory glance at something is not enough. Only that observation in which thinking and reasoning is involved has any meaning. Hence, regarding those people who used to attend the meetings, sermons and gatherings of Rasul-ullah, and used to watch and listen to him perfunctorily while their thoughts were adrift elsewhere, the Quran states:

*If you call them to guidance, they hear not. You will see them looking at you, but they see not. (7:198)*

They appear to you as if they are looking at you but in truth they see not. This subtle difference between *Nazar* (simply looking with the eyes) and *Basr* (comprehending what is being said while seeing) is worth examining. As the Quran states:

*Among them are some who (pretend to) listen to you: But can you make the deaf to hear - even though they are without understanding? (10:42)*

But since they do not listen to your words with their hearts, they do not reflect on what is being said and do not make use of their intellect and reasoning. Therefore, this listening of theirs is not in reality hearing. These are not those who have eyes, but are, in reality, blind:

*And among them are some who look at you: but can you guide the blind - even though they will not see? (10:43) See also (47:16)*

## 4.12 Merely Knowing the Language is Not Sufficient

Some people say that those people whose native language is Arabic (or those who understand Arabic) must be familiar with the meanings of the Quran. It is correct that to understand the meanings of a book it is essential to know the language in which the book has been written. But it does not necessarily follow that by merely knowing the language, the meanings of this book will also be comprehended. In order to understand its meanings, it is necessary to make use of thinking and reasoning, and intellect and mindfulness. This is why, in Surah *Hud*, in reply to the invitation of the messenger Shuaib, his people used to say:

*They said: 'O Shuaib! much of what you say we do not understand'...(11:91)*

Even though it is obvious that Shuaib used to converse with his people in their own language. In the case of Rasul-ullah himself, the first recipients were the Arabs, but from amongst them only those accepted Eimaan who used to ponder over the message of the revelation using their intellect and reasoning. The ones who did not do this were not able to recognise the truth and reality of this message. When the messenger used to reflect on their condition, and see how the wrong path on which they were treading was leading them to the hell of destruction and ruin, his heart would ache like that of a zealous physician, and he wished to somehow or other bring them onto the right path and save them from destruction, even if force had to be used on them for this. In reply to this wish and desire of his, it was stated that Eimaan is only that which is accepted after rational thinking and reasoning.

## 4.13 Eimaan is Only That Which is Based on Rational Thinking and Reasoning

Any argument which is accepted through force is not Eimaan (because Eimaan is accepted with the willingness of the heart and the satisfaction of the mind). See, in this regard the Quran states:

*You would only, perchance, fret yourself to death, following after them, in grief, if they believe not in this Message. (18:6)*

Even though, if the purpose had been to make people Muslims by force, then what difficulty was there for Allah in simply creating man in such a way that he (like other animals) would be obliged to follow a single path only. But he did not do this purposely. He has given man free will and choice, and the inevitable consequence of this freedom to choose is that whichever path he wishes, he can adopt:

*If it had been your Sustainer's Will, they would all have believed - all who are on earth! Will you then compel mankind, against their will, to believe! (10:99)*

It is therefore wrong that you should attempt to make people Momin by force. Eimaan is achieved according to Allah's established laws:

*No self can believe, except by the Will (Law) of Allah, and He will place doubt on those who will not understand. (10:100)*

Those people who do not make use of their intellect and reasoning, remain in doubt and suspicion, and the truth is never made plain to them. In their sight, the matter is never clear, therefore only those who make use of their intellect and reasoning can accept Eimaan.

Here the Quran states that if someone is made to accept something by force, it can never be called Eimaan. Eimaan is only that which is based on intellect and reasoning. It is obvious from this that to coerce someone means that this person is not able to use his intellect and reasoning. One form of such coercion is putting a sword on someone's head and saying to him, accept whatever you are being told, otherwise you will be beheaded. It is obvious that in this situation the question of using one's own intellect and reasoning, and making a decision based on free choice does not even arise. The second form is to suspend intellect and understanding through some other method, so that the individual does not even remain capable of thinking and understanding, and by being thus suppressed by another, rather through fear, accepts whatever he asserts. This is called superstition.

## 4.14 Eimaan Cannot be Accepted by Seeing a Miracle

In several places, the Quran, addressing Rasul-ullah, states that these people demand of you, show us a miracle then we will have Eimaan at your invitation. Tell them that Eimaan means to accept something through the use of intellect and reasoning - to accept something after seeing a miracle cannot be called Eimaan. For example, a person claims that whatever I say to you is absolutely true and its proof is that I can walk on fire. It is obvious that his walking on fire cannot be termed as proof for his first claim. Hence, the Quran has made it clear that Rasul-ullah was not given any miracle other than the Quran. It states in Surah *Al An'am*:

*If their spurning is hard on your mind, yet if you were able to seek a tunnel in the ground or a ladder to the heavens and bring them a sign - (what good?). If it were Allah's Will, He could gather them together unto true guidance: so be not you among those who are swayed by ignorance (and impatience)! Those who listen (in truth), be sure, will accept (it): as to the dead, Allah will raise them up; then will they be turned unto Him. (6:35-36)*

O messenger, if this matter weighs heavily on you as to why these people are rejecting your message, then if you possess the ability to do so, find a tunnel in the earth or erect some ladder up to the heavens, and in this way show them some miracle (you can try doing this but it will not be possible to make them Momin in this way).

If the aim was to make everyone a Momin in this way by force, then Allah could have done this with great ease according to his Law of Will. Therefore, do not become one among those who are ignorant of reality, despite knowing everything that you do. Remember that only those who listen to the message of truth with their hearts say *Labaik* (yes, I accept it).

## 4.15    The Ability to Reason Vanishes

The Quran has also stated that, regarding those people who do not use their intellect and reasoning due to arrogance and prejudice, or due to the following of ancestors blindly and because of ignorance, then after a period of time not even a vestige of the ability to think and reason remains in them. This is a great truth for which the Quran has provided guidance.  Biologists say that when a limb remains unused then after a while, nature, considering it to be redundant, makes it unusable - this species then becomes deprived of this limb forever. This is that reality towards which the Quran has signaled by saying that the people who make this their practice - that 'whatever is presented to us we will reject without thinking and reflecting and having once rejected it, we will continue to keep rejecting' - in them the ability to reason and reflect finishes:

*Indeed, those who disbelieve - it is all the same for them whether you warn them or do not warn them - they will not believe. Allah has set a seal upon their hearts and upon their hearing (as per His Law), and over their vision is a veil. And for them (as a consequence) is a great punishment. (2:6-7)*

For the people who adopt the path of rejection, warning them or not warning them of the destructive consequences of their life is equivalent. Having once rejected, they will never admit the truth. The consequence of their following such a path is that Allah's Law of Requital puts seals on their hearts and ears and their eyes are covered by drapes. Their end is extremely tragic. This is because:

*Then We sent after him messengers to their people, and they came to them with clear proofs. But they were not to believe in that which they had rejected before. Thus We seal over the hearts of the transgressors. (10:74)*

They reject truth and reality merely because previously either they or their ancestors have rejected this – in this way Allah's Law of Requital seals the hearts of these transgressors.

## 4.16  How Are Hearts Sealed?

These seals are the consequences of their very own actions:

*By no means! but on their hearts is the stain of that which they do. (83:14)*

The reality is not that which people think of their own accord, that Allah randomly puts seals on the hearts of people. The actual truth is that the deeds of these people themselves become 'rust' and stains their hearts. Their state is such that:

*Verily We have propounded for men, in this Quran every kind of Parable: But if you bring to them any Sign, the Unbelievers are sure to say, 'You do nothing but talk vanities.' Thus does Allah seal up the hearts of those who understand not. (30:58-59)*

When the Law of Allah is presented to them, they do not arrive at some conclusion by using their intellect and reasoning. Their first reaction is that this messenger giving the message is fraudulent. After this, they totally refuse to accept it; in this way Allah seals the hearts of those who do not make use of their intellect and vision:

*And who does more wrong than one who is reminded of the Signs of his Sustainer, but turns away from them, forgetting the (deeds) which his hands have sent forth? Verily We have set veils over their hearts lest they should understand this, and over their ears, deafness. If you call them to guidance, even then will they never accept guidance. (18:57)*

The sealing of hearts means that their hearts turn away from the truth, and all this because these people do not make use of their thinking and reasoning:

*... Allah has turned their hearts (from the light); for they are a people who understand not. (9:127)*

## 4.17    The 'Eyes' of the Hearts Become Blind

The Quran has made it clear that wherever it is stated that veils descend over the eyes of such people and they go blind, do not think that this means that the eyes on their faces split, and they actually become physically blind. No, this is not the case. The eyes on their faces do not become blind, it is the eyes of their hearts which are losing their light:

*Do they not travel through the earth, so that their hearts (and minds) may thus learn wisdom and their ears may thus learn to hear? Truly it is not their eyes that are blind, but their hearts which are in their chests. (22:46)*

## 4.18    Three Ways to Understand the Quran

In the verse quoted above, the Quran has directed travel through the earth. By this, the mind turns towards that aspect in which the Quran informs us of the method by which to understand it. It states that the technique to assess a message or a system is:

(1) Assess it in the light of the level to which the knowledge of your era has reached, and see what *Fatwa*[86] you get from the court of knowledge.
(2) Or, observe from among the nations of the past, what the consequences were of the nation which lived its life under this system, and what was the outcome of the one which went against it.
(3) And the third method is that, whichever group is following this system, let it work according to this peacefully, and after this its results will demonstrate themselves whether this system is true in its claims or false.

In Surah *Yunus* it is stated:

*Nay, they charge with falsehood that whose knowledge they cannot compass, even before the elucidation thereof has reached them: thus did those before them make charges of falsehood: but see what was the end of those who did wrong! (10:39)*

Reflect how the Quran, by suggesting these three methods, has clasped all aspects of knowledge and action in it. It has stated that either man should look at the Quranic truths via the point of view of knowledge – for this it is essential that he should have access to the latest facts of his era – or, he should ask the pages of

---

[86] *Fatwa* - a legal ruling or learned interpretation. (Ed)

history as to what was the outcome of living life according to such a system. And the third method is a pragmatic test according to which the outcome of any system can be judged to be right or wrong. This method encompasses all three eras – bygone eras through historical evidence[87], the state of development of knowledge of the modern era, and the outcome of actions and their impact on future time.

The third method was the one on which Rasul-ullah had put special emphasis because those people did not wish to learn any lessons from the fates of past nations, nor was their knowledge so wide that they could use it as a basis to check the proclamations of the Quran. Therefore, the messenger used to repeatedly tell them:

*Say: 'O my people! Do whatever you can: I will do (my part): soon will you know who it is whose end will be (best) in the Hereafter: certain it is that the wrong-doers will not prosper.' (6:135)*

It is evident from this that Eimaan in the revelation of the Quran can only be achieved through knowledge and reasoning, whether this is through ideological reasoning or through the evidence which you witness of the results of the system defined through revelation. In any case, the edifice of Eimaan is established on the foundation of knowledge and vision, and intellect and reasoning. Apart from this, there is no other way to understand and accept the truth.

## 4.19    The Blind One and the One Who Has Eyes Are Not Equal

The Quran has declared in very clear terms that the people who do not use knowledge and vision, and intellect and reasoning, can never be like those who make use of their intellect and reasoning:

*... Say: 'can the blind be held equal to the seeing?' Will you then understand not? (6:50) See also (11:24, 13:16)*

In another verse, it is stated:

*The blind and the seeing are not alike; nor are the depths of Darkness and the Light; nor are the shade and heat of the sun: nor are alike those that are living and those that are dead. Allah can make any that He wills (as per His Law) to hear; but you cannot make those hear who are (buried) in graves. (35:19-22)*

---

[87] The Quran puts great emphasis on historical evidence. This aspect is explained in a subsequent chapter.

The only one who can be made to hear (according to the Divine laws) is the one who himself wishes to listen. By condensing this reality into just a few words as follows, it is stated:

> ...Say: 'Are those equal, those who know and those who do not know?' It is those who are endued with understanding that pay attention. (39:9)

For those people who make use of intellect and reasoning, the paths in front of them leading towards Allah will keep opening up:

> And those who strive in Our (cause) - We will certainly guide them to our Paths: For verily Allah is with those who are righteous. (29:69)

Therefore, Eimaan is only acquired through intellect and reasoning, and to whatever great an extent any individual or any nation makes use of their intellect and reasoning, the paths of life before them will keep expanding to just as great a level.

## 4.20 What is the Motive of a Deed?

After Eimaan, the question of deeds comes before us, and regarding deeds it is said instinctively that these are exclusively related to emotions, not to intellect and reasoning. By provoking the emotions, you can motivate man to do ever greater tasks. In this way, he becomes willing for any kind of sacrifice, so much so that he does not even hesitate or waver in laying down his life. If, at this time, a man sits down to consult his intellect, it will never grant him permission for this sacrifice and selflessness. If you converse with anyone on this subject, he will present it as an established fact that only emotions can be the motive for action, not intellect. But in this aspect too, instead of being carried away by emotions, the Quran presents the reality. It states that by inciting emotions you can get someone to act on an emergency basis, but neither strength in actions is developed by this, nor does it help to develop character. It is through steadfastness and perseverance that character is shaped. Hence, in describing the traits of the Momineen, it states:

> Those who, when they are reminded with the Signs of their Sustainer, droop not down at them as if they were deaf or blind...(25:73)

## 4.21 Deeds Should Also be Based on Intellect and Reason

Obviously, when the instruction is to use intellect and reasoning in the case of the Divine commands themselves as well, then how can it be declared admirable to be inclined to act in other matters merely on the basis of emotions. The truth is that trust can never be put in emotive people. It is possible that at one time you may inflame their emotions to the extent of even laying down their life, but on another occasion, they may not be willing to even give you an *anna*[88]. Trust and reliance can only be placed on those who adopt a path based on their intellect and reasoning, and whatever step they take is after due thinking and reasoning. These are the people who will steadfastly tread the highway of life with determination and perseverance, and will thus ultimately reach their desired destination. About them, the Quran says:

*In the case of those who say, 'Our Sustainer is Allah', and, further, stand straight and steadfast, the angels (universal forces) descend on them: Fear you not! nor grieve! but receive the Glad Tidings of the Garden (of Bliss), the which you were promised!*
*(41:30)*

## 4.22   One Doubt

At this point an important and delicate question arises which befuddles the minds of those who think cursorily – they say that all the trouble and suffering prevailing in the world is not due to those who are foolish, but is because of those people who possess great mastery in intellect and reasoning. The world is, in reality, an arena of a battle of wits. Here, from morning till night, a battle continues between intellects: the one who is the greatest master of intellect and intelligence is the most cunning and clever, and snatches away everything from those of lower intelligence by the use of deception. Moving forward from individuals, this is the same situation for nations. The nation which is more astute, enslaves (politically or economically) the nation which has less intellect.

## 4.23   Intellect Itself is Devious

Not only does their intellect continually communicate such tricks to them through which they keep fleecing the nations possessing less intellect, it also provides such reasoning which justifies their political and economic ruses, making these appear very attractive and pleasing in the eyes of the world. So much so that, at times, based on such reasoning, these actions begin to appear admirable in the eyes of these individuals or nations themselves and they unwittingly begin to view themselves as being righteous. In other words, human intellect not only deceives others but also deceives the person possessing this intellect. Professor Joad's remarks deserve careful consideration:

*Reason tends to be exhibited as a mere tool or hand-maid of desire. Its function is to secure the ends which we unconsciously set ourselves, by inventing excuses for what we instinctively want to do, and arguments which we instinctively want to believe...Reason*

---

[88] *Anna* -  an old currency of the Indian sub-continent. Sixteen *annas* equalled one rupee. (Ed)

*is the power of deceiving ourselves into believing that what we want to think true, is in fact true.*[89]

In another place, he says:

*A man's thought follows his desire much as the feet of a hungry dog follow his nose.*[90]

The Quran also supports this reality that if man is overtaken by his emotions and makes these his 'god' (like a drunk), his intellect does not remain capable of guiding him correctly. The Quran states:

*Do you see such a one who takes for his god his own passion? Could you be a disposer of affairs for him? Or do you think that most of them listen or understand? They are only like cattle - nay, they are worse astray in Path. (25:43-44)*

## 4.24   Desires Enslaving Intellect

They do not remain as humans but instead descend to the level of animals, in fact even worse. In another verse, it is further clarified that those people who keep following their desires gradually reach such a state that even the ability to think and reason no longer remains in them:

*... Such are men whose hearts Allah has sealed (as per His laws), and who follow their own lusts. (47:16)*

They possess knowledge and intellect, but just as in an intoxicated state a man's intellect and consciousness is of no use, on being conquered by emotions also knowledge and vision become useless:

*Then do you see such a one as takes as his god his own vain desire? Allah has, knowing (him as such), left him astray, and sealed his hearing and his heart (and understanding), and put a cover on his sight...(45:23)*

The consequence of this then is that (according to the Law of Requital of Allah), despite intellect and reasoning, he strayed from the path, and his ears and heart became sealed, and his eyes were veiled.

---

[89] C.E.M. Joad, *Guide to the Philosophy of Morals and Politics*, p. 239
[90] C.E.M. Joad, *Decadence*, p. 36

## 4.25   The Demise of Nations Possessing Vision

After narrating the condition of past nations, the Quran states that these were not destroyed because they did not possess knowledge and vision – these were destroyed because their emotions of self-interest made their wrong path appear very attractive and pleasing in their eyes and these were destroyed despite possessing intellect, reasoning, vision and knowledge:

*(Remember also) the 'Ad and the Thamud (peoples): clearly will appear to you from (the traces) of their buildings (their fate): the Evil One made their deeds alluring to them, and kept them back from the Path, though they were gifted with intelligence and skill. (29:38)*

In another verse:

*And We had firmly established them in (prosperity and) power which We have not given to you (Arabs) and We had endowed them with (faculties of) hearing, seeing, heart and intellect: but of no profit to them were their (faculties of) hearing, sight, and heart and intellect, when they went on rejecting the Signs of Allah; and they were (completely) encircled by that which they used to mock at! We destroyed aforetime populations round about you; and We have shown the Signs in various ways, that they may turn to Us (to this message). (46:26-27)*

## 4.26   Emotions and the Quran

From these explanations, it seems (apparently) as if, according to the Quran, intellect (which it said had such a high status) is nothing when faced with emotions, and emotions do not permit man to come to the right path. Therefore, man is left completely helpless at this point. The Plato magic (*Vedant* and Mysticism) has prescribed the following solution to this problem, that emotions be destroyed, so that there should 'neither be any bamboo and nor will the flute play'. But the Quran declares this mentality as monasticism, and states that this is a self-created doctrine of men which does not have the authority of Allah (57:27). Firstly, because the Quran recognises that emotions can never be eliminated – the most you can do is suppress them. But the state of emotions is such that if they are suppressed from one side, then to escape and emerge, these create ten other ways to manifest themselves, and these ways are so destructive that the human self becomes severely entangled in them and chaos is created in society. In psychological terms, it means that due to the perversion of emotions, repression is born. Secondly, if it is accepted that emotions are the reason for the destruction of man and the only cure is to eliminate them, then it will mean that Allah has created alongside of man such a thing which is completely evil.

## 4.27    Virtue and Evil

According to the Quran, this concept about Allah is false and misguided. Allah is completely good and He has not created any such thing which is in itself evil and whose solution could only be its own elimination. He has created various types of forces in the world. The way in which these forces are used makes them either good or evil. If the sword is used to halt the hand of a tyrant, then it is virtuous. If this is used to cut the throat of an innocent, then it is evil. Emotions contain tremendous force within them. If this power is left unbridled and rebellious, its consequence is destructive. If it is channeled in the right direction, then it produces constructive results. Therefore, using something correctly is good and using it in the wrong place (even to the extent of wasting it and not using it) is evil.

According to the Quran, emotions are not such a thing from which one should run far away and by declaring them to be hateful, attempt to eliminate them. The Quran states that when emotions are utilised under the guidance of revelation, then constructive results are produced. And if without this guidance, these become rebellious and cross all limits, then the consequences are ruin and destruction. Hence, the Quran states:

> But if they hearken not to you (the Quranic message), then know that they only follow their own desires: and who is more astray than one who follows his own lusts, devoid of guidance from Allah? For Allah guides not people given to wrong-doing.
> (28:50)

If these people do not listen to your message or accept it, (this is not because after using their intellect and reasoning they have reached this conclusion that your message is not worth accepting), it is because these people are following their own desires (emotions), and who is more misguided than the one who follows his emotions without guidance from Allah. Remember, the law of Allah does not guide such people who do not keep the various powers and energies in their rightful place.

## 4.28    Intellect in the Light of Revelation

From these explanations this reality is made clear to us that if emotions are made use of in the light of the Divine revelation, then those results are manifested for which emotions were created. But it is obvious that emotions do not contain the ability to think and understand – this is the task of intellect.[91] In other words, whatever the Quran has declared means that if the intellect functions under the guidance of revelation, then such strength is produced within it, that it causes

---

[91] Metacognition (thinking about thinking) is an exclusive trait of the human mind. (Ed)

emotions to follow behind (instead of becoming the slave of emotions). This means that the intellect which becomes overpowered by emotions and thus ends up becoming its tool, is raw and undeveloped. The intellect which is trained within the guidance of the revelation becomes so strong that it cannot be suppressed by emotions - instead it gets work done by them according to its own will. In summary, it can be understood like this: that intellect alone becomes overwhelmed by emotions, but intellect and revelation both together remain in control of emotions. This is the reason that the Quran has declared in very clear terms that 'Satan'[92] can never overcome those people who tread under the guidance of revelation.

## 4.29    How Intellect is Trained Through Revelation

The question now arises, as to which matter revelation helps the intellect to understand due to which it acquires such strength that, instead of following emotions, it causes these to follow it, and in this way keeps producing constructive results instead of destruction. This question is very important and deserves profound attention and reflection. It is easily understood that the human intellect always adopts that thing in which it views its own interest. The person who considers his own interest is called a wise man. The one who desires his own loss is called foolish, or rather mad by everyone. Hence, the duty of intellect is to think of its own interest and it is that duty from which you cannot prevent it.

You will often have seen that a person is doing some business, and after a period of time, he leaves this and starts some other business. On being questioned, he says that though there was no loss in the previous business, there is more profit in the present one. Therefore, the human intellect discards that work in which there is less benefit.

But this also happens that the intellect takes on a business believing there to be great advantage in it, whereas instead of there being benefit in it, there is loss. It is obvious from this that it is not a must that what the intellect considers to be profitable, is indeed profitable.

From the above, it is evident that:

(i) If the intellect can be convinced that there is a greater benefit in something, then it will adopt it.
(ii) If, after experimenting on some matter, it sees that what was said by an individual is correct, then after that it will trust other things said by that

---

[92] By Satan is meant man's rebellious emotions and that intellect which follows these emotions.

person and will continue to place trust in him until there is a loss in some matter.

## 4.30   Wealth for Life and Life for Honour

Now we will proceed forward. There is a famous quote among us which says, 'Wealth for life and life for honour' – this means that while wealth has its own value, if such a situation ever arose where only one thing could be saved between wealth and life, then for the sake of life, wealth should be sacrificed. At such a time, a person who does this is considered wise. This means that according to the intellect, saving life is more profitable compared to wealth. Therefore, if there is ever a tie between wealth and life, then the human intellect will sacrifice wealth and save life.

And if a situation ever arose where there was a tie between life and honour, then the one who is wise will even sacrifice his life to protect his honour.

Everything which has been said above means that each one of wealth, life and honour has its own intrinsic value. But firstly, there is a difference in their values i.e. life has a higher value than wealth and honour has a higher value than life. Secondly, honour is so valuable that it cannot be sacrificed for anything, but wealth and life are such things which can be sacrificed for the attainment of more valuable things.

## 4.31   Relative and Permanent Values

In other words, wealth and life are relative values, but the value of honour is permanent or absolute. The task in hand is to inform the intellect about the value of a thing in life and which are the things possessing Permanent Values. It is clear from this that until the Permanent Values are not defined and established, it is not only difficult, but in fact impossible to ascertain what thing it is essential to sacrifice in order to protect some other thing. This is the foundation of ethics.

## 4.32   Deen Defines the Different Values

In the previous chapters we have stated that Deen informs us of that way of life, by following which, the caravan of humanity can reach its destination. Or it provides us with that system of life according to which the development of the human self takes place. Now we have reached the point where it can be said precisely, what does Deen give us? In one sentence - Deen defines various values.

We have seen that one concept of life is that man is defined by his physical body. The purpose of life is the satisfaction of the physical needs of the body and all this takes place according to physical laws. Obviously, according to this concept of life, values will be defined from the physical viewpoint. For this, there is neither any need for external guidance, nor any requirement for a source of knowledge beyond the intellect. What are the things that are required to fulfil the physical needs of man (along with physical nourishment, emotive aspects are also included in these needs), and which among these is more important and valuable, and which is less. When there is a tie between two things, then which one of them should be adopted and which one should be abandoned. This can all be determined by the human intellect and experience. Who does not know that, when there is a tie between wealth and life, then in order to protect life, wealth should be sacrificed. For this, there is no need for guidance via revelation. The preservation of life is a natural human instinct (indeed of all animals) which is verified by his intellect, experience, evidence and study.

But (as already stated) the second concept of life is that a human being is not the name for merely his physical body – apart from his body, there is another thing also which is called the human self or ego. Just as there are needs of his body, his self also has requirements. In the same way that nourishment and development of the body takes place, similarly, nourishment and development of his self also takes place. Just as there are laws established for the nourishment and development of the body, in the same way there are also laws established for the nourishment and development of his self.

Be aware that (as noted in Chapter 1), a human being is a single unit which is manifested through the body and the self, therefore, from the Quranic point of view, the human body and its self are not two antagonistic elements which remain in opposition with each other, nor is one of them evil and the other good. A human being is defined by both, and nourishment and development of both is essential.

## 4.33    The Quranic System of Ethics

But in the same way that there is a difference in the values related to the physical body – some value is more important and another less, and in the case of a conflict between two values, the less important value has to be forfeited in favour of the more valuable one - similarly, when there is a mutual struggle between a value of the body and that of the self, then, since the human self is more important when compared to the body, therefore the value related to the body has to be given up in favour of the value of the self (as at the time of a conflict between honour and life, life should be sacrificed to protect honour). Those values which help to nourish and develop the human self, enabling it to achieve infinite life, are superior and invaluable compared to those whose relation is only with the protection and nourishment of the body. This is the foundation on which the edifice of the Quranic System of Ethics is raised.

## 4.34 Only Revelation Can Provide the Permanent Values

The question is, can these Permanent Values be ascertained through human intellect and reasoning? The Quran declares that this is not a matter within the remit of human intellect – these can only be ascertained through revelation. This verdict of the Quran is one that is also supported by philosophers and ethical scholars of the West. On this point, we cannot do better than quote the words of Martin Buber:

*The absolute values...cannot, of course, be meant to have only subjective validity for the person concerned. Don Juan finds absolute and subjective value in seducing the greatest possible number of women and the dictator sees it in the greatest possible accumulation of power. 'Absolute validity' can only relate to universal values and forms, the existence of which the person concerned recognises and acknowledges.* [93]

Rashdall makes the same point:

*That there is one absolute standard of values, which is the same for all rational beings, is just what morality means.* [94]

In the following passage, Rashdall contends that what is controversial is not the existence of an objectively valid Moral Law, but only the manner of its existence:

*We say that the Moral Law has a real existence, that there is such a thing as absolute morality, that there is something absolutely true or false in ethical judgements, whether we or any number of human beings at any given time actually think so or not. Such a belief is distinctly implied to what we mean by Morality. The idea of such an unconditional objectively valid Moral Law or ideal undoubtedly exists as a psychological fact. The question before us is whether it is capable of theoretical justification. We must then face the question where does such an ideal exists, and what manner of existence we are to attribute to it. Certainly, it is to be found, wholly and completely, in no individual human consciousness. Men actually think differently about moral questions and there is no empirical reason for supposing that they will ever do otherwise. Where then and how does the moral ideal really exist?* [95]

Having reached the conclusion that the moral standard must be based on a universal and absolute system of values, Rashdall proceeds to tell us that such a system can have its source nowhere but in the Divine Mind:

---

[93] Martin Buber, *Between Man and Man*, p. 108.
[94] Hastings Rashdall, *The Theory of Good and Evil*, Vol. II. p. 286
[95] Ibid., p. 211

*An Absolute Moral Law or moral ideal cannot exist in material things. And it does not (we have seen) exist in the mind of this or that individual ...A moral ideal can exist nowhere and nohow but in a mind; an absolute moral ideal can exist only in a Mind from which all Reality is derived. Our moral ideal can only claim objective validity in so far as it can rationally be regarded as a revelation of a moral ideal eternally existing in the mind of God.*[96]

Regarding revelation, we have seen that the *Nabi* gets this from outside – it does not gush forth from the depths of his own heart i.e. it has objectivity. The Quran uses the term *Nazool* (descending) for this. Bergson discusses the question whether it is possible for human intellect to reach reality and gives a negative answer:

*Not through intelligence...or at least through intelligence alone, can (man) do so: intelligence would be more likely to proceed in the opposite direction; it was provided for a definite object and when it attempts speculation on a higher plane it enables us at the most to conceive possibilities; it does not attain any reality.*[97]

Einstein had written a book titled, 'Out of My Later Years' in the later part of his life and he writes:

*For science can only ascertain what is, but not what should be, and outside of its domain value judgments of all kinds remain necessary... Representatives of science have often made an attempt to arrive at fundamental judgments with respect to values and ends on the basis of scientific methods and in this way have set themselves in opposition to religion. These conflicts have all sprung from fatal errors... For the scientists, there is only 'being' but not wishing, no valuing, no good, no evil, no goal.*[98]

These values can be received through revelation, the characteristics of which, according to Joad who prefers the term 'Intuition' to 'Revelation,' are:

*(Intuition) is its own authority and carries with it the guarantee of its own authenticity. For those truths which we know intuitively no reason can be adduced, simply because they are not reached by a process of reasoning. Reason no doubt may be enlisted later to produce arguments in their favour.*[99]

As the following passage shows, Professor Cassirer, too, does not credit reason with the power of apprehending the highest values:

---

[96] Ibid., p. 212
[97] H. Bergson, *The Two Sources of Religion and Morality*, p. 201
[98] Albert Einstein, *Out of My Later Years*, p. 152
[99] C. E. M. Joad, *Philosophical Aspects of Modern Science*, p. 215

*(In Greek philosophy) the power of reason was extolled as the highest power of man. But what man could never know, until he was enlightened with a special Divine Revelation, is that reason itself is one of the most questionable and ambiguous things in the world.*[100]

From these explanations, it is evident that the source of the Permanent Values is Divine Knowledge and their availability is through revelation.

## 4.35   The Permanent Values Affect the Human Self

Let us now take a further step forward. In the example which we quoted earlier (i.e. wealth for life, life for honour), it will be clear to everyone that to save life one should spend wealth, because life is related to the human body. Everyone knows and feels what harm is sustained by the loss of life.  But not every individual can feel what harm is sustained if honour is lost. This does not result in any material loss to man – this loss is related to something which is non-material, and this is human personality. If some individual does not accept the existence of the human self, then for him the loss of honour will not be any loss. The most we can say is that this will result in damage to a reputation within society. But a stain on a reputation only occurs in that society in which honour is considered a valuable commodity. But the question of loss of honour does not even arise in a society in which honour is not held as a valuable commodity. For example, among us if some unmarried girl (unfortunately) becomes pregnant, then for her this is something worthy of such condemnation that she would prefer to die. But since in Europe such a pregnancy is not viewed as wrong, there is no question of dishonour.

This makes it clear that the Permanent Values are those whose benefit or loss (directly and intrinsically) affects the human self. Therefore, for the Permanent or Absolute Values it is essential to recognise the existence of the human self, and with it to recognise this truth that by neglecting these values, (though the human body does not suffer any loss) the human self suffers a loss. In other words, it is essential to accept that every deed of man does have a consequence, and that no deed of his can remain without an effect – this is called the Law of Requital. Those deeds which benefit the human self provide support in its development. And when the human self becomes developed, then it attains infinite life.

## 4.36   The Need for Eimaan

For this it is necessary that after the physical death of a human being, the existence of the continuity of life should be accepted (this is called having Eimaan in the hereafter). In other words:

---

[100] E. Cassirer, *An Essay on Man*, p. 9

(1) Eimaan in Allah
(2) Eimaan in the human self
(3) Eimaan in the continuity of life (the hereafter)
(4) Eimaan in the Law of Requital
(5) And Eimaan in this fact that the creation of the universe and of man himself is with a particular purpose as part of a special programme.

See how beautifully the Quran describes in two verses all that has been said above. In Surah *Al Jathiyah* it states:

*Allah created the heavens and the earth for just ends, and in order that each self may find the recompense of what it has earned, and none of them be wronged. (45:22)*

After this it states:

*Then see you such a one as takes as his god his own vain desires? Allah has, knowing (him as such), left him astray, and sealed his hearing and his heart (and understanding), and put a cover on his sight. Who, then, will guide him after Allah? Will you not then receive admonition? (45:23)*

Such a person can only come to the right path in the event that he desists from worshipping his emotions, and follows the Divine laws.

The people who follow their emotions are those who consider human life to be merely a physical life and do not believe in the existence of the human self and its life in the hereafter:

*And they say: 'What is there but our life in this world? We shall die and we live, and nothing but time can destroy us.' But of that they have no knowledge: they merely conjecture. (45:24)*

But this belief of theirs is not based on knowledge, it is merely based on conjecture. The only verdict which will be received from the font of knowledge will be that there is definitely something within man which is not annihilated with his death - it holds within it the potential to endure and the ability to continue forward.

In another verse it is stated:

*Therefore shun those who turn away from Our Message and desire nothing but the life of this world. That is as far as knowledge will reach them. Verily your Sustainer knows best those who stray from His Path, and He knows best those who receive guidance. (53:29-30)*

You should stay clear of the individual who avoids Our Laws, because he only has the interests of physical life in his view. He is in no way convinced of the continuity of life and the immortality of the human self. Their total knowledge is confined only to physical laws.

## 4.37    Who Can Have Eimaan in the Permanent Values

The Quran has made it clear in these verses that only that individual can have Eimaan in the Permanent Values who does not consider life to be a physical life only, but is also convinced of the existence of the human self, the Law of Requital and the life in the hereafter. For the one who is not convinced of these facts, neither having Eimaan in Allah has any meaning for him, nor is he convinced of any code of morality. This is because the code of morality is indeed the other name for the Permanent Values. And only he can believe in the Permanent Values who is convinced of the human self, the Law of Requital and the continuity of life.

When, in this way, human intellect and vision accepts the Permanent Values, then instead of following after emotions, it directs these to follow it, and then intellect itself treads in the light of the Divine revelation.

This combination of revelation and intellect is declared by the Quran as being the characteristic of the Momineen:

*Behold! in the creation of the heavens and the earth, and the alternation of night and day - there are indeed Signs for men of understanding - men who keep in view the Laws of Allah, standing, sitting and lying down on their sides, and contemplate the (wonders of) creation in the heavens and the earth, (with the thought): 'Our Sustainer! not for naught have You created (all) this!...(3:190-191)*

These are the men of vision about whom it states:

*Say: 'Not equal are things that are bad and things that are good, even though the abundance of the bad may dazzle you; so fear Allah (stay within the Laws of Allah), O you that understand; so that you may prosper.' (5:100)*

They are the ones it declares as being the holders of Eimaan when it says:

*...Therefore fear Allah (keep in view the Laws of Allah), O you men of understanding - who have believed (have Eimaan)! (65:10)*

In other words, according to the Quran, Momin and *Mutaqee* can only be men of vision. In another verse it states:

*But those endued with knowledge and Eimaan will say: Indeed you did tarry, within Allah's Decree (as per His Law), to the Day of Resurrection, and this is the Day of Resurrection: but you - you were not aware! (as you never considered it a possibility). (30:56)*

In other words, Eimaan, knowledge and vision are essentially bound up with each other. Without knowledge, man cannot reach Eimaan. Belief is only that belief which an individual has acquired through his own vision and evidence. The following statement of Locke is commonly quoted among people who are philosophers and possess knowledge:

*He that takes away reason to make way for revelation, puts out the light of both.*[101]

But see how many centuries before Locke the Quran had already proclaimed this reality that knowledge and Eimaan (revelation and intellect) are essentially complementary to each other. As has been stated above, Eimaan is only that Eimaan which knowledge and evidence support. The result of acquiring Eimaan in this way is that the emotions of these people follow their intentions. If it ever happens that some wrong idea comes to them while out and about, then they immediately bring to mind the Divine laws and inquire of them as to which is the correct path – the moment the Divine laws come before them, all darknesses immediately vanish and the right path emerges clearly before them:

*Those who fear Allah (remain within the Divine Laws), when a thought of evil (from Satan) assaults them, bring Allah to remembrance (bring these Laws to mind), when lo! they see (aright)! (7:201)*

As soon as the light of the revelation appears before them, the whole environment is brightly illuminated and they immediately make a decision in its light as to what they should do.

This is that technique of the Quran through which it causes the intellect to accept the importance of the Permanent Values, and when in this way the intellect accepts these facts, then its treads in the right direction in the light of the revelation and human emotions follow along behind it. The name of this remarkable combination of revelation, intellect and emotions is Life Based on Islam. In this, every individual with the full conviction of his mind and the full gladness of his heart, sells his life and wealth into the hands of Allah and his intellect congratulates him on this transaction of his:

---

[101] John Locke, *Essay Book*, IV (XIX, 4) quoted by Brightman, op, cit., p. 104

*Allah has purchased of the Believers (Momineen) their persons and their goods: for theirs in return is the garden (of Paradise)...(9:111)*

This is because, based on his vision and on evidence, he has satisfied himself that obedience to those Permanent Values which have been defined through revelation will result in profit only, and that there is not even an iota of any possible loss:

*To the righteous (when) it is said, 'What is it that your Sustainer has revealed?' they say, 'All that is good.' To those who do good, there is good in this world, and the Home of the Hereafter is even better, and excellent indeed is the Home of the righteous. (16:30)*

When the intellect understands the truth and importance of these values, then, instead of going towards those destructions to which rebellious emotions beckon, it follows the voice of the revelation which is in reality profitable for him. This is because the propensity of the intellect is always to go towards that direction which appears profitable to it.

## 4.38    Conclusion of the Discussion

You can comprehend everything which has been said in the previous pages regarding revelation, intellect, and emotions in the following brief summary:

(1) The status of human intellect is like a force which will result in consequences according to whichever way it is used.

(2) When human intellect (dissociated from emotions) researches and investigates the secrets and hidden treasures of the external universe, then it reaches the correct conclusion through its own empirical technique. This is called the scientific method of research. The Quran places great emphasis on the importance of this method because through this the forces of nature are harnessed and only through the harnessing of nature does man attain the status of a human being.

(3) However, in the case of mutual relations between humans, when this same intellect follows emotions (i.e. when this force is used by human emotions), then a battle of wits erupts in this world which results in 'the spilling of blood and creating mischief on earth' (2:30). In the terms of the Quran this is called the obedience of Satan.

(4) Emotions instigate human actions and so these are also a great resource and power for man. But this power can only produce constructive results in that situation where it is not allowed to overwhelm the intellect.

(5) The technique for this is to make the intellect the protector of the Permanent Values, which man receives through revelation. When man, having dissociated himself from his emotions, thinks and reasons using his

intellect and knowledge, the importance of these values springs before him, and in this way his intellect declares their protection and supervision to be its responsibility. To be thus convinced by the human intellect about the significance of the Permanent Values is known as Eimaan.

(6) In this way, man's emotions and his intellect (both of which are exceptional forces) become the means of attaining the defined objective set by Eimaan; and in this way the forces of nature, instead of causing the destruction of humanity, result in becoming the continuing basis for development and civilisation. This is the status of a Momin i.e. a human being who keeps his emotions within the control of his intellect and keeps his intellect in the service of the revelation. Through the application of this technique, by achieving balanced development, his self is enabled to tread the evolutionary stages of life. This is the very aim of the Quran.

From these explanations it is evident that the edifice of Deen is established on the Permanent Values. Details of these values will be found in a later chapter.

# 5 IMPLEMENTATION AND FUNCTIONING OF THE 'LAW'

We have seen in Chapter 1 that one concept of god is that which the human mind coined, and the other which Allah Himself provided through revelation. The god invented by the human mind belongs to that era when his consciousness was undeveloped and his intellect was in the embryonic era. In that era, the greatest authority in front of man was a king, ruler or sultan, therefore he also put god into the same category as a king. He could not think of god as being anything other than this. He observed that kings are not bound by any rules or laws; whatever they wish they command and everyone has to obey. No-one can even ask them this much, as to what is the aim and purpose of this order. If anyone does even pick up the courage to ask them such a thing, and if they are in the mood to reply to him, then their answer will be no more than that, this is our wish, and we desire it like this. This is that 'royal attitude' which has already been noted. Sometimes their state is such that, if someone greets them they may become annoyed with him, and sometimes their state is such that, if someone swears at them they may bestow a treasure on him.

## 5.1   God – An Absolute Dictator

It is obvious that when god is viewed in this form and together with this, there is such a belief that (in comparison to a king) god's powers are limitless, then such a god will be an absolute dictator and it will be considered an insult (and for such a god a cause for humiliation) to even imagine that he is constrained by any rule and procedure. It will be said, what kind of a god is that who is limited by some rule. Being tied down by rules is against the stature of godliness. He himself is an absolute sovereign and there is no other ruler above him, how can he be constrained by some law and procedure. His every command will be law and his every gesture an order. He can do whatever he wants and give whatever order he wishes. He can destroy and obliterate whoever he wishes and bestow gifts and riches on whoever he desires. The one who gains his pleasure, will reap all and the one he becomes angry with, will be left desolate. The natural consequence resulting from such a belief regarding god was also that man should remain constantly fearful of him, as he could never know when he might become angry and destroy and ruin him.

The second consequence of such a belief was that, in order to seek the pleasure of god, (just as various means and techniques are adopted to please kings), similar techniques required to be also invented and similar means to be pursued. The way in which to please kings is to recite praises in their honour, sing songs in their appreciation and flattery, and present gifts in their courts. If even these tricks do not work, then it was necessary to seek intercession through their close courtiers (ministers and aristocrats) in order to reach them and in this way, manage to get their job done.

Consider the history of mankind. The concept of god which the human mind had evolved was this very same one. And this was that same concept which was prevalent throughout the world at the time of the revelation of the Quran. We have noted above that the concept of Allah which was received through revelation (via *Anbiya*[102]) was different from this concept. But the revelation from Allah (in different times), which came to different nations, was not present in its original form (and unadulterated) anywhere at the time of the revelation of the Quran. Therefore, the concept of god which these nations (who were claimants of heavenly guidance) had, was similar to that which the human mind had carved.

## 5.2   The Quranic Concept

The Quran arrived, and it refuted in every nook and cranny the concept of god carved by the human mind and in its place, presented the accurate concept of God. This is that very concept of Allah on which the whole structure of Deen is erected and through which every aspect of human life is influenced. This is the reason it has declared 'Eimaan in Allah' as being the 'first brick' in that foundation and has declared the correctness or wrongness of this concept as being the criterion between *Kufr* (denial) and Eimaan (acceptance). In other words, if an individual upholds that concept of Allah which the Quran has put forward, the Quran declares him to be a Momin (the one who has Eimaan in Allah). Contrary to this, if an individual's concept of God is not the one which the Quran presents, then according to the Quran, he will not be declared a Momin even if in his own mind he considers himself to be a devout worshipper of God. It is clear from this how much significance the concept of Allah holds in Deen (the Islamic System of Life).

Now let us see what the Quran says in this respect. According to the Quran, there are three spheres of operation of Allah, each one of which has its own unique characteristics. We will first of all discuss the first domain.

## 5.3   First Domain – His Will

By observing the system which is working in the universe at this time, this reality will become evidently clear that there is a system of cause and effect working in it i.e. for any event to appear in the universe there has to be a cause for it – without a cause no event can take place. If we extend this series of cause and effect backwards, then ultimately a point will be reached where it will have to be accepted that the first link in this chain appeared somehow or other without a cause. This

---

[102]. (Ed).

is termed as something coming into existence from non-existence. How did this happen? This matter cannot be comprehended by man. The Quran only tells us this much about it, that Allah has created the heavens and the earth from nothing (2:117) i.e. the One Who brings all the system of the universe into existence from nothing. It is obvious that for something to begin at the point where cause and effect simply do not exist, the question of any law or process being present there does not even arise. Cause and effect is the very name for law and procedure. The Quran has termed this stage as *Alm-e-Amr* - the universe of *Amr* - and has only stated this much about what takes place there:

*Verily, when He intends a thing, His Command is, 'be', and it is. (36:82)*

In this respect, the *Amr* of Allah works in such a way that when He makes an intention about something and says 'Be!' then it happens.

It is also obvious that when something is to be brought into existence from nothing, then this will also need to be determined regarding it, as to what it should be – what it is to finally become after traversing through the various stages of life. What will be its characteristics? What will be its traits and effects? This is also clear that when the existence of something takes place according to the *Amr* (Absolute Authority, Intention, Will) of Allah, its traits etc. will also be established according to His Will. Why did honey receive sweetness and salt saltiness? Through the chemical reaction of a specific proportion of hydrogen and oxygen, why does a water drop form? Why does water flow downhill? Why is water an elixir of life for us and why does poison cut down on life? These are those matters which we cannot comprehend. The properties of things are established according to the Will and Intention of Allah – in these matters the question of 'why' does not arise.

This is that aspect i.e. creating the universe from nothing and establishing properties and their effects, about which it is stated that Allah does whatever He wills. 'Allah does whatever He wishes as per His intention' (22:14). 'Allah does command according to His Will' (5:1). No one has the right to ask Him why He made something as He did, and why He made a certain decision as He did. He cannot be questioned as to why He did this and why He does such and such (21:23). Apart from Him, all others can be questioned.

This is that sphere of Allah's *Amr* in which His Intention and Will operates as an absolute authority and where He is not constrained by any law and procedure.

## 5.4   Second Domain – Laws of Nature

Now we come to the second sphere in which the universe is busy in carrying out its functions. We saw, (in the first domain), that Allah has established the characteristics and effects of things in the universe using His absolute power, and all this has taken place through His *Amr*. But, after establishing the characteristics and effects of things in the universe, Allah has modified the state of His *Amr*. Under the first domain, His *Amr* was not constrained by any laws, but now the same *Amr* is encircled by laws:

> ...And the command of Allah is a decree determined. (33:38)

The *Amr* of Allah has become constrained by defined scales.[103] In another verse, it is stated that He has fixed a scale for everything:

> ...verily, for all things has Allah appointed a due proportion. (65:3)

These measures and scales are those things which are called the laws of nature, and which are immutable. For example, the characteristic that was fixed for water is that, under normal conditions, it remains liquid. When it is cooled, on reaching a certain temperature, it changes into a solid (ice) and similarly, when heat is provided to it, then on reaching a particular level, it vapourises. When its chemical analysis is carried out, it splits into hydrogen and oxygen etc. These laws (scales) for water are so absolute and immutable that there will be no change or modification of any type in them. Wherever man wishes, he can experiment on this and he will find no variation in it. Allah has called these established laws *Sunnat-ullah* (Habit or Practice of Allah) and has stated about these:

> ...No change will you find in the practice of Allah. (33:62)

Note that the same Allah Who, under the first domain, declared that He does whatever He wishes, and whatever he intends He decides according to it, is now saying that you will not find any change in His practice, habit, law or *Sunnat*. How big a constraint is this which Allah has imposed on His Own absolute authority. Remember, if a man imposes a constraint on himself through his own volition, then there is no aspersion cast on his freedom to choose and intent. When Allah Himself has confined His *Amr* and Will within the scales of laws, by this there is no diminution in His intent and Will in any way. Nor, by His declaring that 'We will not make any change in the constraints We have imposed on Our *Amr*, can we construe Him as being captive and trapped. This is His Own decision that the universe should be actively functioning according to defined and established laws, and that there should be no change in them. All this is happening according to His Own well-defined programme. He has done this so that the universe continues to function with organised discipline and excellent balance. Just think, that if it was ever the case that water sometimes extinguishes fire, while another time it bursts

---

[103] The term used in Arabic is *Qadr* which means scales and measures.

into flames itself, fire sometimes boils water, and sometimes freezes it, then the whole system of the universe will be in tatters.

From the above discussion, this reality has come to the fore that under this second domain (i.e. external universe), the *Amr* of Allah works in the form of an immutable law. But since these laws also operate according to the *Amr*, intention, and Will of Allah, the working of these laws is also referred to as His Will and *Amr*. It is apparent from this, that when it is said in this regard that, 'Allah does so', then this will mean, 'Allah does so according to His law' or 'the law of Allah does so'. For example, in the Quran it is stated:

*He has made subject to you the Night and the Day; the sun and the moon; and the stars are in subjection by His Command...(16:12)*

It is clear that the stellar bodies (moon, sun, stars) are busy in dynamic movements within the natural immutable laws. These laws are so immutable and precise, that by the use of very simple mathematics, it can be determined hundreds of years in advance as to when there will be an eclipse of the moon or sun, and at which time a certain planet will be at a certain distance from the earth. These are those immutable laws on the basis of which the enthralling edifice of the science of astronomy is constructed. But for these laws the term *Amr* is used which commonly means 'command'. In another place, the term *Azn* is used for this (22:65) which is commonly taken to mean 'by His leave'.

Hence, wherever in relation to the working and functioning of the external universe the terms *Amr*, *Azn*, *Mashiat* etc. have been used, these will mean the immutable laws of nature.

At this juncture, another point is worthy of attention. In the external universe, there are immutable laws established for all things which is called the *Taqdeer* (destiny or purpose) of this thing i.e. its characteristics, properties, effects, role and assignment. This law is unalterable, which means that nothing in the universe has the potential to change its *Taqdeer*. It has simply not been given this choice that if it wishes it can obey these laws, or if it wishes it can rebel against them; or if it wishes it can obey these laws up to a certain extent, and for the remaining part follow some other law – absolutely not. Everything in the universe is created so that it is obliged to obey this law which has been established for it by the Creator of the universe:

*And to Allah do obey all that is in the heavens and on earth...(16:49)*

From the above discussion it is evident that:

(1) In the first sphere, through His unconstrained free intention and Will, Allah creates things of the universe and establishes laws for them. In this sphere, He does everything according to His Will and intent.

(2) In the second domain, the laws established by Allah take on an absolute, immutable and unalterable form. In this category, everything functions according to these established laws. Right from the start, nothing is given the choice to go against or disobey these laws. Man can acquire knowledge of these laws, and according to this, can bring the things of the universe into his use. This is called 'harnessing of nature' which is the fundamental requirement of being human. The prostration of 'angels' before Adam refers to this fact (2:34).

It is obvious that in this domain the rule of Allah is not like that of a dictator, but instead becomes the rule of law[104], though the things of the universe are obliged to follow this law.

## 5.5   Third Domain – The Human World

We now come to the third category i.e. human life. One part of human life is that which is related to the physical laws. In this domain, only one type of laws are applicable to man and animals. But the second part of human life is that which is referred to as 'the universe of humanity'. This is related to human personality. In the same way that Allah has established laws for the nourishment of the physical life of man (and animals), He has also established laws for the development of the human self (these laws are received through revelation and are called Permanent Values). This means that whether it is man's physical life, or the life of his self, even on these Allah's working is through the application of His established laws, knowledge of which has been given to man. Knowledge about physical life is through the use of intellect, reasoning, evidence and experience, and knowledge about the human self is through revelation.

## 5.6   Man is Responsible for His Actions

In the case of man there is another characteristic as well. We have seen that the things of the universe have been created enforced to follow the laws which have been established for them. But man has been given choice in this matter, as to whether he wishes to spend his life according to these laws, or if he wishes he can transgress or rebel against them:

---

[104] Unlike the universe of *Amr* (21:23), in the universe of *Khalq* (creation) Allah is answerable for his promises (laws) (25:16).

*Say, 'The truth is from your Sustainer': Let him who will, believe, and let him who will, reject (it is their choice)...(18:29)*

Say to them that an established and immutable law of life has been revealed before you from your Sustainer. Now from amongst you, whoever wishes can adopt it and whoever wishes can reject it.

You will have seen how in these three domains a fundamental difference has been emerging. Under the first domain, the absolute authority of Allah was operative and He was not constrained by any law or procedure. There, the Divine *Mashiat* (Will of Allah) meant that whatever Allah wished, He did. Under the second domain the Divine *Mashiat* imposed restrictions on Himself of His Own accord, and these restrictions acquired the form of immutable laws. On the other hand, the things to which these laws are applicable have also not been provided with the freedom to go against these laws. Under the third domain, the Divine law remained unchanged, but man was given the freedom to choose whatever path he wishes.

## 5.7   Man Cannot Alter the Effects

But within man's freedom to choose, there is an aspect of limitation as well. Man certainly has the freedom to choose whether he puts a pellet of poison or of sugar in his mouth, but he does not have the freedom to change the consequences of eating the poison. That Divine law of Allah's through which poison has been made to cut life short, will definitely ensure its effect is delivered. Therefore, wherever He told man you can do whatever you wish, alongside this He also stated that Allah's law observes closely what you do (41:40). Though the choice of taking an action is in your control, changing its consequence is not in your control – you can neither change it, nor can you save yourself from it:

*Truly strong is the Grip (and Power) of your Sustainer. (85:12)*

Indeed, the grip of the Law of Requital of your Sustainer is very strict.

From the above discussion, it is clear that there are innumerable laws of Allah dispersed throughout the universe. It is man's own choice to follow whichever type of law for himself that he wishes. Allah never interferes in this choice of man.[105] When I am standing at any crossroads in life, Allah's Law of Requital awaits to see which path I will adopt, and whichever path I set foot on, the law related to that path sets off behind me and begins to yield the effects of my deed.

---

[105] In the words of Iqbal, 'God Himself cannot feel, judge, and choose for me when more than one course of action is open to me'. *The Reconstruction of Religious Thought in Islam*, Chapter 4, *The Human Ego – His Freedom and Immortality*, p. 100

## 5.8   The Meaning of *Taqdeer* (Destiny)

In other words, in human life the initiative is in human hands. The Quran states:

*... Then when they went wrong, Allah let their hearts go wrong...(61:5)*

In another verse it is stated:

*Through which are deluded (away from the Truth) such as would be deluded. (51:9)*

The law of Allah protects the individual who wishes to remain protected from destruction, and destroys the one who wishes to be destroyed (2:284). Whatever a person desires for himself, the law of Allah does that for him. Whatever a person becomes, his destiny (*Taqdeer*) becomes the same.

When the situation is such, then it is obvious that if we fall into those circumstances which are unfavourable for us, then there is nothing to cry about; we should bring about change within ourselves and make the circumstances favourable, and by doing this, another of Allah's laws will become applicable to us, and our destiny will change.

The question is, where can man find these laws and scales? The Quran has stated that these are available through revelation. This is why revelation is:

*That is the Command (Amr) of Allah, which He has sent down to you...(65:5)*

In other words, it is the same *Amr* which was operating as an absolute authority of Allah under the first domain. Then, under the second domain it was implemented as the absolute destiny of different things of the universe (and whose knowledge can be acquired through human intellect, reasoning, and through observation and experiment). Under the third domain, that same *Amr* is given preserved in the Quran in the form of Divine revelation. It is the same *Amr* which in the first domain is called *Mashiat*, becomes the destiny of things of the universe under domain two, and under domain three is declared as the Divine Commandments.

## 5.9   The Quranic Concept of Allah

From the above discussion this truth becomes evident that the concept of Allah given by the Quran is completely different from the concept which the human mind had invented and which different religions had adopted (by ignoring the guidance provided by Allah). According to this concept, Allah (Allah forbid) like an absolute despot (dictator) did whatever he wished and man was helpless in front of Him. According to the concept of Allah which is presented by the Quran, the law of Allah is operating in the universe, and He never makes any exemption in this law, nor does He make changes or modifications in it. He has established an effect for every deed and has kept its control in His Own hand so that the deed assuredly produces the defined effect.

'That Allah Who is running the affairs according to laws' – this is the concept bestowed by the Quran. According to this concept, you will see how strictly the nation which has Eimaan in this type of belief in Allah will be following the laws both in the external universe and within the human world itself. In the external universe, the functioning of these laws is termed as 'science'. From the stage of religion, the voice of the Quran was a unique one which proclaimed that the functioning of the great machinery of the universe is tied down in precise laws. In this way, it invited the attention of the world towards scientific research.[106]

The religion given by the Quran is *Al-Deen* which does not falsify science, instead places great emphasis on it. This is the clear evidence of its truth. As far as the falsifying of religion by science is concerned, so far scientific research has verified whatever the Quran has stated about the universe, and has not refuted it. Only that religion can meet this criterion in which the concept of Allah is one which is 'to govern according to the law', and this concept cannot be found anywhere apart from the Quran.

This, then, is the concept of the working of the law in the universe. As far as the human world is concerned, the degree to which the nation which has Eimaan in such a Deity whose every decision is according to law, will have respect for the law, and obedience of justice and righteousness, does not require further elaboration. This is the practical outcome of the concept of Allah which the Quran presents i.e. scientific research and material progress in the external universe, and in the human world, respect for law and the prevalence of justice and righteousness.

*Al-Deen* is the name of such a system of life which is based on this concept of Allah.

---

[106] Ouspensky said, '…the religion which falsifies science and the science which falsifies religion – both are wrong'. *Tertium Organum* by P.D. Ouspensky.

# 6 THE LAW OF REQUITAL

We have seen in the previous chapter that the whole concept of Deen revolves around the focal point that man's every deed (even a passing thought crossing his mind) gives rise to an effect, and these effects are produced according to the Divine laws. In other words, whatever the Divine law has stated will be the particular effect resulting from any action, that same effect will always be the result of that action. There can never be any change in it e.g. a person who swallows poison will die. This is because Allah, according to His physical law, has made poison harmful, so it can never happen that you swallow poison and it should have no effect on you, or that it becomes a life giver for you.[107]

## 6.1   What is the Law of Requital?

A similar system to the one of cause and effect, which is functioning in the physical world, is also established within the human world as well. This law, according to which every deed and intention of man produces an effect, is called Allah's Law of Requital.

In human life, the Law of Requital is of such fundamental importance that without it the system of the world cannot continue. In an uncivilised savage society, 'might is right' is the accepted law (whoever has the whip, owns the buffalo), whereas in a civilised society this issue as to who owns the buffalo is settled according to the law and whoever goes against this decision is punished accordingly.

## 6.2   The Law of Requital within the Human System

But within the human system there remain many flaws. For example:

(1) An individual commits a theft but does it in such a way that no-one finds out about it so he cannot be punished for his crime or
(2) if he is apprehended, he gets the police onto his side, or manages to gain 'access' to the court, and in this way, too, he can escape punishment or
(3) the government or the legislature makes such laws which simply do not declare the particular misdeeds of a special class of people to even be crimes, just as in the capitalist system[108] such laws are formulated according to which not giving full wages to workers is not considered a crime or

---

[107] Some people who use drugs in low doses over long periods of time become habituated to these, and these doses therefore do not kill them immediately and their end is thus gradual. But if they ingest higher doses than these then they will also die instantly. Similarly, the dose administered by doctors is controlled and so that gives a positive result but a greater dose than this can prove fatal.
[108] This commonly happens in a system when the majority of the parliament consists of representatives from a special group of people.

(4) a nation formulates such laws according to which exploiting and looting other nations cannot be declared as being a crime. In the present era, when human beings are divided by nationalism, every nation of the world formulates those kinds of laws according to which the welfare of their own people is a 'praiseworthy' deed even if they have to go to any lengths to deal with other nations – modern 'Machiavellian politics'[109] is fundamentally based on this principle; according to this type of politics, the greatest man is that patriot who will even go to the lengths of fleecing other nations in order to protect the vested interests of his own nation.

Hence, in this connection, Cavour, a thinker of Italy, used to say, 'If we did for ourselves what we do for our country, what rascals we should be'.[110] And it was a belief of Walpole that a principled man can never save a great nation because an honourable man can never go to that extent to which it becomes necessary in order to do this.

## 6.3   The Law of Requital in the Divine System

Under the human system this is the state of the Law of Requital, but in the Law of Requital under the Divine system, this kind of error or omission does not remain. We see how in the physical world a man, in the solitude of his room, eats poison; he was not seen or caught by the police nor was he punished by a court, but the effect of the poison on him was automatic. For the outcome of this action of his, there was no requirement for either a witness or a prosecutor or a court. This action leads to its result automatically according to the Law of Requital of Allah. It is declared in the Quran that the purpose of the functioning of this awe-inspiring system of the universe is to ensure that the precise result of every deed continues to manifest itself:

*Allah created the heavens and the earth for just ends, and in order that each self may find the recompense of what it has earned, and none of them be wronged. (45:22). See also (53:31)*

Everything which is in the lowest and highest parts of the universe is pursuing the goal of completing the programme of Allah, and the aim of this is that those people who adopt a wrong path in life should receive the recompense of their deeds, and that those who live a righteous life should receive a pleasant recompense in return.

In another verse, it is stated:

---

[109] N. Machiavelli, *The Prince.*
[110] Cavour, *Foreign Affairs,* July 1952

*He it is Who created the heavens and the earth in six stages - and His control is over the source of life (water) - and this is to see which of you is best in conduct...(11:7)*

For this aim, 'forces of Allah' are present in the whole universe (48:4) which keep an eye on the deeds of every single individual. In Surah *Al Ra'd* it is stated:

*He knows the unseen and that which is open: He is the Great, the Most High (so His system of accountability is free from interference). It is the same (to Him) whether any of you conceal his speech or declare it openly; whether he lies hid by night or walk forth freely by day. For each there are (such forces) in succession, before and behind him (to note down details): They guard him by command of Allah. Allah does not change a people's lot unless they change what is within their own selves...(13:9-11)*

You can understand it as follows:

*But verily over you (are appointed forces) to keep watch on you, honourable, Writing down (your deeds). (82:10-11)*

Not only the visible deeds, but even the deepest innermost thoughts which cross our hearts:

*It was We Who created man, and We know what dark suggestions his self makes to him: for We are nearer to him than (his) jugular vein. (50:16)*

The name of this personal record is the 'book of deeds' which remains glued to each individual:

*Every man's fate We have fastened on his own neck: On the Day of Judgment We shall bring out for him a scroll, which he will see spread open. (It will be said to him:) 'Read your (own) record: Sufficient is your self this day to make out an account against you.' (17:13-14)*

## 6.4   Every Deed Establishes its Mark

We have already mentioned that the meaning of the Law of Requital is that the effect of every deed of man continually affects his self. It is possible that under the human system a man may somehow or other shroud his crimes, but under the Law of Allah the effects of these crimes which affect his self will not be able to be hidden by anyone when the time comes for the manifestation of results:

*Nay, man will be evidence against himself, Even though he were to put up his excuses. (75:14-15)*

*(It will be said:) 'You were heedless of this; now have We removed your veil, and*
*sharp is your sight this Day (nothing can obstruct your vision)!' (50:22)*

At this time, every veil of intellectual deception is lifted, and vision becomes so sharp that even the greatest obstacle cannot cause any obstruction in its path.

## 6.5   Reward and Punishment of Deeds

From these explanations, whereas this reality has become apparent that, according to the Law of Requital of Allah, no deed of man can remain without being accounted for, it has also become evident that the reward or punishment for deeds does not come from outside, but is the natural and essential consequence of these deeds themselves. For example, you can understand it as asking a labourer to deliver a note to a certain individual whose home is three miles away and paying him eight *annas* for this task. This labourer has no interest in this note, nor any concern as to the reason why you are sending this note to this individual. He is only concerned with the remuneration for his labour, which is obtained externally. In such matters, a deed and its consequence has no internal connection or relation.

Contrary to the above, you go out for a walk every morning for three miles. This results in a beneficial effect on your health. This is the natural consequence of this action (i.e. the three mile walk). In other words, you do not receive the recompense for this deed from the outside, this result is intrinsically hidden within the deed.

As another example, a student becomes absent from school and the teacher fines him. The effect which this absence from school has on the student's educational ability has no relation or connection to the fine. It is also possible that the student will pay the fine by taking money from his father, in which case the punishment was received by the father, and not the student. But if a child puts his finger into a fire, then the pain he experiences will be the natural and necessary consequence of his action. This pain of his cannot be transferred to his father, or for that matter, to anyone else. The recompense of this deed of his was hidden within the deed itself and he has to bear it himself.

A third example can be understood as follows. A person earns some money by his effort and labour and from this income buys some *ghee*[111] which he consumes. It is obvious that by eating this *ghee* his body will gain strength. Contrary to this, another person steals *ghee* and eats it. The effect of this *ghee* on his body will be exactly the same as the effect on the individual who eats *ghee* bought from the income earned as a result of his own hard work. This means that as far as the physical laws are concerned, ethics has no effect on them. But this does not mean

---

[111] A type of cooking oil. (Ed)

that in the case of humanity as well, there is no difference between the purchasing of *ghee* using earned income from personal labour, and acquiring it through stealing. The effect of this action affects the human self, and this is that very point where the sphere of the Law of Requital commences which is related to the world of humanity.

From this discussion, the following truth is apparent:

(1) No deed of man can remain without producing its effect.
(2) The consequence of living life according to the Permanent Values is that it results in the development of the human self.
(3) Going against these values results in the human self becoming destroyed.
(4) These effects are hidden within human deeds i.e. these are their natural and essential consequences.
(5) These effects cannot be transferred to someone else.

## 6.6  The Effects of One's Deeds Cannot be Borne by Another

In this connection, the Quran has clearly stated:

*And if any one does something which affects his self. He earns it against His own self...(4:111)*

In another verse:

*If you did well, you did well for yourselves; if you did evil, (you did it) against yourselves...(17:7)*

In other words:

*Whoever works righteousness benefits his own self; whoever works evil, it is against his own self...(41:46)*

This was the reason that the voice of revelation declared in very clear words:

*Now have come to you, from your Sustainer, clear and manifest evidences: if any will see, it will be for (the good of) his own self; if any wishes to remain blind, it will be to his own loss: I am not (here) to watch over your doings. (6:104)*

The truth is that (as noted in Chapter 2) the individuality and uniqueness of human personality means that those effects which are imprinted on it cannot be shared or participated in by anyone else. The personality of every individual is exclusive in its own right. This is its individuality because of which his being exists. This is why its effects cannot be transferred to anyone else.[112] The Quran has stated:

*...no bearer of burdens can bear the burden of another...(6:164)*

And this is such an established and immutable law on which the whole structure of Deen is raised. For this, let us once again look at the example which has just been quoted. You put your hand into fire and your hand is burnt due to which you are in severe pain. If you have ten compassionate friends by your side who would not hesitate to lay down their lives for you, even then none among them can share your pain. It cannot be that your hand is burnt and the pain is experienced by your friend. Similarly, it is impossible that by giving a bribe of thousands of rupees you can become free of your pain, or that, through the highest of intercessions, a decision be made in your favour so that your pain can be removed. By putting your hand into fire, you have disobeyed a law, and you will have to face the punishment for this. This is that Law of Requital about which it is stated:

*Then guard yourselves against a day when one self shall not avail another nor shall intercession be accepted for him, nor shall compensation be taken from him, nor shall anyone be helped (from outside). (2:48)*

You should always bear in mind the manifestations of the consequences of your deeds when the situation will be such that no individual will be of any use to another, nor will anyone's intercession be accepted, nor will anyone be able to escape by offering compensation, nor will anyone be able to help a criminal. This is the immutable law of Allah in which there is no change or alteration.

## 6.7   Deeds of Nations

So far, we have discussed that part of the Law of Requital which relates to the individual life (self) of man. But as has already been mentioned, on the one hand the development of the self of an individual takes place within a collective life, and on the other hand these individuals shape a society which fulfils the duty of taking humanity to its intended aim. Therefore, the Law of Requital, as with individuals, also encompasses nations within its sphere. Those nations, which remain steadfast in respecting and pursuing the Permanent Values, are bestowed with prosperity and successes in life, and those which work against these values are humiliated and destroyed (details of this will be covered later). The effects and marks imprinted on the self of an individual are not visible and felt by others (though his character and behaviour become a reflection of these), but the results of the conduct of nations become both visible and are felt by others. Hence, the Quran (as noted in

---

[112] Leaving aside the effects and imprints on the self, no-one can transfer even another's headache to himself.

Chapter 4), in order to verify the truth of its recommended programme, suggests this procedure, that one group should establish this programme in its practical form and after this observe whether this has produced the same results which are promised by the Quran or whether they falsify its claim. The Quran, addressing Rasul-ullah, says:

*Say: 'O my people! Do whatever you can: I will do (my part): soon will you know who it is whose end will be (best) in the Hereafter: certain it is that the wrong-doers will not prosper.' (6:135)*

Tell them, 'You work according to your programme in your place, and I will work according to my programme in my place. It will become apparent to you from the results themselves who is the recipient of success in the end'.

## 6.8    Pragmatic Test

The method to recognize the Law of Requital according to its results, which is known as the pragmatic test, is the best technique of all. There cannot be any more precise and definite technique other than this. However, a difficulty arises in this which has been noted in Chapter 1 (Basis of Deen) i.e. if we leave this law to operate at an evolutionary pace, then for the deeds and their result to manifest takes a very long time which, according to our calculation, could be thousands of years or more.

The way to reduce this time period is for the human *Jamaat* to become the companion and helper of the Divine law. In this way, those results will become manifest according to the human timescale.

As far as the self of an individual is concerned, no matter how long the time period lasts between the commission of a deed and the manifestation of its effect, this makes no difference, because human life does not end with the death of the physical body as it continues on even after this. Therefore, if these effects do not manifest here in this life, then these manifest after death. This is that point where having reached it, certain such beliefs and concepts appear before us which are generally cited in the world of religion e.g. salvation, *Sawaab*, forgiveness, repentance, paradise, hell etc. This will be discussed in the next chapter.

## 6.9    The Concept of Mercy (*Rahm*)

At this stage, it is important to clarify one point. We have seen that the Law of Requital of Allah functions solely on the principle of absolute justice in which there is no room for any concession or intercession. The question is, whether there is even any possibility for 'mercy' (or forgiveness) in it or not. There is definitely a possibility, but the concept of 'mercy' is different. One concept of 'mercy' is this, that according to the law the punishment for his crime has been meted out to a criminal, but he wails and implores, and the ruler, taking mercy on his condition, forgives him. This is the emotive concept of 'mercy' which has nothing whatsoever do with the Law of Requital of Allah. The other concept (and correct one) is that you are in severe pain as a result of having burnt your hand. That same Allah Who has made this law that fire burns and that burning will cause pain, has also created such medicines which can give relief from this pain. If, after the first crime (of putting your hand into fire), you turn to the second law of Allah and make use of those medicines which he has created, then you will receive 'forgiveness' for your crime. This is the concept of 'mercy of Allah' according to the Quran. In other words, for the recovery of the loss suffered due to going against the law of Allah, you have to turn to another law of Allah. Just as Allah's first law is universal and not individual, in the same way this second law of His is universal as well. After transgressing against any law, turning towards that law of Allah through which that loss is compensated, is called *Tauba* (repentance). And by following this second law, acquiring protection from the destructive effects resulting from disobedience of the first law, is called *Maghfirat* (protection). The very meaning of *Maghfirat* is protection – according to the law of Requital of Allah, the concept of, 'Go, you are forgiven' is wrong.

This law of *Tauba* and *Maghfirat* of Allah is applicable to nations in the same way that it is to individuals. If a nation goes against some law of Allah, then the technique to protect itself from the destructive effects of doing this is that it should obey that law of Allah whose effects are constructive and profitable, with even more determination and enthusiasm. The constructive results of this law will provide the means of protection (*Maghfirat*) from the destructive effects of the former mistake.

At this point this summary is considered sufficient. Further details will be covered in the following chapter.

# 7 SALVATION (*NAJAAT*)

Ask anyone in the world, why does he tolerate so much suffering and trouble in the pursuit of religious rituals and commands? Why does he wake up in the later part of winter nights, bathe in freezing waters and sit on bare floors for *Bhakti*[113]? Why does he tolerate the trouble of hunger and thirst during the season of summer in which the days are as long as the height of a mountain? Despite his poverty and deprivation, why does he keep himself in privation by giving charity from his income? Despite the lack of sufficient resources, why does he journey hundreds of miles to perform a pilgrimage to some specific sacred destination? In the end, what is the ultimate purpose of going through these life threatening troubles and privations and tests of patience?

## 7.1 The Objective is Salvation

You will see that from every corner of religion (i.e. from the followers of every religion) you will only receive one answer for these questions, and that will be that we do all this so that we can get *Najaat*, so that we can get *Mukti*[114], so that we can get salvation. Due to the differences of language, these words vary but their meaning is the same i.e. man endures such hardships in the obedience of religious commands so as to achieve salvation. Salvation from what?

## 7.2 The Meaning of Salvation

According to Hindu *Shaster* (*Shariah*), every human child at the time of his birth brings with him the burden of his sins from his previous life. For the whole of his life he tries to get rid of the contamination of these sins, but the case is, more often than not, that there is a further increase in this contamination. Then he dies, and subsequently, together with the burden of these contaminations, he takes birth again. This process is continuous and is called the circle of *Avagown* (*Tanasakh*). The aim and ultimate purpose of life is that man should achieve *Mukti* from this circle of *Avagown*. The extreme hardships of religious commands and rituals are undertaken for this.

As per (Hindu) *Vedant* (i.e. through mysticism), the human soul (*Atma*) is part of the soul of God (*Parmatma*) which has become separated from its whole and is trapped in *Prakarti* (material) impurities and is constantly entangled in anguish and suffering. The purpose of life is to free this *Atma* from the constraint of matter and this purpose cannot be achieved without going through the hardships and privations of *Yug*.

---

[113] *Bhakti* - a Hindu ritual. For more details see Wikipedia. (Ed)
[114] *Mukti* - Hindu concept of salvation. (Ed)

According to Buddhism, every desire of man becomes the precursor for a new hardship. The purpose of life is to free the human heart from the deception of the desires of the heart - in this way he achieves *Nirvan*, which means complete annihilation.

According to Christian belief, every human child is born with the burden of sin on his back from his first parents (Adam and Eve). The purpose of religion is to provide him with salvation from the burden of this sin which can be achieved by believing in the 'crucifixion and atonement' of Christ.

The belief of the Jews is that every child of Bani Israel gains paradise following circumcision, but as a result of some sins having been committed by their ancestors in a bygone era, this nation will be sent to hell for a period of time. To be freed from the punishment of this hell is called salvation.

Keep this concept of salvation in mind and see how at a fundamental level one element is a common value i.e. that man was hale and hearty somewhere, and for certain reasons he was sent to the prison of the world. After toiling at the grindstone in this prison, once he has proven himself to be a 'gentleman', he will then be extricated from the prison and sent back to his original position. This is what salvation is. Using an ordinary example, you can comprehend it as a person who awoke in the morning feeling well and then became feverish around ten o'clock in the morning. All day he remained feverish, the doctor administered medicine and by dusk he received salvation and his fever subsided i.e. he became as he had been in the morning prior to falling ill. He achieved nothing from the exertion and hardship of the whole day - he only became the same as he was previously. This is that concept (i.e. as you were) which is the basis of salvation. The cloth was white, it became dirty with dust and grime, the *dhobi* (washerman) laundered it, the dirt was removed and the cloth became white as before. This is the meaning of salvation.

Now reflect as to whether this explanation appeals to intellect and reasoning - that this great system of the universe, the awesome programme of human creation, such an eminent process of Divine revelation and guidance, was brought into being merely so that man can become the same as he was previously. From this, there is no progress, no achievement, no constructive purpose intended. Every man of vision will declare that this is child's play which cannot be attributed to Allah, the Wise, All-knowing:

*Exalted is Allah from the things they ascribe. (37:159)*

## 7.3 The Purpose of Human Life According to the Quran

According to the Quran, the purpose of human life is not *Mukti*. The aim of Deen is not *Najaat*. Man is neither trapped in the prison of this world toiling at a grindstone, nor is salvation the aim of his endeavours in this life. Neither has his soul become detached from its whole and is now trapped in material impurity, nor is he born bearing any burden of sin on his back from his previous birth, nor is he sent here as a consequence of the crimes of his first parents. The Quran declares that every human child arrives in the world with a clean and untainted slate. He is given some realisable possibilities, the development of which is the purpose of his life.

According to the Greek philosophers, the dynamics of the universe was cyclical i.e. it was going around in a single circle like a merry-go-round. During this continual journey, it was not taking any step forward. If we examine it more closely, then it becomes evident that the Hindu concept of the circle of *Avagown* or the belief of salvation, is the outcome of this cyclical belief about the universe. The Hindu philosophy of life is mostly borrowed from Greek philosophy. The Quran came and rejected this doctrine as false and declared that life does not go round in a circle, instead it advances straight ahead and is on a balanced path:

> ...Indeed, my Rabb (Sustainer) is on a path that is straight. (11:56)

Say to them that my Sustainer is on a path which is balanced and straight i.e. Allah is directing His universe along a straight path according to His law. In another verse, it is stated:

> The path of Allah, to Whom belongs whatever is in the heavens and whatever is on the earth...(42:53)

This is the path of that Allah for the completion of Whose programme the whole universe is in action. Therefore, the universe is also proceeding along a straight and balanced path, and not only a straight and balanced path, but one which is ascending as well – the path of that Allah Who is:

> (From Allah), Owner of the ways of ascent. (70:3)

Hence, the universe is progressing forward on a straight and balanced path and alongside this is also ascending. It is traversing through its evolutionary stages and heading towards its destination. In other words, according to the Quran, the universe is progressive and dynamic. It is not static and not going round in a single circle. This is that same path on which man is invited to tread. Therefore, in Surah *Al Fatihah* mankind is taught this very *Dua* (prayer):

*Guide us to the straight path. (1:5)*

From this, this reality becomes evident that according to the Quran the purpose of the endeavours and hardships of human life is not to achieve salvation from some difficulty and become 'as you were', but is to progress forward on the highway of life and to ascend higher – this is called evolution. As has already been noted, according to the Quran:

(1) Man does not arrive into life with any kind of burden; he comes with a clean and untainted slate.
(2) He is bestowed with many realisable potentials by nature.
(3) The purpose of his life is to actualise these possibilities, to manifest his latent potentials and to develop his self, and in this way, from this life, become worthy of living a more eminent life at a higher plane.

## 7.4   The Evolutionary Stages of Life

About these evolutionary stages of life, the Quran has stated:

*You shall surely ascend stage by stage. (84:19)*

Hence the purpose of life is not to gain freedom from some trap – it is to ascend ever higher by traversing through evolutionary stages. For this, Deen provides a practical programme. It is obvious that there are two parts for every programme. One is that doctrine, law or formula which is the foundation of this programme, and the second is that technique through which the programme can reach its completion. The first condition for the success of the programme is that the formula on which it is based should contain within it the potential to progress forward. If the formula itself only has the potential to produce wrong or negative effects, then the programme which is dependent on it can never succeed. Next, this technique should possess the ability to make this formula blossom further. Note in what a beautiful and balanced way the Quran, in a few words, has explained this foundation and the structure raised on it. It states:

*If any do seek power - then to Allah belongs all power. To Him mount up words of Purity, and it is He Who exalts each deed of righteousness…(35:10)*

The prosperous and pleasant doctrine of life (which is received through revelation) contains the potential of ascension and progression, and righteous deeds raise it high. The Quran explains this abstract reality through the practical metaphor of a farm (this is a common technique in the Quran). On a farm, the fundamental item is the healthy seed which contains the potential to germinate, sprout and bear fruit.

## 7.5    Eimaan and Righteous Deeds

This is that ideology which, according to the terminology of the Quran, is called Eimaan. After this, is that process through which the growth and development of this seed occurs in such a way, that at its appropriate time, it prospers and flowers and bears fruit. If this seed remains buried deep under a pile of earth, not even a seedling will sprout from it. Using this metaphor, regarding the aim and objective of human life the Quran states that:

*He has succeeded who develops it, and he has failed who suppressed it. (91:9-10)*

The one who developed his self, his crop reached fruition, but the one who suppressed his self, he became ruined and destroyed. Therefore, (as noted in the previous chapter) there is not even a question of man receiving reward or punishment externally in return for his actions – reward or punishment of deeds is concealed within the deeds themselves and is their natural consequence. The result of righteous deeds is the development of man's self, whereas the result of wrong deeds is weakness and decline in his self, or the disintegration of the self. This is that reality about which the Quran has stated:

*…Can they expect to be rewarded except as they have wrought? (7:147)*

Their deeds themselves become their recompense and confront them.

## 7.6    Confrontation Between Truth and Falsehood

In the development of the human self, or we can say, in the process of implementation of the Permanent Values within human society, destructive forces and vested interests stand up as an obstruction in its path. It is essential to confront these forces and this is what is called the struggle between *Haqq* (Truth) and *Batil* (Evil). It is obvious that to remove these rebelling elements from the path, power will be used. Now, if the situation is such that the accumulated power is continually being used and new power is not being produced, then after a period of time, man will not have any strength left with which to confront these destructive forces. The Quran states that inherent in the system of action proposed by it, is the ability that whatever force or power is utilised in the achievement of this objective, it can replenish it. In Arabic terminology, this is called *Sawaab*[115].

---

[115] *Sawaab* - this term is explained in more detail in the book titled '*The Life in the Hereafter; What Does the Quran Say*' by the author.

## 7.7   The Meaning of *Sawaab*

The word *Saub* means to return; whatever has been spent has been returned in full. The English translation of the word *Istasaab* will be restoration. Therefore, under the Quranic System whatever energies are expended in the defence of *Haqq* and to defeat *Batil*, these are restored simultaneously.

Let us consider another example. In the case of infectious diseases (e.g. influenza) you may have seen that some people succumb to it immediately, whereas others remain unaffected. The reason for this is obvious. People who have reduced immunity are quickly overwhelmed by the germs of disease, whereas those in whom immunity is greater, are not affected by these germs.

What does the doctor do in such cases of infectious diseases? He suggests such measures due to which the immunity of people improves and they become capable of fighting the infecting germs.

## 7.8   The Meaning of *Maghfirat* (Protection)

Similarly, when some person falls ill due to these germs, the doctor helps to improve his immunity and this increase in immunity assists the patient against the destructive elements. In Quranic terms this process is called *Maghfirat*. The meaning of *Maghfirat* is protection. The term *Maghfir* is used to denote that helmet which soldiers wear in order to protect their heads in a battlefield.

In this connection, let us look at another example. You are heading to some village. On the way, the road divides into two at a junction from where you step in the wrong direction. After travelling for a mile, you come to realise that you are on the wrong path. It is obvious that whatever energy and time was spent in travelling this journey of a mile, all went to waste. About such travellers on these wrong paths in the journey of life, the Quran states:

*...so their deeds have become worthless...(18:105)*

These are the ones whose works remained fruitless and were wasted.

## 7.9   The Meaning of *Tauba* (Repentance)

After realizing your mistake, what do you do? You again return to that same junction where you stepped in the wrong direction. In Arabic terminology such a return is called *Tauba*. But it is obvious that the result of this return of one mile on the same path is negative. Its positive outcome will commence at that point in time when, after having reached the junction, you start treading in the right direction.

If you were previously walking on foot and now you take some method of conveyance, then whatever time and energy was consumed in going in the wrong direction, will be saved. The Quran terms this whole process as *Taba wa Aslaha* i.e. to desist from the wrong path and to produce an increased ability within oneself to follow the right path.

If we wish to understand it using the example of disease, then it can be said that *Maghfirat* is a preventive measure and *Tauba* is a curative action. Or, after suitable treatment following the attack of a disease, gaining protection from the destructive effects of the disease will also be called *Maghfirat*. It is apparent that the whole foundation of this process is based on the fact that, if measures which produce constructive results are more effective, then these will overcome the elements which produce destructive results, and will eradicate and compensate for their harmful effects. This reality is specified in the Quran in the following words:

> *...Indeed, good deeds do away with misdeeds...(11:114)*

Remember that deeds which create balance compensate for deeds producing damaging effects. In another verse, it is stated:

> *If you avoid the major wrongs which you are forbidden, We will remove from you your smaller errors and admit you to a noble entrance. (4:31)*

If you continue to avoid the big wrongs from which We have forbidden you, then We will compensate for the harmful effects of your minor mistakes and admit you into an eminent place.

From these explanations it is clear that, according to the Quran:

(1) The aim of life is not to be rid of some punishment (i.e. to gain salvation), but by developing the human self, is to ascend and evolve towards a higher plane of life from the current level of existence in life.
(2) For this aim, a human being is not conceived as an angel who cannot make a mistake. He (Allah) keeps an eye on the weaker aspects of man and says that if the balance of your righteous deeds is kept heavier, then He will compensate for your weaknesses and you will ascend one step higher on the ladder of life. In this regard, He says in very clear words:

> *And those whose scales are heavy (with good deeds) - it is they who are the successful. But those whose scales are light - those are the ones who have lost their self, in Hell, abiding eternally. (23:102-103)*

Whoever has a heavier scale (of righteous deeds), his orchard will bear fruit. The ones whose scale remains light will be those people in whose self there is a deficiency and thus they will not be capable of moving on to the next stage, and so will remain in hell.

This reality should be understood by relating the example of a student. If the marks required to pass an annual exam (for example) are sixty percent, then the student who achieves sixty percent will be successful in moving on to the next class. His forty percent of mistakes do not obstruct his progress. But the student who gains only fifty percent marks does not get promotion. The marks achieved are of no benefit to him because he does not meet the criterion fixed for promotion to the next stage. He is halted wherever he is, with this proviso, that, in the example of a school, he is given an opportunity by staying in the same class to achieve success in the following year. But in the case of the human self, this is not possible. The basic condition in this case is that whichever individual in this earthly life has attained competence to such a degree with which he becomes capable of journeying through the next life, he will achieve promotion. Whoever has not achieved this much competence, will stagnate forever.

## 7.10 *Jannat* and *Jahannum* (Paradise and Hell)

The Quran has called the state of the ones who are able to progress forward as *Jannat* and the state of the ones who have halted as *Jahannum*. *Jahannum* is a Hebrew word (which means that valley in which human beings used to be sacrificed). In the Arabic language, the Quran has used the word *Jaheem* for *Jahannum*, whose basic meaning is of halting someone. This is also what happens in the universe according to the theory of evolution. The species which, after having reached a certain stage loses the ability to move forward, halts at that stage. Hence, this belief that criminals will be sent to hell for a period of time to be given punishment and, after completing their period of punishment, they will enter paradise, is a non-Quranic concept. According to the Quran, the question of getting out of *Jahannum* does not even arise. In Surah *Al Hajj* it is stated:

*Every time they want to get out of Hellfire from anguish, they will be returned to it…(22:22)*

Contrary to this, the dwellers of *Jannat* will be kept far from this right from the start. They will not be able to hear even a whisper from *Jahannum* (21:101-102). In other words, those people who give so much development to their self that it will become capable of living in the next life from the present life, they will be the dwellers of paradise. The ones in whom there is not this much capability, will be halted from progressing forward, and they will be called the denizens of hell.

From the above discussion, this reality becomes apparent to us that, according to the Quran:

(1) This belief is wrong that the purpose of human life is to gain freedom from some punishment.

(2) This concept of reward and retribution is also not correct that reward means to be given something from outside and retribution means punishment. Reward and retribution are natural consequences of deeds and their effects are imprinted on the human self.

(3) *Jaheem* means that man will not be capable of traversing the evolutionary stages of life. This is why his development will stop. And since he will feel the consequences of this loss intensely, therefore his life will be in hell.

(4) The dwellers of paradise will be those who will have developed within themselves the ability to traverse ever more evolutionary stages of life. This will be such a massive and successful achievement seeing which will give rise to immense delight in their beings.

According to this philosophy of reward and punishment, someone gaining exemption through another's intercession, or atoning for another's sins, or getting salvation by merely accepting Eimaan (without deeds), or the 'forgiving' of sins by Allah, is a non-Quranic concept. Successes and prosperities of life are the name given to the natural consequences of human deeds. These cannot be obtained as a 'charity' from anywhere.

The concept of *Safarish* and *Bakhshish* (intercession and forgiveness) is the product of that mentality according to which God is conceived as an earthly king. The concept of God which is presented by the Quran is One Whose every act is according to law and order, and in law and order there is never any question of intercession and forgiveness. If we sow wheat, we will reap wheat, and if we sow barley, we will reap barley – this is an immutable law which always remains in force.

According to this law, you can gain *Maghfirat* but not *Bakhshish*. And as has already been stated, *Maghfirat* means that man through large, righteous deeds protects himself from the consequences of minor mistakes. Therefore, that which is commonly known as *Bakhshish* is also the result of man's own righteous deeds. (It would be more correct to call this protection instead of *Bakhshish*, in fact it should never be called *Bakhshish*, it should be called *Maghfirat*, meaning protection.)

At this juncture, it is important to clarify this much that the Quran has also used the word *Najaat*. But the meaning of *Najaat* is not only to escape from some punishment, it also means to remain fully protected from some destruction, and this is the actual meaning of *Najaat* as per the Quran i.e. man remaining protected from destruction through righteous deeds.

The Quran has also called the life of paradise as 'life forever'. This will be discussed in the next chapter.

# 8 LIFE FOREVER (IMMORTALITY)

No human being in the world, (apart from those who have lost their mental balance), wishes to die. He wishes to live forever. Preservation of the self is an intrinsic animal instinct. Since animals do not possess any concept even of death, the thought of living forever therefore does not even arise in their heart. They only want self-preservation. Man possesses consciousness about death, therefore the desire to live forever frequently enters his heart.

## 8.1   Desire for Life Forever

In the story of Adam, the Quran has stated that *Iblees*[116] exploited this motive in man. This much should also be understood that the narrative of Adam as explained in the Quran is not the story of a particular individual (i.e. a man named Adam). This is the metaphorical account of man himself. This is the story of his human condition, emotions, problems and the mutual conflicts of his psychological and social life, which is presented by the Quran in extremely beautiful metaphors which appeal deeply to the heart. In this narrative, *Iblees* represents those emotions of man which prevent him from bowing to the Divine laws (or Permanent Values) and in this way yank him towards the ruin and destruction of hell.[117] In relation to this story, the Quran has stated metaphorically:

> *Then Satan whispered to him; he said, 'O Adam, shall I direct you to the tree of eternity and possession that will not deteriorate?' And Adam and his wife ate of it, and their private parts became apparent to them, and they began to fasten over themselves from the leaves of the garden...(20:120-121)*

*Iblees* said to Adam – shall I tell you of the whereabouts of a tree from which you will get immortality, and such a kingdom on which decline will never descend? Adam and his wife ate of the fruit of this tree, from this their sexual awareness was aroused due to which they felt shame, and they began to cover their bodies with leaves from the trees in the garden.

## 8.2   Immortality in the Form of Offspring

In this metaphor, the Quran has stated that the desire to live forever always remains alive in the human heart. He never wishes to die, but despite his thousands of endeavours he cannot escape the grip of death. Therefore, in order to satisfy his greed to live after death, he achieves this in the form of his offspring. He says that after my death, my name will remain bright through my children. The flowers

---

[116] *Iblees* or Satan – these terms represent human emotions and desires.
[117] Further details are covered in the book titled *'Iblees and Adam'*, by the author.

and fruits of this tree will be my own flowers and fruits (hence the very name of the map of an ancestral chain is called the 'ancestral tree').

The Quran declares that this is a deception through which man satisfies his own heart. The life of every human being is an individual one. Therefore, an individual can never remain alive by another's remaining alive, even if the other person is own son. Immortality is achieved through the development of the human self.

It is important at this point to clarify this much, that what the Quran has said about immortality not being achievable through offspring, does not mean that the Quran declares the love of wife and children as something to be despised - not at all. It states that these things are a cause for attraction. In Surah *Al Imran* it states:

> *Beautified for people is the love of that which they desire - of women and sons, heaped-up sums of gold and silver, fine branded horses, and cattle and tilled land. That is the enjoyment of worldly life, but Allah has with Him the best return (in the following of Divine Laws). (3:14)*

For humans the love of wife and children, wealth and possessions, well-bred horses, cattle, ranches (i.e. all worldly things which are attractive), is made a cause for lure. (But this much should be understood that these things are not the ultimate aim and objective of life, these are the needs of physical life). But the pleasant abode of real life is achieved through the Divine laws (not through physical laws).

The Quran wishes to make it clear from this that the father cannot gain immortality through the life of his son. The method for achieving immortality is different.

## 8.3    Immortality Through Development of the Self

This is achieved through the development of the human self and death is its test. The Quran states:

> *Who created death and life to provide you opportunities to develop your self and to see (for yourself) which of you is best in deed...(67:2)*

We created death and life so that you could receive opportunities to develop the self and so that it could be seen who amongst you does such good deeds due to which his self becomes developed.

Death disintegrates the human body, but if the human self becomes suitably developed, then it does not finish with the physical death of the body. In Surah *Al Naml* it is stated:

*Whoever comes with a righteous deed will have better recompense than his deed, and they will be protected from the terror of that Day (death will not affect them).*
*(27:89)*

There is no doubt in this that the shock of death is a massive one. Through this, the process of the physical life of man is severed forever (as there is no return to this world). But regarding those in whom the potentials of the self have awakened, this shock cannot affect them adversely:

*They will not be grieved by such a great revulsion...(21:103)*

From these explanations, it is clear that immortality is achieved through intention and deeds. Every individual does not just receive it as a right. Righteous deeds and intention (i.e. living life willingly within the remit of the Permanent Values) are not an issue of life at the animal level, therefore the question of immortality at this level of existence does not arise. In this connection, Professor Galloway writes:

*That every creature formed in the semblance of man, however brutish and undeveloped, is destined to immortality, is more than we dare affirm. To do so would require a deeper knowledge of divine economy than we possess. We agree with Lotze, 'that every created thing will continue if and so long as its continuance belongs to the meaning of the world: that everything will pass away which had its authorized place only in a transitory phase of the world's course'.*[118]

Life after death is an established reality according to the Quran, but what kind of form or state this life will take cannot be understood at the existing level of human consciousness. In Surah *Al Waqi'ah* it is stated:

*We have decreed Death to be your common lot, and We are not to be frustrated from changing your forms and creating you (again) in (forms) that you know not. (56:60-61)*

We have established the scales of death among you and We are not in any way limited from changing your existing form into such a form of which you have no knowledge.

---

[118] G. Galloway, *The Philosophy of Religion*, pp. 572-573.

## 8.4 Life Following Death

The decomposition of the human body does not affect the human self in any way, because the human self is neither part of the body nor under the control of physical laws. Hence the Quran, presenting the material concept of life, declares:

*They say: 'What! When we are reduced to bones and dust, should we really be raised up as a new creation?' Say:  be you (even) stones or iron, Or created matter which, in your minds, is hardest (to be raised up), (Yet shall you be raised up)! Then will they say: 'Who will cause us to return?' Say: He who created you first time...(17:49-51)*

These people say that when we have decayed into a skeleton of bones and thus will disintegrate into particles, what, will we still be re-created? Say to them, that (leaving aside being bones), if you were stone or iron or something even tougher than this of which you can conceive as being very difficult to bring to life, even then you will be brought to life. They say, who will create us anew? Say to them, that same Allah Who brought you into existence from nothing the first time.

It is obvious that life did not come into existence according to physical laws from nothing the first time. This came into existence according to that plan which is related to Allah's universe of *Amr* i.e. life is not the product of physical laws. This came into existence through the *Amr* of Allah. Similarly, the life after death will not come into existence according to physical laws – it will come into existence according to the *Amr* of Allah. This is the next link in the evolutionary process, in which greater strength and ability will develop in the human self and it will become free from dependency on the present supports. In Surah *Nuh* it is stated that Allah has created you by passing you through various stages. Now, after the present stage of life, why are you not desirous of more *Waqar*[119] in this? The messenger Noah says to his people:

*'What is the matter with you that you place not your hope for attaining solidarity from Allah, Seeing that it is He that has created you in diverse stages?' (71:13-14)*

This thing (*Waqar*) is acquired by living life according to the Permanent Values i.e. this will be the outcome of man's own righteous behaviour.

## 8.5 Intention and Deed

With regard to a 'deed', it is important to understand this much that a deed is the name given to the manifestation of an intention. The one who has no intention, his deed is not even a deed; in other words, an individual is not responsible for the

---

[119] *Waqar* – this means heaviness i.e. crystallization or solidarity of the human self.

consequence of a deed behind which there is no intention. Similarly, righteousness under compulsion is not righteousness, nor is evil, evil. Therefore, for the one who does not possess intention, the question of strengthening or weakening his self does not even arise. The one who, with intention through his own volition, selects the wrong path and in this way development of his self does not occur, will also be alive after physical death. But as was noted in the previous chapter, he will not have the ability within him to evolve further. This is declared to be the life of hell about which the Quran states:

*In which they will then neither die nor live. (87:13)*

In this, they will be counted neither among the dead, nor among the living. Neither death will come to them, nor will they have life. No death, because after physical death they were made alive, no life, because life is only the name of progression and evolution itself. The life in which there is no growth and development is not life. It is stated in the Quran that such a person will say with regret, 'I wish I had sent something forward for my life' (89:24). Contrary to this, the occupants of *Jannat* will be the possessors of immortality and will say:

*'We shall not die, except our first death, and we shall not be among those who are punished'. (37:58-59)*

We, after the first death (which we face in the world) shall not die. They will be alive and active and ever more evolutionary stages of life will keep lighting up in front of them:

*One Day you will see the believing men and the believing women - how their Light runs forward before them and by their right hands...(57:12)*

In other words, the life of the occupants of hell will be mere survival after death, and the life of the dwellers of paradise will be immortality, which every individual will not receive as a right, but will have to achieve through his own righteous deeds. Survival is the state of the intense regret caused by the destructive effects of following the wrong path of life; and immortality is the name of the state of continuing ahead while progressing through further extremely pleasant evolutionary stages of life.

This is what the material concept of life tells man:

*And they say: 'What is there but our life in this world? We shall die and we live, and nothing but time can destroy us'...(45:24)*

But the Quranic concept of life teaches that, if you awaken the powers of your self, then you can remove yourself from the confines of these 'materialistic four walls' and can progress very far ahead (55:33).

## 8.6   Both Lives Are Not Alike

This is the fundamental reason why neither the life nor the death of those who possess these two contradictory ideologies can be the same. The Quran states:

*What! Do those who seek after evil ways think that We shall hold them equal with those who believe and do righteous deeds - that equal will be their life and their death?...(45:21)*

Do those people, who create inequities, sit thinking that We will make them like the ones who have conviction in the Permanent Values and tread on Our proposed potential enhancing programme of life? Not at all! Neither can their life be as one, nor can their death. How false and evil is that judgement which these people make for themselves.

## 8.7   A Momin (Believer) Does Not Fear Death

This is the reason that for a Momin death is not something to fear. He knows and maintains conviction in the fact that with the cessation of breathing, man does not die - the doors of further paths of evolutionary stages of life open up before him. For him, therefore, death is the stairway to further ascendency and this is the reason that the Quran has declared death to be a criterion for truth. It asks the Jews (opponents):

*...then seek you for death if you are truthful. (2:94)*

If you are truthful in your claim, then show us your desire for death in the defence of truth. Only he can lay down his life for the preservation of a Permanent Value who is assured of this fact, that death in this manner will result in immortality for man. These are the very ones about whom the Quran declares:

*And say not of those who are slain in the way of Allah: 'They are dead.' Nay, they are living, though ye perceive (it) not. (2:154)*

This is that technique through which the human desire to live forever is fulfilled. At this point it is important to understand that the 'immortality' of man is not infinite in the same way as that of the Divine Self. But at the level of our present consciousness, we cannot even say what will be the ultimate end of the human self. And when it is not infinite like the Divine Self, and neither is it a part of the

Divine Self, then what will be its end? In this connection, the Quran only tells us this much that after the disintegration of the human body, human life progresses forward traversing through its further evolutionary stages. Regarding the states of existence after this, the Quran neither discusses this nor can we make any comments. This question is beyond the limits of our present level of cognitive comprehension, just as the issue of the beginning of life itself and the universe is beyond the bounds of our intellectual comprehension.

But as has already been noted, life after death is a reality, to have Eimaan in which is a basic requirement of Islam. This is, in reality, an extension of the Law of Requital. If life is only confined to the life of this world then the whole ideology of Deen becomes meaningless. Its structure only rises on the human self, the Law of Requital and Eimaan in the continuity of life.

## 8.8   Paradise and Hell in This World

So far, we have been discussing that part of life which is concerned with the world after death. But the Quran says that the manifestation of the results of human deeds begins in the life of the present world i.e. the process of building of Paradise and Hell commences right here. By living a life according to the Divine laws, a paradise like society is established here in this world and this is that paradise which the Quran does not consider of lesser importance. But this is established through the hands of those people whose abilities of the self begin to manifest here. Therefore, in the next chapter we will discuss how the human self develops and how a paradise-like society is established through the hands of those people whose self begins to manifest itself.

# 9 THE PRINCIPLE OF DEVELOPMENT OF THE HUMAN SELF

In the previous chapters we have seen that the focal point of Deen is conviction in the human self and its aim is the development of this self. In the Arabic language, nourishment and development is called *Rabubiyat*. This refers to that technique or method through which a thing is taken from the point of its beginning and slowly and carefully it is gradually taken to its point of completion. If you look at the outer universe, you will see the functioning of the law of *Rabubiyat* everywhere.

## 9.1 The Law of *Rabubiyat*

In the example of a farm quoted in the Quran, a seed stores that kind of potential of becoming a tree of which it is the seed. If suitable nourishment is provided to this seed (*Rabubiyat*) then these latent potentials will keep manifesting themselves. From the seed, there will sprout a seedling and from this seedling a plant will grow. This plant will grow and become a tall strong tree. After this, (we need to understand the differences between various seeds), the end objective of the seed of a poplar tree is to become a poplar tree in which there are only leaves; in a jasmine plant there will be flowers in addition to leaves; in a mango tree there will be fruit as well. The ultimate objective of such a process will be that seeds are reproduced in these trees from which this process remains continual. This means the ultimate aim of a seed is to produce another seed like itself. Moving forward from plants, animals also have a similar condition. The objective of an animal life is also to produce another animal like itself. So, up to the animal level, a cyclical order remains established. This is the final end of this process. Nothing can exceed this constraint. The Quran states:

*Say: Everyone acts according to its own disposition...(17:84)*

Every single thing can go to that extent to which it is destined. This constraint is what is termed the destiny of this thing. As far as man is concerned, when his life remains merely at the animal level, then in that too, in the process of procreation, a cycle becomes established, in which the ultimate objective of the life of every individual is confined to procreating a person (son or daughter) like himself.[120]

---

[120] As already written, procreation is important for the nourishment and continuation of human generations. What we wish to note here is that the ultimate aim of human life is not procreation – its aim is the development of the human self.

## 9.2    The Aim of Human Life

But when life, (by raising up from the animal level), is brought to the human level, the ultimate aim is not to procreate and produce another person like us, it is to develop the human self and to progress forward and keep ascending. When Allah had declared about Himself that He neither produces another like His Own Self through the process of procreation, nor is He Himself the product of the process of procreation[121], by this it was to point to this same characteristic of the self. Therefore, when life reaches the human level, then the caravan of life does not travel in a circle. It keeps progressing forward in a straight path (a path which is straight and balanced).

In the universe, with regard to the system of *Rabubiyat*, another point merits attention. For the nourishment and development of a seed, soil, water, air and temperature is required. However, if you put a seed to one side on a table and on the other side leave some soil and fill a bowl with water, with air and heat (sunlight) already being present in the room, despite the presence of all of these elements a seedling will not sprout from this seed. For this it is essential that these elements become amalgamated. It is evident from this that, in the system of *Rabubiyat*, for the nourishment and development of something, mutual co-operation of different elements, indeed amalgamation, is essential.

## 9.3    Development of the Self Takes Place Within a Collective System

The development of the human self also cannot take place in the individualistic life of monasticism. This is a completely non-Quranic concept. According to the Quran, the *Rabubiyat* of the self of an individual takes place while residing in a society through mutual cooperation and help, indeed the coming together of hearts (by merging into one another). In this regard, the Quran states:

> And hold fast, all together, by the rope of Allah (the Quran), and be not divided among yourselves; and remember with gratitude Allah's favor on you; for you were enemies and He joined your hearts in love, so that by His Grace, you became brethren (to each other); and you were on the brink of the pit of Fire, and He saved you from it. Thus does Allah make His Signs clear to you: That you may be guided. (3:102)

For this purpose, the Quran shapes an Ummah:

> Thus, have We made of you an Ummah justly balanced, that you may be witnesses over the nations...(2:143)

---

[121] 'He begetteth not, nor is He begotten' (112:3)

And in this collective system the self of individuals develops.

## 9.4    The Need for Balance and Proportion

Regarding the process of the nourishment and development of things in the universe, another point is worthy of attention. In the example of a seed, if too much soil is applied, insufficient or too much water is given, the wind blows too strong, if the temperature is either too high or too low, even then development of the seed will not take place. For this, it is essential that there should be a specific balance and proportion among these elements.

This is also the condition for the nourishment and development of the human self. By examining it closely, this reality will become evident, that the human self is the sum of many attributes. Not just the human self, but the self of Allah Himself, the image of Whose attributes are reflected on a smaller scale in the human self, possesses many attributes. In other words, numerous attributes remain concealed in the self. It is essential to have specific balance and proportion within these attributes. The Quran has used the term *Al Asma ul Husna* (proportionate attributes) for the Divine attributes. *Husn* is the best proportion, therefore these are declared the most beautifully proportionate (*Al Husna*). From this respect, the Quran has declared those deeds through which the attributes of the human self manifest themselves with a specific proportion, as righteous deeds or *Al Hasnaat*.

## 9.5    The Basic Principle for the Development of the Human Self

The law for the development of the physical body is that every individual grows with whatever he himself eats. This is impossible that I should be the one who eats healthy food but the growth should be of the body of my brother. This is that 'selfishness' on which physical life is completely dependent. At the physical level, no individual can be exempted from this. But contrary to this, the human self develops from that thing which he gives for the nourishment and development of others. This is that point from where there becomes a glaring difference in the paths of animal (i.e. physical) life and human (i.e. concept based on the self) life. In the physical life, 'taking' is essential for the human body, but the principle for the development of the human self is that of 'giving'. In the case of the former, preferring yourself over others is essential. If you and your neighbour are hungry and there is only one piece of bread, until you give yourself preference over your neighbour and eat that bread, nourishment of your body will not occur. But for the development of the human self it is imperative to prefer others over yourself. Regarding those people who spend their lives along these lines, the Quran states:

*...but give them preference over themselves, even though poverty was their (own lot). And those saved from the covetousness of their own self, they are the ones that achieve prosperity. (59:9)*

Regarding those who prefer others over themselves, even if by doing so they have to live in hardship, the truth is that these individuals who are saved from preferring themselves over others are the ones whose fields will flourish.

## 9.6  What is *Shu'ha Nafs* (Covetousness of the Heart)

In the above verse, it is stated that only the one who saves himself from *Shu'ha Nafs* can be successful. What does *Shu'ha Nafs* mean? In order to understand this, bring to mind this scenario. It is the season of extreme heat and the water tap will only be open for two hours and the water will run from it with a much reduced flow. If you look towards the people waiting to get water you will see a queue of empty utensils from here far into the distance. In this situation, the desire (rather effort) of every individual will be to push another back and to advance forward and take his fill of water. This motive is called *Shu'ha Nafs*. The Quran states that the individual who remains protected from this motive and instead of pushing others back, himself steps back and allows those who are more needy to take water first – his fields will bloom. According to physical law, the one whose land receives timely water will be the one whose farm bears fruit, (in a village they will go to the extent of murder for this), but according to the Quranic System of *Rabubiyat*, the person who is successful is the one who turns the direction of water towards the fields of others.

## 9.7  For the Good of Mankind

'Others' here does not just mean people of his own group, own party, own tribe, own nation, own religion – in this are included all of those people from the whole of mankind (irrespective of religion, colour, language, tribe, nation) whose need is greater. For this, the fundamental principle of the Quran is this:

*... What is good for mankind remains on earth...(13:17)*

According to the Quran, this is the core value for the development of the human self. According to this principle, the Quran shapes such a society in which every person is busy in the effort of work towards the development of others and prefers others over himself. And he does all this because his Eimaan is that, by doing so, development of his self will take place. And this is the sole objective and purpose of his life.

## 9.8  Support from Western Thinkers

This is that very reality which Western thinkers and researchers are now presenting with great emphasis. In this regard, Rashdall writes in his book on ethics:

*'It may be urged that the ideal is that I should be producing something for another and find my good in doing so; while he is working in turn for my good, and finds his good in doing so.'*[122]

The well-known historian of human civilisation, Robert Brifault, writes in his renowned book, 'The Making of Humanity':

*'The peculiar means and conditions of human development necessitate that development shall take place not by way of individuals, but by way of the entire human race; that the grade of development of each individual is the resultant of that ecumenical development.'*[123]

He says further:

*'The making of humanity! That is the burden of man's evolution; and that is the solid, nay, somewhat hard fact, of which the 'moral law' is the vaguely conscious expression. It is not throbbing impulse of altruism, no inspiration of generosity for its own sake, but a heavy weight of necessity laid upon man's development by the unbending conditions that govern it.'*[124]

With reference to how important the development of others is, this thinker writes in another place:

*'In the natural scale, that action is good which contributes to the process of human development, that act is evil which tends to impede, retard, oppose that process: that individual life is well deserving which is in the direct line of that evolution, that is futile which lies outside the course of its advance; that is condemned which endeavours to oppose the current. That is the natural, the absolute and actual standard of moral values. Nature does not value the most saintly and charitable life which brings no contribution to human growth, as much as a single act which permanently promotes the evolution of the race... The only measure of worth of which nature takes any account — by*

---

[122] H. Rashdall, *The Theory of Good and Evil*, Vol II, p. 77
[123] R. Briffault, *Making of Humanity*, p. 260
[124] Ibid., p. 261

*perpetuating it – is the contribution offered towards the building up of a higher humanity.'* [125]

## 9.9   Evolution of the Whole of Mankind

As has been already written, the Quran only declares that deed as worthy of survival which is for the good of the whole of mankind. The truth is that the addressee of the Quran is the whole of mankind itself. The objective of this programme is to make the whole of mankind one Ummah:

*Mankind was but one Ummah...(10:19)*

This is the revolutionary proclamation and life-giving aim of the Quran. It declares the whole of mankind to be as one individual and states in clear words:

*And your creation or your resurrection is in no wise but as an individual self...(31:28)*

In order to achieve this aim, regarding the map of the system of *Rabubiyat* which it presents, it states about the centre (Ka'bah) that it is established for the security and asylum of mankind (5:97). Therefore, when it says that the human self can only develop when it concerns itself regarding the development of others, then this development is not restricted to its own group. This includes all people of the whole of mankind (without any distinction of religion or nation and without any discrimination of colour or race).

Professor Whitehead has pointed to this very reality when he said:

*'The perfection of life resides in aims beyond the individual person in question.'* [126]

Mason in this regard says:

*'Man, in his individual capacity, self-develops his personality as he satisfies his desires, and his self-conscious interpretation of his subconscious knowledge of his origin in Pure Spirit may influence his activities. But, racially, man ought to engage only in such activities as tend to extend creative freedom to the utmost through the self-creativeness of all personalities to their uttermost limits. Man may turn from this second movement while holding to the first. Man, therefore, may be moral individually and immoral racially. The highest personalities unite the two moralities.'* [127]

---

[125] Ibid., p. 352
[126] A. N. Whitehead, *Adventures of Ideas*, p. 373
[127] J. W. T. Mason, *Creative Freedom*, p. 226

With regard to the programme which the Quran proposes for the development of the human self, this is not at all possible that an individual becomes so absorbed in the development of his own self that he neglects the development of others. Its programme is purely this, that an individual's self develops proportionally to the same degree to which he works for the development of others. Kant has said:

*'Act in such a way as to treat thyself and every other human being as of equal intrinsic value; behave as a member of a society in which each regards the good of other as of equal value with his own, and is so treated by the rest, in which each is both end and means, in which each realises his own good in promoting that of others.'* [128]

But the Quran goes a step further than this and states:

*...but give them preference over themselves, even though poverty was their (own lot). And those saved from the covetousness of their own self, they are the ones that achieve prosperity. (59:9)*

Huxley, a great scientist who holds no brief for religion, writes to the same effect:

*'I believe that the whole duty of man can be summed up in the words: more life for your neighbour as for yourself. And I believe that man, though not without perplexity, effort and pain, can fulfil this duty and gradually achieve his destiny. A religion which takes this as its central core and interprets it with wide vision, both of the possibilities open to man and of the limitations in which he is confined will be a true religion, because it is conterminous with life; it will encourage the growth of life, and will itself grow with that growth. I believe in the religion of life.'* [129]

Who can tell Huxley that he cannot get this type of religion in any way other than through *Wahi*. His difficulty was that he considered the self-created religions of men to be based on Divine revelation.

## 9.10 New Life

Today, under this heaven, Divine revelation in its pure and true form cannot be found anywhere outside the Quran. The message of Allah is only for those who possess the ability to live:

*That it may give warning to any who are alive. (36:70)*

---

[128] Quoted by H. Rashdall, *The Theory of Good and Evil*, Vol I, p. 133
[129] Julian Huxley, *Religion without Revelation*, p. 113

For the admonition of those in whom the flame of life exists. And by following its given programme this life keeps multiplying. The Quran states:

*O you who believe! Give your response to Allah and His Messenger, when He calls you to that which will give you life...(8:24)*

But (as has already been noted) only he can get life who concerns himself with providing sustenance of life for others and for which he does not desire any recompense. Leaving aside recompense, he is not even desirous of any gratitude. To those for whom he provides means of sustenance, he says in no uncertain terms:

*We feed you for the sake of Allah alone: No reward do we desire from you, nor thanks. (76:9)*

He should tell them that to fulfil others needs was my duty and once I fulfilled someone's need, then that need was met. After this, how is there any question of any reward or recompense? As the Quran states:

*Is there any reward for good – other than good? (55:60)*

What can be the recompense of meeting someone's need and in this way restoring his distorted balance other than that his balance was restored. The people who make this the sole aim of their life keep the outcome of their hard work available for the *Rabubiyat* of mankind. And for the people that they help:

*Those who spend their substance in the cause of Allah, and follow not up their gifts with reminders of their generosity or with injury, for them their reward is with their Sustainer: on them shall be no fear, nor shall they grieve. (2:262)*

Never mind asking for recompense, this thought does not even arise in their hearts that people should see what we are doing so that we will be admired. According to the Quran, the people who seek such admiration cannot be members of such a *Jamaat* which declares the *Rabubiyat* of mankind as their aim and objective. Hence, Allah addresses the Momineen:

*O you who believe! cancel not your charity by reminders of your generosity or by injury, like those who spend their substance to be seen of men, but believe neither in Allah nor in the Last Day...(2:264)*

This is the reason that the messengers of Allah who were the first proclaimers of this system of *Rabubiyat* used to announce unambiguously to their people:

*I do not wish any reward from you, my reward is from the Sustainer of the Worlds.*
*(26:109)*

From the above explanation, the following reality has come before us that according to the Quran:

(1) The purpose of life is to develop the human self and
(2) the procedure for the development of the human self is that man keeps the results of his hard work (wealth and possessions) accessible for the development of others, and in this way, should give others preference over himself.

At this point the question arises (as noted in Chapter 4) that the requirement of the human intellect is that it fulfils the needs of life of that individual (and his progeny) who is the possessor of this intellect. If this intellect is told that you should desist from attending to the nourishment of this individual (and his progeny) – if he dies let him die and if his progeny suffer from hunger, let them suffer – you should worry about the nourishment and development of others, then the intellect will never be prepared to do this. If it is forced to follow this practice (firstly, it will not even tolerate this and if it is somehow forced under duress) then the psychological consequences which will result are obvious.

## 9.11  The Way to Satisfy the Intellect

Therefore, the question which we have referred to above is this – how can the intellect be made to accept that it should give priority to the needs of others over itself? Not only to accept it but be happily contented with this? The solution to this issue devised by the mysticism of sainthood (monasticism) was to declare the human body and its demands as worthy of loathing and the elimination of these to be accepted as the aim and objective of human life. But firstly, this concept and philosophy of life is impractical to implement because the demands of human life cannot be eliminated; secondly, the history of monasticism is a witness to the way in which the neck of humanity is strangled as a consequence of this, whether this is in the caves of Christian priests or in the fire temples of Zoroastrians, the ashrams of Hindu yogis or in the isolated habitats of mystics. The Quran does not suggest that the solution to a headache is to sever the head. For the development of the human self, it does not ignore nourishment of the human body but assigns great importance to it. For an exemplary life, it emphasizes the abundance of both 'body and knowledge' as being essential (2:247). According to the Quran, wealth and possessions, wife and children, splendour of attire and appearance are a reason for attraction (3:14). It challenges the holders of the doctrine of monasticism and declares:

*...Who has forbidden the beautiful gifts of Allah which He has produced for His servants...(7:32)*

Therefore, after juggling with this we return to the same question to which we have pointed earlier. For the nourishment of the body, the demand of the intellect is that it should derive maximum benefit from the means of sustenance (and the Quran also supports this). On the other hand, the requirement for the development of the human self is that he should give priority to the needs of others over himself.

The question is how to persuade the intellect to accept that it should prioritise the needs of others over its own. For this, the Quran formulates such an arrangement so that not only does the intellect become inclined towards this eminent goal, but feels full contentment and satisfaction in doing so.

The details of this system will be covered in the next chapter.

# 10 THE SYSTEM OF *RABUBIYAT*

In the previous chapter we have said that the Quran makes this type of arrangement by which the intellect of every individual is satisfied to prefer others over itself, and considers this to be the correct responsibility of life. Obviously, human intellect cannot achieve this type of satisfaction until it is fully contented that by doing so his own needs and those of his progeny will not be affected. We need to see what programme the Quran proposes for the achievement of this objective. The structure of Deen is dependent on the assuredness of contentment in this programme, therefore, in this matter, this link in the chain is extremely important.

It has been noted in previous chapters that people who believe in the Permanent Values, as defined through revelation, establish a society. By a society is meant a social order in which the Permanent Values are implemented on a practical basis. In modern terms, this is called a State. It is obvious that (as in all other systems), in this system there will be certain people who will be responsible for the establishment and consolidation of the system. The remainder of the citizens of this society will be their hands and arms in carrying out these responsibilities. In this society, there will be no distinction between the ruler and the ruled because, according to the Quran, no man possesses this right that he should subject other human beings to his government.[130] In this system, every individual will follow the Divine laws. But this is also obvious that even obedience of the Divine laws themselves is only possible within a practical system. This is called the machinery of government. In this government, the presence of an executive body is essential, and this should implement the laws in the State (you can term it as the Centre of the System). The practical form of obedience of the Divine laws will be in the obedience of the orders implemented by this executive. The citizens of this society will follow the orders of this Centre, and this Centre will fulfil the whole of those responsibilities which Allah has taken upon Himself and whose promise (or *Zikr*) has been made in the Quran.

## 10.1 Covenant

After this introduction, it should be understood that the establishment of the Quranic system is via an agreement between the Centre and the citizens. This agreement is:

> *Allah has purchased of the Believers their persons and their goods; for theirs (in return) is the garden (of Paradise): ...then rejoice in the bargain which you have concluded ...(9:111)*

---

[130] Further details of this are available in Chapter 12.

This covenant of 'buying and selling' has four elements which should be part of every business deal related to buying and selling i.e.:

(1) The buyer – Allah
(2) The seller – the Momineen
(3) The asset which is sold – the life and possessions of the Momineen
(4) The price of the sale – *Jannat*

In these, a Momin and his life and possessions are tangible elements about which everyone can understand what these are. But the other two elements (i.e. buyer - Allah, and buying price - *Jannat*) are abstract. It is clear that this matter of buying and selling cannot be viewed as tangible until is clearly understood what is meant by these two abstract elements e.g. if an individual says that I have sold my life and possessions into the hands of Allah, then this will be merely an ideological or intellectual matter. His life and possessions will continue to remain with him and this business deal will stay merely at the level of a belief. On the other hand, if he says that in return for this Allah will bestow *Jannat* on me, then this matter (the selling price) will also be (as far as this world is concerned) confined to a belief. Since Islam is a practical system of life, these matters cannot stay merely at the level of ideology or belief. Their practical and tangible form should become apparent. The reality as to what these mean in practical terms has been clarified by the Quran.

## 10.2 Aim of *Al-Jannah*[131]

First of all, let us understand the selling price (i.e. *Al-Jannah*). The Quran has termed the evolved state after the death of the developed personality as the life of *Jannat*. But since human consciousness at its present level cannot comprehend what the conditions and circumstances of the life after death will be, it has therefore stated in clear terms that all the statements about the paradise over there are metaphors. In Surah *Al Ra'd*, the Quran states:

*The parable of the garden which the righteous are promised, beneath it flow rivers...(13:35)*

In another verse, it declares about this garden:

*... And for a garden whose width is that of heavens and of the earth...(3:133)*

Alongside these types of metaphorical statements, it also states:

---

[131] *Al-Jannah* – the paradise on earth which is created through human hands as per the Quranic system. (Ed)

*Now no person knows what delights of the eye are kept hidden for them as a reward for their deeds. (32:17)*

But - and this but is very important - He (Allah) has declared the life which is achieved in this world in accordance with the Quranic system also as being the life of *Jannat* and has described such details of this life of *Jannat* from which it becomes clear what are its aim and outcomes. First of all, we should understand that the Arabs who were the first addressees of this message, and in whose language the Quran was revealed, were a nation of desert dwellers. For them, pleasing gardens, fresh and cool water springs, shady trees, abundance of fruits, flowing streams of milk and honey and other similar things - what could be better than these comforts of life. How great the importance of orchards was for them can be gauged from the objection raised by the opponents of Rasul-ullah, that if he was really a pious human being and a messenger of Allah, then:

*Or why has not a treasure bestowed on him, or why has he not a garden for pleasure...(25:8)*

In reply to this the Quran answered, wait awhile. Let this system become established. He will bestow upon you not just one garden but many orchards beneath which streams of water will be flowing, and He will bestow upon you a palace in which to live (25:10). Here, apart from orchards there is mention of palaces as well. The Arabs were a nomadic nation who mostly spent their lives in tents. To their right and left were empires such as those of Persia and Rome, which were heirs of great civilisations of the world. Their living standard was far higher than the nomadic Arabs. These States (at the very least a large part of them) were very soon going to come under the control of the Arabs, as a consequence of the Divine system. This is why, in the details of earthly paradise, the Quran had also included their goods of comfort and adornment. With this background, you can see how the Quran has narrated details of *Al-Jannah* (i.e. paradise on earth). First of all, it states with certainty and surety that the consequence of Eimaan and righteous deeds will be a government and nation State in this world. In Surah *Nur* it states:

*Allah has promised to those among you who have Eimaan and work righteous deeds that He will of surety grant them in the land power as He granted to those before them, that He will establish in authority their Deen – the one which He has chosen for them; and that He will change their state after fear in which they lived to one of security and peace. (And then) They will follow Me alone and not associate (other*

*laws) with Me. If any do reject (My laws) after this, they are rebellious and wicked.*[132]
*(24:55)*

## 10.3  Establishment of Government in the World

From these verses, it is clear that Allah had promised these people that the consequence of their Eimaan and righteous deeds will be acquisition of power in the land. So, when they overcame their opponents, it was stated to them:

> *And He made you heirs of their lands, their houses, and their goods, and of a land which you had not frequented. And Allah has power over all things. (33:27)*

Seeing the promises of Allah being fulfilled in this way, those people used to rejoice and proclaim in excitement and exhilaration:

> *They will say: 'Praise to Allah, Who has truly fulfilled His promise to us, and has given us land in heritage: We can dwell in the garden as we will; how excellent a reward for those who work righteousness'. (39:74)*

## 10.4  Basic Necessities of Life

Have you seen at which point the Quran has made use of the term *Al-Jannah*? This *Al-Jannah* first of all fulfilled the basic necessities of their lives which were so deficient among them. This is that first characteristic of *Jannat* which is mentioned to 'Adam' in these words:

> *'There is therein enough provision for you not to go hungry nor to go naked. Nor to suffer from thirst, nor from the sun's heat'. (20:118-119)*

This means that in this *Jannat* there is complete certainty of things to eat and drink, clothing, shelter etc. And certainty such that:

> ... *'And eat of the bountiful things therein as you will'...(2:35)*

And after fulfilling the basic needs of life, all the accoutrements of luxury and adornment:

---

[132] It is also implicit from these verses that: (1) The essential and definite consequence of Eimaan and righteous deeds is the establishment of government in the world. (2) For the establishment of Deen, having one's own government is absolutely essential because Deen is the very name of the collective system of life in which the Divine laws are followed. (3) For *Ibadat* of Allah and to avoid Shirk it is necessary to have one's own government. From this, the meaning of the word *Ibadat* becomes clear i.e. to be governed by the Divine laws.

*...adorned therein with bracelets of gold and pearls...(22:23)*

*To them will be passed round, dishes and goblets of gold...(43:71)*

*Upon them will be green garments of fine silk, And heavy brocade, And they will be adorned with bracelets of silver...(76:21)*

*And the flesh of fowls, Any that they may desire (56:21)*

*Among tall trees, With flowers (or fruits) piled one above another - In shade long extended, By water flowing constantly, And fruit in abundance. (56:29-32)*

Reflect on these details and if no more than this, at least look at the war bounty which came into their hands in the victory of Madayn (part of Iran). Look at this list in the books of history, and it will be very apparent how the things of *Al-Jannah* which were promised were present in this pile. And this was not confined to Iran only, the evergreen orchards of Syria, the rich as gold agricultural land of Egypt, the spring laden breezes of Iraq (which was part of Iran at that time) – all this was the renowned *Tafsir* (interpretation) of this same *Al-Jannah* which they saw before them. And then the Quran states that in this:

*...no toil nor sense of weariness shall touch us therein. (35:35)*

In this society, because the Divine Laws were prevalent everywhere, no vain talk was therefore heard by their ears and from everywhere life-giving salutations and discourses of peace and security arose (19:62). In this society, everyone lived like real brothers with full sincerity and affection (15:47). There was neither any rancour in anyone's heart nor were there any hidden emotions of jealousy and vengeance (7:43).

Up to this point, only that aspect of this *Al-Jannah* has been presented according to which the means of sustenance for the human body are available in abundance. But, according to the Quran, the purpose of life is not solely physical nourishment, the real purpose is development of latent human potentials (development of the human self). Therefore, all means and resources for this too are available in this *Al-Jannah*:

*A Fountain where the Devotees of Allah do drink, making it flow in unstinted abundance. They perform (their) vows...(76:6-7)*

Such a fountain of life which men of Allah cause to gush and flow through their efforts from the depths of their hearts. They fulfil all those responsibilities which they have taken upon themselves. In this wide sphere of worldly life, they are left free - the one who wishes can advance forward and the one who wishes can lag behind (74:37). There is no impediment of any kind in the path of anyone – there are equal opportunities for all. The radiant light of the foreheads of those advancing forward points straight ahead and to their right (and left) and their desire is that there should continue to be further increases in this light (66:8). The ever increasing heights of evolutionary stages keep appearing in front of them – those heights below which the means of sustenance of life flow continuously like a stream (39:20).

This is that *Al-Jannah* which the citizens of a Quranic society get in return as the 'price for selling' their life and possessions. From this it is made clear that in this matter of buying and selling which has been previously mentioned, the third element (i.e. price of selling) is not merely intellectual and conjecture, or purely ideological and a belief - this is a concrete reality which every person can witness with his own eyes.

## 10.5  What Does 'Allah' Mean in Practical Terms

Now we come to the fourth element of this agreement. In this covenant, it is stated that the Momineen sell their lives and possessions into the hands of 'Allah'. The question is, what does this mean in practical terms? Into whose hands do the Momineen sell their lives and possessions? And in exchange, who gives them *Al-Jannah*? Those individuals in whose selfs development commences, become companions of Allah in the system of the universe, and in the human world the Divine laws are implemented through them. These are the individuals through whose hands those responsibilities are fulfilled which Allah has related to Himself (we have termed them the Centre of the Divine system). Hence, in the matter of buying and selling which is currently under discussion, this selling on behalf of Allah in this society is done through those responsible individuals at the helm of affairs, or in other words through the hands of the Centre of the Divine system. During the time of the last messenger, this Centre was Rasul-ullah himself. Therefore, selling by the citizens of the society was into the hands of Rasul-ullah. This is that reality which the Quran has stated in these words in Surah *Al Fath*:

*Verily those who plight their fealty to you do no less than plight their fealty to Allah; the Hand of Allah is over their hands...(48:10)*

O Rasul, those persons who are selling their lives into your hands, they are indeed doing their deal with Allah. At the time of sealing this deal, it looks as if your hand is over their hands, but in truth, it is the hand of Allah Himself. This is because the Centre of the Divine System does not decide matters in a personal capacity but does so as a Divine representative of Allah. In other words, in all these matters the Quranic system of a society becomes a stand-in for Allah. In connection with the Islamic system, this point holds great significance (which we will discuss in detail in a later chapter on the political system and government). From this, this reality also becomes apparent as to what is meant when the Quran instructs to spend in the path of Allah:

*...and loan to Allah, a balanced loan...(73:20)*

'Giving a balanced loan to Allah' – what is meant by this? From this is meant the Centre of the Quranic System. That same Centre which receives all this from the citizens of the society, and the same one that then spends it on working for the welfare of the whole of mankind.

## 10.6  Responsibility for Sustenance

Now all of the four elements of selling and buying in relation to that matter, (with which we began this discussion), are in front of us in a tangible and concrete form. In other words, according to this covenant, citizens of this society hand over their lives and possessions to the Centre of the Divine system and it, then, with their possessions (and lives if required), establishes society on these lines, as a consequence of which all the citizens of the society receive their sustenance of life in abundance and over and above this, their self also keeps developing in such a way that in the life after death it becomes capable of traversing further evolutionary stages. In this way, they achieve paradise both in this world and in the life in the hereafter:

*...Our Sustainer! Give us good in this world and good in the Hereafter...(2:201)*

This is that system which proclaims with certainty and surety to the citizens of this society:

*...We are responsible for your sustenance and also of your progeny...(6:151)*

Because of this, you should not have any kind of worry regarding means of sustenance, you should be assured that neither you can die of hunger nor your progeny.

This is that practical methodology due to which the intellect of the people becomes assured about the matter of the means of sustenance and devotes its full attention to the nourishment and development of mankind. By this, the self of every individual continues to develop and thus the development of both the body and the self is arranged – i.e. prosperity in this world and joys in the hereafter also. The present becomes prosperous and the future perpetually bright and this is a great achievement (5:119).

## 10.7  Responsibility for the Sustenance of Every Living Thing

The sphere of responsibility of the Quranic system does not remain confined to the sustenance of its own citizens, since it is the system of that Allah Who is Sustainer of the Worlds (1:2) i.e. the Giver of Sustenance to all nations of the world. That is why, as this system gains in strength, its sphere of action keeps broadening i.e. firstly this system takes responsibility for the development of those citizens who reside within its domain, whether they are Muslims or non-Muslims; after this its *Rabubiyat* keeps encompassing other peoples of mankind - irrespective of religion, nationality, and without differentiating on the basis of colour and creed. Making this *Rabubiyat* commonplace in the whole world is the focused aim of this system. In this respect, this great proclamation of the Quran becomes apparent as a reality:

*There is no living creature on earth but its sustenance depends on Allah...(11:6)*

The Quran has used the word *Da'abba* in this proclamation, which encompasses within it all human beings and animals. Because of this, responsibility for the sustenance of all living things lands on the head of this system of *Rabubiyat* and it fulfils this responsibility.

## 10.8  What Was the Motive to Work

At this point this question arises, that when the basic needs of life of all the citizens of this society will continue to be automatically fulfilled (through the system of the society), then what will be the need for these individuals to work? Even if you put them to some work, why would they expend their full effort? For example, if a worker knows that he will get remuneration proportionate to the amount of work he does in a day, he will work the whole day with maximum effort so that he can receive an even greater amount of remuneration. But if he knows that, for example, if he does work daily worth ten rupees, but his needs are met with two rupees and the remaining eight rupees will be given to someone else, then why would he do the work of ten rupees? Indeed, this question is of fundamental importance in economics.

## 10.9  An Important Question of Economics

Such people have existed who desired that the distribution of sustenance should be according to the needs of the people, so that those who are not capable of earning more but whose needs are greater (i.e. their needs are not being met from their earnings), should also continue to receive full means of sustenance. What form could this take other than that the excess earnings of those who are capable of working more but their needs are less, is utilized to meet the needs of other individuals. As a consequence, in some places experiments were also done in relation to this (first of all Plato himself did an experiment around this). But these experiments always failed and these were the failures on the basis of which experts on economics reached the conclusion that, till someone is not declared as the sole owner of the remuneration for his work, he will never put in his full effort. This is called private enterprise[133] and this is the very foundation of the capitalist system.

## 10.10 Communism[134]

In our times, communism raised its head against this system (of capitalism). The pioneers of this movement provoked the poor and deprived, by telling them to rise up and snatch the wealth of the rich. Hence, they rose up and snatched the wealth of the rich. As a consequence, the revolution succeeded on an emergency basis. But after this, the same question now faces them as to how people can be persuaded to work to their maximum ability. What motivation and incentive should be created due to which they will work to their maximum, and in recompense only take enough earnings from which their necessities are fulfilled and the remainder is handed over to the government? In the philosophy of life on which the structure of communism is erected, there is no concept even of any other life for man other than the physical one. Therefore, apart from the laws of physical life the question of any other law or value does not arise. This is why they cannot find that motivation and incentive anywhere. Hence, they have no other alternative except to extract work from people by force.

## 10.11 Soviet Union[135] and Democracies

The capitalist democracies have created the concept of the welfare State within them, in which the State takes measures to provide the maximum assistance to the needy, but it is obvious that until the State has ample wealth, how will it fulfil the needs of the people? For this they have placed emphasis on taxation. Hence, the situation is that in these countries nearly eighty percent of the income of an individual is consigned to various taxes. Obviously, nobody gives this much tax willingly. The Government extracts it through the force of law while the people continuously hatch and devise all kinds of ruses to avoid these taxes. It is therefore a similar coercion here with the difference that under communism this coercion is evident and plain, while under democracies it is concealed within the veils of the eyes of the law. The matter is the same under both systems because any system

---

[133] In economics the term 'laissez faire' is used for this which means that in business matters the government should not intervene.
[134] This book was written when Communism was in place in many countries in the world. (Ed)
[135] The USSR (Union of Soviet Socialist Republic) was based on Communism and split into republics in 1991 when it ceased to exist as a Communist State. (Ed)

which is based on coercion cannot survive for long. This is why, as with communism, there are continuing cracks developing in the palaces of the governments of democracies.

Contrary to this, let us look at the Quran. Its philosophy of life is:

(1) Man is not defined by his body alone, other than a body he has been given a self as well.
(2) The purpose of human life is to develop the human self.
(3) The development of the human self occurs by what he does for, and gives for the development of other human beings. The greater the extent to which an individual gives for the nourishment and development of others, the greater the degree to which his self will continue to develop.

The Quranic system is based on those individuals who have Eimaan in this philosophy of life. It is obvious that when human beings are made free from the worries of meeting the necessities of life, then they will make efforts day and night to earn ever more so that the development of others can take place to a greater extent, and so that in this way the development of their self occurs as much as possible. This is that motivation because of which man, after maximum hard work, is willing with his full heart to make his all available for the nourishment of others. There is no requirement in this for any coercion or persuasion. Coercion aside (as has already been stated) they are not even desirous of any thanks from others.

Professor Hawtrey has said, 'What differentiates economic systems from one another is the character of the motives they invoke to induce people to work'.[136]

If you compare the motive which the Quranic system provides with those of other economic orders, and reflect, is it possible that any system can compete with the Quranic system? As you continue to ponder this point, this reality will keep becoming clear that the solution for this important problem cannot be availed from anywhere else other than the Quranic Philosophy of Life. The day that the nations of the world understand this truth, the caravan of humanity will tread on the path of achievement and prosperity.

## 10.12 Mysticism (*Ta'sawwaf*) and Islam

Before ending this chapter, it is felt necessary to clarify an additional point. We have said from the beginning that the purpose of human life is to develop the self and the procedure for this is that which is described above. Mysticism also makes the claim that its purpose is *Tazkiya Nafs* (purification of self) or is the 'spiritual

---

[136] Quoted by E. H. Carr, in *The New Society*, p. 60

development' of man. But for this it suggests the procedure for man to be that he adopts for himself dissociation from worldly issues, and kills his desires and dreams. *Tazkiya Nafs* means to purify the soul from material comforts and impurities and its procedure is that man should run far away from the material world.

What is *Ta'sawwaf* (mysticism) actually, and what is its history? This matter is outwith our current subject. At this stage, we feel it is sufficient to say only this much, that its source is the Platonic doctrine of life and not only has this no relation to the Quran, but it is the complete opposite of the Quranic philosophy and concept of life. In other words, these are the claimants of *Tazkiya Nafs* about whom the Quran declares:

> *Have you not turned your vision to those who claim sanctity for themselves? Nay – but Allah does sanctify (as per His law). But never will they fail to receive justice in the least little thing. (4:49)*

Have you also reflected on the state of those who are claimants of *Tazkiya Nafs* (say to them that *Tazkiya Nafs* does not happen like this). It can only be attained by the one who wishes to achieve it according to the Quranic laws and its code of life. There will not be the slightest reduction in the results of the efforts and deeds of whoever wishes to attain it through this method.

In another verse:

> *…Therefore justify not yourselves: He knows best who it is that is righteous. (53:32)*

Do not think of your own accord that *Tazkiya Nafs* is happening to your self. Allah knows who is righteous. Here, we are clearly informed that those who have *Tazkiya Nafs* (development of the self) are called *Mutaqee* (righteous). At another place, it is clarified as to who is *Mutaqee*:

> *Those who spend their wealth for increase in self-purification. (92:18)*

It is clear from this that according to the Quran, *Tazkiya Nafs* takes place for him who earns with his full effort and then keeps giving his all for the nourishment and development of others. *Tazkiya Nafs* does not take place for the one who lives on the earnings of others. No matter how far the claimants of spiritual growth may run from the world, as long as they are alive they need food and drink for the nourishment of their body, which is (obviously) being provided by other people. How is the *Tazkiya Nafs* going to take place of the individual who is dependent on others for his own needs. Then, according to the Quran, *Tazkiya Nafs* takes place while living within the confines of a human society, it does not occur by living an isolated life. Therefore, the individual who is seeking *Tazkiya Nafs* in the isolated corners of monasteries is going in the opposite direction to the Quranic path. This is that monasticism about which the Quran has stated:

> ...*But the monasticism which they invented for themselves, We did not prescribe for them...(57:27)*

As for the institution of monasticism which you see prevalent among them, they have invented it from their own minds, We did not ordain it for them. *Tazkiya Nafs* (development of the human self) can only take place through the establishment of the system of *Rabubiyat* – earning the maximum through hard work and then handing it over to the system of *Rabubiyat*.[137] From this, that system will fulfil the needs of these people themselves (i.e. the ones earning) and with the surplus wealth it will provide for the nourishment of other peoples of mankind. This system is the practical sign (manifestation) of the attribute of Allah which is called *Rabb-ul-Alameen* (Sustainer of all Worlds).

In summary, we can say that the outcome of the system presented by the Quran is that man should harness the forces of nature to the greatest extent possible, and the benefits obtained from these forces should be made available for the nourishment and development of the whole of mankind – in this, there should be no difference or discrimination between man and man.

---

[137] It does not mean that if the system is not yet established, one cannot develop his or her self. The Quran directs us to have Eimaan and do righteous deeds wherever we are. However, we should continue to make efforts for the establishment of the Quranic system of *Rabubiyat*. (Ed)

# 11 INTELLECTUAL RATIONALES FOR THE SYSTEM OF *RABUBIYAT*

It has been noted in the previous chapter that the system of *Rabubiyat* is established by that group of people who have Eimaan in this truth, that by establishing this system, their selfs can develop. And development of the self is the very purpose of life. But the Quran also presents intellectual reasons in support of this system, so that members of this group can also have conviction in this reality on the basis of evidence, and they can present it before others also through evidence and reasons.

## 11.1 Basis of the Capitalist System

The foundation of the capitalist system is based on the concept that every individual considers that whatever he earns through his expertise and cleverness, ability and skill, is his property. No other person can have any right over it. From the narratives about previous nations, the Quran has presented (Bani Israel's) Qarun as the representative of this (capitalist) system. In Surah *Al Qasas* it is stated that when it was asked of him why, in all this (surplus) wealth which he has accumulated in this way, he does not consider the right of others, he replied:

> ...This (wealth) has been given to me because of certain knowledge which I have...(28:78)

I have received this wealth due to my skill - I have earned it through my knowledge and personal ability, therefore there is no question of the right of anyone else in it. In another verse, the Quran states that this reply is not specifically confined to one Qarun only; wherever there are upholders of the capitalist system this same answer will be heard from them. This is the mentality of these people which is the root cause of the problem:

> ...He says, 'This has been given to me because of a certain knowledge (I have)'. Nay, but this is but a trial, but most of them understand not. (39:49)

But most among them do not know the truth of how mistaken this mentality is and how baseless their claim is. Let us see what rationale the Quran presents in this connection. If you examine it closely, then this truth will become apparent, that the earning of a man is the collective outcome of the following factors i.e.:

(1) Intellectual ability which every child gets at birth
(2) Initial environment, education and effects of upbringing
(3) Opportunities for the use of ability and skills
(4) The personal hard work of a man

## 11.2 The Verdict of the Quran

The first of these factors i.e. intellectual ability, which is of basic importance in this regard, is bestowed (free as a gift) by nature at birth. It has neither been bought nor can it be bought by an individual. The second and third factors are related to the society within which the child is brought up. Over this also, he has no personal control. Only the fourth factor i.e. the personal hard work of an individual is such a thing which the person utilises by employing his own intent and choice.

From this brief analysis, it is clear that whatever an individual earns, his right can only be over that portion which is the result of his personal effort. This is that truth to which the Quran has drawn our attention by stating:

*That man can have nothing but what he makes effort for.*[138] *(53:39)*

As a result of this basic principle, the Quran gives the verdict on this conflict between work and capital which has, from the beginning of time till today, been a source of disgruntlement for human society, and has remained a cause for thousands of discords and continues to be so.

## 11.3 Why are Abilities Different?

As far as the difference in intellectual ability of different individuals is concerned, the Quran states that this variance is for the distribution of work. Within a society there are diverse types of work which require different abilities. If there is no difference in the abilities of different people, then the business of a society cannot function. The Quran has stated:

*...And we raise some of them above others in ranks, so that some may command work from others...(43:32)*

The difference in abilities among people is so that different types of work can be obtained from one another. There is no doubt that through scientific research efforts are being made to remove these deficiencies, on the basis of which intellectual ability remains low in a child. It is possible that gradually such a time will come when there is not much difference left in the intellectual abilities among children. Obviously, when man progresses to such a degree in these matters then the economic map of this society will become different. But as long as there

---

[138] This principle is to make man understand that it is not legitimate in any way to seize the earnings of others using the force of capital, otherwise, as noted in previous chapters, in the Quranic System the responsibility for fulfilling the needs of life of every individual belongs to the state, therefore in this there is no question of division of sustenance in proportion to work and capital.

remains a difference in abilities - and it seems that some difference will continue to remain, because man is not a machine moulded from metals such that there is not the slightest difference from one machine to the next one (man is a wide-awake living holder of choice and intent, influenced by hundreds of different factors) - the Quran has directed that this difference is only for the distribution of work, not for the distribution of sustenance. The distribution of sustenance will be according to needs. Those people who have a greater ability to earn more should not consider that the whole of whatever they earn is their right and portion. The excess of their earnings is based on those factors in the acquisition of which their personal choice was not involved. Therefore, they have the right to take according to their needs out of these earnings based on these factors. The remainder is the right of those people who, due to lesser intellectual ability, work under their supervision. In Surah *Al Nahl* it is stated:

*Allah has bestowed His gifts of sustenance more freely on some of you than on others: those more favoured are not going to throw back their gifts to those whom their right hands possess, so as to be equal in that respect. Will they then deny the favours of Allah? (16:71)*

Allah has bestowed on some among you a greater ability to earn more sustenance as compared to others. Those individuals who have received more of this ability do not return the excess sustenance to those people who work under them, so that they should not all become equal in sustenance. This means that these individuals deny the fact that their ability to earn more has been received by them as a blessing from Allah, and is not the product of their own personal effort and skill, though they should know that whatever they have received as a blessing is all from Allah:

*And you have no good thing but is from Allah: and moreover when you are touched by distress unto Him you cry with groans...(16:53)*

Therefore, whatever is earned on this basis should also belong to Allah, and not be the personal possession of man.

The Quran has made this reality clear (that sustenance should be distributed according to need and not according to the ability to earn) in a very powerful way in the verses associated with verse (16:71) quoted above.

## 11.4 Home as a Model

The conclusion of everything it has stated is that you should pay attention to the situation within your home. In it are both children and old people, women and men, and also those who are low earners. Now see whether the distribution of sustenance for every member of the family in the home is according to need or according to the ability to earn? If it is according to the ability to earn, then the children should be kept totally deprived but you do not do this. You fulfil the needs of the children first of all, similarly with regard to the elderly folk. So why do you not establish the principle that you observe within the four walls of your home, in your society (and for universal mankind)? Why do you not base the distribution of sustenance there on needs, rather than on earning ability? This difference of us and them is the product of your short-sightedness and not of Allah. Allah holds the position of the 'head of the family' (Sustainer of the Worlds) for the whole of mankind. Therefore, His law is that the distribution of sustenance among all the individuals of mankind should be done according to need and not according to the ability to earn.

## 11.5  Sources of Production

There is another factor which is included in the ability to earn which is known as the source of production. In this matter, the Quran gives fundamental importance to land (and its status is in fact fundamental). During the time of the revelation of the Quran, there was no industry prevalent, which is why it did not mention it specifically. But it is obvious that the basis of industry is also founded on raw material which is itself obtained from the land. Therefore, the principle which is applicable to land will also be applicable to all its derivatives.

## 11.6  There Can be No Private Ownership of Land

In relation to *Ard* (land), the Quran has stated in principle that it is created for the benefit of the whole of creation:

*It is He Who has spread out the earth for His creatures. . .(55:10)*

This is a means of earning a livelihood:

*And We have provided therein means of subsistence – for you and for those for whose subsistence you are not responsible. (15:20)*

And in it We have created sources of sustenance for you and for those that you do not provide sustenance to. In it, there is the wherewithal for subsistence for you and for your cattle (79:33). You can take advantage from this i.e. can benefit from it. Private ownership cannot be declared over it. Whatever means of subsistence are bestowed as a blessing from nature (e.g. air, water, light, heat etc.) they should remain equally available for the needs of all of mankind. 'Ownership' over them is only for Allah. Whichever individual claims 'ownership' over them makes himself a god along with Allah. This reality is detailed by the Quran in very clear words:

*Say; is it that you deny Him Who created the earth in two periods? And do you join equals with Him? He is the Sustainer of the Worlds. He set on the earth mountains standing firm, high above it, And bestowed blessings on the earth, and measured therein all things to give them nourishment in due proportion, in four periods, in accordance with the needs of those who seek sustenance. (41:9-10)*

Tell them, do you deny the Sovereignty of Allah who has created the earth in two stages, such that it became suitable for you to inhabit. Allah did this so that the nourishment of the whole of mankind continues but you create rivals with Allah. For this *Rabubiyat* (universal sustenance), he raised mountains from within the earth so that they became the source of flowing water and created the ability to produce subsistence from the land. Then, by alteration of the seasons, scales for four harvests were set up. Therefore, the land should remain free forever for the equal use of all those who are needy and should not become the private property of anyone.

Just as He had said about other matters that your share in sustenance is only equivalent to the amount of work you do, similarly in relation to the land He has stated that its produce consists of different elements and efforts. If you reflect on this, then this reality will automatically become evident as to how much should be your share in it and how much for 'Allah'. In Surah *Al Waqi'ah*, this reality is explained in a very beautiful way where it is said – have you paid any attention to that which you are sowing? You plough the land and sow seeds (56:63) – after that is it you who converts that seed into crop or is it We that do it? (56:64). If Our Divine law was not like this and had been different, We could have obliterated it into pieces and then you would have been left shocked and stunned and would have groaned in grief – we have been visited by ruin, far from harvesting a crop, we have been left destitute of our seeds as well (56:63-74).

Proceed forward and contemplate this water on which the whole of sustenance depends. Is it you that rains it down from the clouds or do we pour it down (56:68-69)? If our Divine law was not functioning in the way it is now, but had been of a different kind, and if we had made water extremely salty instead (like the water of the seas which evaporates and transforms into the shape of clouds), then you could have neither drunk it and nor would your fields have bloomed – you do not even appreciate this either (56:70).

And proceed further – have you even considered this fire which you light and through which the warmth of life is maintained. Is it you that makes the trees grow from whose wood this fire burns, or do We make them grow! (56:72).

If you pay attention to all these different things which provide the basis to life, then this truth will dawn on you that all this is received from Allah as a free gift, none of your skills and efforts are involved in it (56:73). These exist in their own right, and are not indebted to your effort and labour. Now the question is, why did Allah bestow these without anything in return or recompense from you? What is their purpose? The purpose is - so that these become resources of sustenance for the hungry, and become the means to fulfil the universal responsibility of Allah as Sustainer (56:73). Therefore, you should make full endeavours to accomplish Allah's great programme of *Rabubiyat* (56:74). This is a joint business in which the capital is from Allah and the exertion is yours. Then divide the 'profit' (the resulting produce) of this business in the same proportion. Take the portion due to your hard work and give the portion which belongs to the 'capital' to Allah. Now the question arises, who to give Allah's share to because He does not appear in front Himself. This is why Allah has declared that His share should be passed to those hungry ones whose needs are greater.

Iqbal has explained the subject of these verses in the following beautiful words:

*Who nourishes the seed in the soil which no ray of light penetrates?*
*Who raises clouds from the waves of the oceans?*
*Who drove hither favourable wind from the West?*
*Whose is the soil, Whose the light of the Sun?*
*Who has filled the ear of corn with pearly grain?*
*Who has taught the seasons to change with regularity?*
*Landowner! This land is neither thine nor mine;*
*Thy forefathers did not own it, nor dost thou nor I.*[139]

All this is material for sustenance for the servants of Allah (50:11). Referring to this truth in another verse, it is stated:

*Or who is there that can provide you with sustenance if He were to withhold His provision? Nay, they obstinately persist in insolent impiety and flight (from the truth).*
*(67:21)*

In another verse:

*Then let man look at his food. For that We pour forth water in abundance, And we split the earth in fragments, And produce therein corn, And grapes and nutritious plants, And olives and dates and enclosed gardens, dense with lofty trees, And fruits and fodder – For use and convenience to you and your cattle. (80:24-32)*

---

[139] M. Iqbal, *Bal-e-Jibreel*, p. 161

All these consumable things are for your use and for the use of your cattle. But there is a clear difference between you and your cattle. The state of the cattle is that when they eat their fill, then they do not carry the remaining fodder around, they do not hoard it, they do not hold back sustenance so that unlawful advantage can be taken of the needy:

> *How many are the creatures that carry not their own sustenance? It is Allah Who feeds them and you, for He hears and knows all. (29:60)*

But it is human beings who hoard whatever is beyond their needs, in order to accumulate material and wealth from this. This is the basis of the capitalist system, through which man kindles the fire of hell in the world, and then burns both himself and others in it. In Surah *Tauba* it is stated:

> *...And there are those who hoard gold and silver and spend it not in the way of Allah – announce unto them a most grievous penalty. On the Day when heat will be produced out of that (wealth) in the fire of Hell, and with it will be branded their foreheads, their flanks, and their backs, 'This is the (treasure) which you hoarded for yourselves, so taste then the (treasures) you buried.' (9:34-35)*

## 11.7  The Capitalist System is Evil

The Quran uses the term *Bukhal* (miserly) for this system (in which the surplus means of sustenance is held back as material or financial capital) and declares in very clear terms that this system is not good, but is evil. In Surah *Al Imran* it is stated:

> *And let not those who covetously withhold of the gifts which Allah has given them of His Grace, think that it is good for them: Nay, it will be the worse for them; soon shall the things which they covetously withheld be tied to their necks like a twisted collar, on the Day of Judgement (Results) to Allah belongs the heritage of the heavens and the earth; And Allah is well acquainted with all that you do. (3:180)*

The people who hold back this material of sustenance which Allah bestows for the economic conveniences of mankind should not think that this conduct of theirs is good for them. Nay – it is evil for them. When the consequences of this wrong economic system manifest, this hoarded material will become a chain around their necks. They should know that all that is in the highs and lows of the universe is in the ownership of Allah. And whatever it is that you do, Allah knows about it. He says that this system and the nation which sustains it cannot continue to exist in the world. This system will be destroyed in the end, and the nation holding this system will be replaced by another nation, which will be the holder of a different system:

*Behold, you are those invited to spend (of your substance) in the Way of Allah: But among you are some that are miserly. But any who are miserly are so at the expense of their own selfs. But Allah is free of all wants, and it is you that are needy. If you turn back (from the Path) He will substitute in your stead another people; then they would not be like you! (47:38)*

History is a witness that those nations which implemented the capitalist system in their lands were destroyed and ruined. They were far greater in power and wealth than you (21:11). Their ultimate end will be yours too, because a wrong system of life produces the same outcome everywhere. The correct system of life is that you should expend maximum effort to produce maximum sustenance, and retain only whatever meets your needs from it, making the remainder available for the nourishment of others.

## 11.8  Say: Whatever is Beyond Your Needs

*…They ask you how much they are to spend; Say: 'What is beyond your needs'…(2:219)*

They ask of you as to how much we should keep available for the needs of others. Say to them, all that is beyond your needs, because the means of sustenance are for fulfilling the needs of life, not for hoarding and taking unlawful advantage of others in this way. This is that system of life which the Quran proposes.

## 11.9  Orders for the Interim Period

But the Quran takes this system gradually to its complete and final form. The orders given in the Quran in relation to charity, donations, inheritance, (*Sadqa, Khairat, Warassat*) etc. are for this interim period when the system is not yet fully established in its final form. Even in these orders during this interim period, you can see how the Quran gradually and unconsciously takes the society towards the complete system of *Rabubiyat* - charity and donations, being kind to parents and relations, through the division of inheritance into smaller and smaller parts, prohibition of usury in giving loans, offering every concession in the return of a loan, injunction regarding wealth that it should not just circulate among the upper strata of a society (59:7). On the one hand, the Quran makes way for general *Rabubiyat* through these orders, and on the other hand, it keeps emphasizing the establishment of the system of *Rabubiyat* – in this way, through the process of motivation and direction, it shapes its system.

When this system is established in its complete form, then neither is anyone left with surplus wealth, nor is there a need for orders of the interim period. There will be no need to say to the one who gives his all (which is beyond his needs) in the path of Allah, that he should give a certain percentage as 'Zakat' out of his possessions. This was the reason that throughout his life Rasul-ullah did not give Zakat (because he never retained any surplus wealth), nor did he leave any inheritance which could be distributed among his heirs. This was the final and complete form of Islam in which Rasul-ullah presented himself as a balanced model (*Uswa Husna*), and to which the aim was to take the Ummah gradually. In this system is hidden the secret of the emancipation and eminence of mankind. Emancipation from this *Jahannum* (hell) in which humanity is ensnared and suffering due to a wrong system of life. The Quran states that the vested interests of the custodians of the capitalist system can do whatever they will, this revolution is bound to come:

*The Hour (period of the Divine System) will certainly come; Therein is no doubt: Yet most men believe not. (40:59)*

In that era, 'the way that the sovereignty of Allah is in the heavens, similarly His Throne will spread on the earth as well' - at that time man will see this reality in front of him in a tangible form:

*It is He Who is Allah in heaven and Allah on earth; And He is full of wisdom and knowledge. (43:84)*

Undoubtedly, in the outer universe it is His Sovereignty and law which is functioning, and in the human world it is His law which is functioning. This is the objective and aim of Islam i.e. the establishment of the system of *Rububiyat* based on evidence and observation. The foundation of this system is based on this ideology (Eimaan) which has been discussed in the previous chapters, and this is that fundamental difference which makes it unique and different from the Western democracies and the (former[140]) communist system of the Soviet Union.

---

[140] This is added as the system has since collapsed. (Ed)

# 12  THE POLITICAL SYSTEM

When human beings began living together, their interests clashed with each other. From these clashes, mutual conflicts emerged. As a result of this, the need was felt for a solution to be devised which would prevent this from occurring, so that if a conflict did arise, these mutual frictions and clashes could be amicably resolved so that society could remain protected from wars and turmoil. The concept of a political system started from this. The beginning arose from this need, but those people who undertook responsibility for conflict resolution and decision making, perceived that getting others to obey their orders gives rise to great pleasure. Therefore, they started to devise those techniques through which the power which had come into their hands was not snatched away. As a consequence, two classes emerged within society. One class was that which got their orders obeyed by others, and the second class was the one which obeyed these orders of theirs. Sometimes, to seize authority and rule from the governing class, another rival group would stand up; and it would sometimes even be the case that the ruled class became prepared to rebel against the governing class.

## 12.1  Struggle Between the Rulers and the Ruled

If you look closely, you will find that the whole history of mankind is a tale of this struggle i.e.:

(1) The effort of the ruling class was that the chains of their authority and rule keep becoming ever tighter and stronger.
(2) The desire of the opposing class was that government should fall into their hands.
(3) The effort of the ruling class was to keep suppressed any rebellion by the ruled class.
(4) And the effort of the people possessing vision and wisdom was, what solution can be devised so that both the political system remains in position, and there is also no conflict between ruler and ruled in society.

Before we examine the solution which the Quran presents for this problem, it is necessary that certain important pieces of this story are brought to the fore, and it should also be seen what kind of efforts and attempts were made in this regard by men of intellect and vision.

## 12.2  Tribal System of Government

In the beginning, man lived a tribal life i.e. members of one family all lived together. This was called their tribe. The elder of the tribe was considered worthy of respect, therefore the responsibility for solving mutual conflicts was his. His decision was to be obeyed by everyone. With the passage of time, the desire to also govern began to awaken in the hearts of these 'elders of the family' and they started to think of ways in which to retain and sustain their rule. To achieve this, the belief was invented that obedience of the elders was compulsory in all circumstances i.e. it was essential that the elders should be approached for decisions on all matters, not only for children, but for any man no matter at what stage in life he was. These verdicts of the elders used to gradually transform into tribal culture and tradition, contravention of which was considered a severe crime. In this way, obedience of both categories of elders, whether alive or dead, used to become such an obligation against which no individual could transgress – this was the first face of government.

## 12.3  Belief in Divine Authority

In the early life of man, priests enjoyed a very high status (even now, wherever ignorance and superstition is prevalent priests are worshipped). They were considered holders of supernatural powers and the offspring of gods or their deputies. Every individual was fearful of them and trembled, and could not allow even the passing thought in his heart of opposing any of their commands. These religious priests took advantage of the veneration of the people and extended their sphere of control beyond the four walls of their places of worship to the palaces of worldly government. For this, they invented the belief that they are the possessors of Divine rights i.e. God has created them in order to govern and their orders are the orders of God Himself. Obedience to them is obedience of God, and disobedience to them is the disobedience of God, the penalty of which is both exemplary punishment in this world and consignment to hell in the next life. When 'worldly' leaders saw that this is an extremely easy and successful technique by which to gain obedience of the public – because by this rule is over hearts and souls rather than over bodies, for which neither police nor armies are required – they joined forces with the priesthood. In this way, Rajah, a dictator or a king (as God's shadow on earth), started having his orders and wishes obeyed as if they were the orders of God. The self-created religion of men provided great strength to this type of rule. The bloodstained pages of history bear witness to this; the tyranny to which mankind was subjected to in the name of God via the hands of these 'Divine wardens' - the portion of poor Satan would not have been even a tiny fraction of a fraction of this.

## 12.4  Theocracy

This political system is called theocracy, which was especially promoted by Christianity. Discussing Christianity, Viscount Samuel writes:

*'It (Christianity) has supported the doctrine 'Divine Right of Kings' and must bear*
*responsibility for all the evil consequences of that doctrine in the history of Europe.'[141]*

This was to maintain own rule by different ruses. Contrary to this, it also happened at times that in some tribe or nation the individual who possessed the greatest physical prowess, or the one who had acquired the most material power, would take rule into his own hands by overpowering and suppressing the rest.

## 12.5  Might is Right

A little reflection will make this truth glaringly evident, that this doctrine of government continues to be prevalent from the beginning till today. Variations in the forms, appearances, and causes and means keep occurring but the 'principle' everywhere remains the same, that 'might is right'. This happened during the era of ignorance and barbarism of man and is still happening in the era of civilization and development today.

When those individuals possessing intellect and vision, who kept a close eye on affairs, understood the reason why the need for a collective system arose in society and what advantage was being taken of this, they tried to reorganise (according to their judgement) the system on correct lines.

## 12.6  Theory of Contract

They stated that the citizens of a society should decide through mutual agreement what the rights and duties of the individuals in the state will be, and what the duties and liabilities of the government will be. The ratification of these rights and duties between the parties should be agreed via a contract. This doctrine is termed as the Theory of Contract. This doctrine was continuing since Greek times, but in the eighteenth century in Europe, Hobbes, Locke and Rousseau especially promoted it. The foundation of modern democracy is based on this doctrine i.e. 'government through the mutual agreement of the people'.

## 12.7  Sovereignty

The second question which arises in the case of the political system is, who should have final authority in deciding matters. This is called ultimate authority or sovereignty. When the reins of power were in the hands of religious priests or kings, this question did not even arise (in our times dictators have replaced kings therefore this question does not arise in the case of their rule either). Religious priests, king or dictator, are themselves sovereign. But when the form of

---

[141] Viscount Samuel, *Belief and Action*, p. 39

government became democratic, then this question acquired importance. According to Rousseau, 'sovereignty' is shared jointly by all the people of a State. But according to Locke this sovereignty should belong to the majority of the people, and democracy has adopted this same principle. Contrary to this, the doctrine of Marx is that sovereignty belongs to that class which has control of the sources of production – in the capitalist system it will be the capitalist class, and in the communist system it will be the labour class. In our times, the doctrine of democracy has acquired great significance and most among the developed nations have adopted this system.

## 12.8  System of Democracy

As we have seen, the basis of this doctrine is on the following assumptions:

(1) In this form of government, no difference remains between the ruler and the ruled. In this, the principle is 'government of the people, by the people, for the people'.
(2) The will of the people can be determined through their representatives.
(3) The criteria for right and wrong in any matter is based on the majority decision of these representatives.
(4) The minority has to accept the decisions of the majority as correct.

This is that system of government which man has reached after centuries of his experiments, and according to Western thinkers, a better system than this is impossible to conceive. This system is considered a blessing and guarantor of thousands of benedictions and benefits. Those who support it are declared witnesses of truth and benefactors of humanity, and those who oppose it are considered to be criminals.

The question is, whether after practical experiments in the West, this system of government has in fact been proven to be such, or have those thinkers and philosophers reached a different conclusion. Thinkers and scholars here refers to the politicians and higher officials of those countries wherever democracy is established as a system.

## 12.9  The Failure of Democracy

In his book, *The Crisis of Civilisation*, Professor Alfred Cobban of London University, discussing the causes of the decline of Western civilization, says:

*'Considering politics in terms of actual facts and not of abstract theories, it must be acknowledged that the identification of ruler and the ruled, assumed in the theory of the sovereignty of people, is a practical impossibility. The government is one set of*

*people and the governed another. Once society has developed beyond the smallest and the most primitive communities, they never have been and never can be the same. The pretence that they are can only lead to the worst excesses of power in the state.*[142]

Professor Ewing of Cambridge University has discussed democracy in his book, *The Individual, The State and World Government.* The following quotation from the book shows the trend of his thought:

*'Had Rousseau written now, and not, as he did, prior to any experience of democracy in the modern world, he could not have been so optimistic.'*[143]

A similar view has been expressed by another thinker, Rene Guenon, in his book titled, *The Crisis of the Modern World.* The relevant passage, though long, deserves to be quoted in full:

*'If the word 'democracy' is defined as the government of the people by themselves, it expresses an absolute impossibility and cannot even have a mere de facto existence in our time any more than in any other. It is contradictory to say that the same persons can be, at the same time, rulers and ruled, because, to use the Aristotelian phraseology, the same being cannot be 'in act' and 'in potency' at the same time and in the same circle of relations. The relationship of the rulers and ruled necessitates the joint presence of two terms; there could be no ruled if there were not also rulers, even though those be illegitimate and have no other title to power than their own pretensions; but the great ability of those who are in control in the modern world lies in making the people believe that they are governing themselves, and the people are the more inclined to believe this as they are flattered by it and as they are in any case, incapable of sufficient reflection to see its impossibility. It was to create this illusion that 'universal suffrage' was invented. The law is supposed to be made by the opinion of the majority but what is overlooked is that this opinion of the majority is something that can very easily be guided and modified; it is always possible by means of suitable suggestions to arouse in it currents moving in this or that direction as desired.'*[144]

Before proceeding, it is necessary to understand this fact again, that the weakness of the democratic system which these thinkers are criticising so severely, is the assumption of this doctrine (i.e. the unconditional and unlimited right to legislate), that the people are holders of sovereignty. And that this right of the people is implemented through the majority of their representatives. In other words, according to this doctrine, this is assumed as fact that whatever laws are drafted by the majority of the representatives of the State are the collective decision of all the people of the nation, and that they are based on truth and fact in every respect.

---

[142] Alfred Cobban, *The Crisis of Civilisation*, p. 68
[143] A. C. Ewing, *The Individual, The State and World Government*, p. 116
[144] Quoted by A. C. Ewing in his book, *The Individual, The State and World Government*, pp. 106-109

According to these thinkers, this is the fundamental weakness of this doctrine and the cause for ruin.

In this regard, Mencken writes in his book, *Treatise on Right and Wrong*:

*'Under all such failures there is a greater one; the failure of man, the most social of all the higher animals and by far the most intelligent, to provide himself with anything, even remotely described as good government. He has made many attempts in that direction, some of them very ingenious and others sublimely heroic, but they have always come to grief in the execution. The reason surely is not occult; it is to be found in the abysmal difference between what government is in theory and what it is in fact. In theory it is simply a device for supplying a variable series of common needs, and the men constituting it (as all ranks of them are so fond of saying) are only public servants; but in fact, its main purpose is not service at all, but exploitation.'* [145]

## 12.10 Investigation by UNO

In 1947, UNESCO[146] the cultural organ of the UN[147] set up a research committee in order to study and report in a scientific manner on the working of the democratic system in different countries. The committee obtained articles on democracy from the great scholars and thinkers of the world and published them in the form of a book. All shades of opinion were represented in the volume which was published under the title, *Democracy in a World of Tensions*. The very first question posed by this committee was, 'What is the meaning of democracy?' In response, it was admitted that this word was extremely vague and to date its precise sense has not been determined. A few went so far as to call it 'one of the most ambiguous words in current usage'.[148]

The next question asked was, 'Is the majority vote always correct, and a protest against it is a protest against democracy'? The answer was:

*It does not, however, imply that the judgement of the majority is inerrant; and it, therefore, allows freedom to minorities to agitate and vote for the reversal of previous majority decisions. (p. 504)*

What we have written so far in the previous pages against democracy does not mean that in our view the different systems of government which are presently established in the world are any of them better than the democratic system. Not at all. What we wish to say is that the best system which human intellect has

---

[145] H. C. Mencken, *The Treatise on Right and Wrong*, p. 234
[146] UNESCO – United Nations Educational, Scientific and Cultural Organisation
[147] UNO – United Nations Organisation
[148] *Democracy in a World of Tensions*, p. 460

devised throughout all its history has been shown by experience to also have failed badly. This failure is, in reality, not the failure of democracy, nor does it mean that according to these thinkers and scholars, or in our view, that dictatorship or monarchy are successful systems of government as compared to democracy. The real cause of this failure is that ideology which is called the secularization of State. This ideology means that whether it is a king or dictator, the majority of a democratic parliament, or the president of a State, they have absolute right of legislation – they can formulate whatever type of law they wish. Whenever they wish, they can alter or revoke it and implement another law in its place. In this freedom of theirs there is no constraint. There are no such immutable limits which they cannot cross. There is no external criterion to evaluate the rights or wrongs of their legislation. This is the fundamental reason for the cause of the failure of whatever system of government human intellect has devised up till the present time. And while this fundamental reason remains, no system of government will be successful.

## 12.11 What Harm Does This Cause

The question arises that, if there is no permanent criterion to judge between right and wrong, and the decisions made by the majority of the representatives of the state become the laws of the nation, what harm results? This question needs profound attention indeed. In this connection, first of all bear in mind this reality, that whether it is the common people of a nation or their representatives, and whether these representatives are in the majority or minority, they will in any case be human beings – and whatever weakness one man can have, this can be present in a group of men as well. Therefore, it is impossible to imagine - and the one who assumes this deceives himself - that a majority of representatives will become free from those attractions, desires, inclinations and feelings which makes the limbs of a man shake. In the words of Lord Snell:

'Governments are always composed of men who share the general imperfections of mankind, with the result that they can never be more noble or more enlightened than are the human beings who administer their laws and shape their policy.'[149]

Aldous Huxley makes the same point in his book, *Science, Liberty and Peace*, when he says:

'There has never been a time when too much power did not corrupt its possessors, and there is absolutely no reason to suppose that in this respect, the future behaviour of

---

[149] Lord Snell, *The New World*, p. 17

*human beings will be in any way different from their behaviour in the past and at the present time.*[150]

Therefore, if the majority is also given the authority to legislate without any limits or restrictions, then the rights of other human beings can never be safeguarded through its hands. This will certainly be the fate of the people living within the boundary of the state itself, but as far as the human beings of other nations are concerned, they will not even be considered to be human.

The beginning of human social life commenced with divisions into tribes. A tribe was in actual fact the name for the extended form of a family, but the consequence of this differentiation and division was that one tribe became bloodthirsty in relation to another tribe. The fire of mutual rivalry and conflict would keep smouldering among them and would spark at the slightest provocation. Then it also used to happen that some tribes would join together and in this way the warring groups would become wider. No matter how much progress mankind makes in other fields, from the point of view of this division and fragmentation, it still stands today at the same juncture where it was during this era of ignorance. Today, man is still divided into those tribes, with the difference that the tribe is now called a nation. In some places, a nation is based on the sharing of race and in others on sharing the same State i.e. people of one race or one nation belong to one group, and people of another race or nation belong to another group. If this division and differentiation had been merely for administrative purposes, even then it could have been tolerable, but the same rivalry and enmity is present between different nations which used to be prevalent between different tribes – in fact far more deep and intense than that. Prof. Cobban's remarks on this point should be noted:

*'Nationalism is a feeling which is born out of hatred and lives on enmity. Nations become aware of themselves by their conflicts with other nations and their feelings of hostility do not cease with the completion of national unity. No sooner has a nation asserted its own right to self-determination than it sets about oppressing other nations that make the same claim. For all these reasons it may be concluded that nationalism is a very dangerous foundation for a state.'*[151]

Fredrick Hertz, the historian of nationalism, writes as follows in his book, *Nationality in History and Politics*:

*'History shows us that for the greater part the quarrels between several nations had scarcely any other occasion than that these nations were different combinations of people and called by different names. To an Englishman, the name of a Frenchman,*

---

[150] Aldous Huxley, *Science, Liberty and Peace*, p. 41
[151] Alfred Cobban, *The Crisis of Civilisation*, p. 166

*Spaniard, or an Italian raises, of course, ideas of hatred and contempt. Yet the simple name of man, applied properly, never fails to work a salutary effect.*[152]

In his book, *New Hopes for a Changing World*, Bertrand Russell has expressed the view that in the present age, the thing which stands in the way of social contacts extending beyond the limits of the nation and which therefore poses the most serious threat to the human race, is the cult of nationalism. But the irony is that every man accepts that the nationalism of other nations is a very evil thing but that the nationalism of his own nation is a very good thing.

A fundamental difference also between the tribal division of olden times and the national division of modern times is that nationalism is no longer just a political ideology but has adopted the form of a belief system instead. Though it is understood as if the West has removed the garb of religion and discarded it, and has now become totally irreligious, it has not become devoid of religion; it has converted its religion - now its religion is nationalism.

In the words of Aldous Huxley[153], nationalism has taken on the form of an idolatrous and pagan religion. Such a religion which is so powerful in the manufacture of chaos and division in humanity, that no monotheistic religion can compete with it for the welfare and unity of mankind. Nationalism or racist sentiments are indeed the dogma of the insane.

Huxley's comment on this is worth noting:

*'Nationalism leads to moral ruin, because it denies universality, denies existence of a single God, denies the value of the human being as a human being; and because at the same time, it affirms exclusiveness, encourages vanity, pride and self-satisfaction, stimulates hatred and proclaims the necessity and rightness of war.'*[154]

Huxley makes the following remarks at another place:

*'Twentieth century political thinking is incredibly primitive. The nation is personified as a living being, with passions, desires, susceptibilities. The national person is superhuman in size and energy, but completely sub-human in morality. Ordinarily, decent behaviour cannot be expected of the National Person, who is thought of as incapable of patience, forbearance, forgiveness and even of common sense and enlightened self-interest. Men, who in private life behave as reasonable and moral beings, become transformed as soon as they are acting as representatives of a National Person, into the likeness of their stupid, hysterical and insanely touchy tribal divinity. This being*

---

[152] F. Hertz, *Nationality in History and Politics*, p. 328
[153] Aldous Huxley, *The Perennial Philosophy*, p. 184 and 203
[154] Aldous Huxley, *Science, Liberty and Peace*, p. 34

so, there is little to be hoped for at the present time, from general international conference.[155]

A thought-provoking passage by Adam de Hegedus is quoted below:

*'At the bottom of these two wars, there was the same anarchic division of the world into sovereign independent nation states, which by their very nature, are forced to compete and conflict with each other and are unable to create a mutually healthy economic organization. The worst feature of this situation is not so much the recurrence of war as the absence of peace.*[156]

## 12.12 Motive of Patriotism

The outcome of nationalism becoming a religion is that patriotism has been declared to be the highest virtue and the patriotic motive a great value. The 'slogan' of this religion is – 'whether my country is right or wrong I will support it regardless'. Rumelin, Chancellor of Tubingen University, wrote (in 1875) that:

*'The State is autarchic. Self regard is its appointed duty; the maintenance and development of its own power and well-being. Egoism – if you call this egoism – is the supreme principle of all politics. The State can only have regard to the interest of any other State so far as this can be identified with its own interest. Self devotion is the principle for the individual; self assertion for the State. The maintenance of the State justifies every sacrifice, and is superior to every moral rule.*[157]

Professor Joad makes the following comments:

*'The practical effect of idealist theory in its bearing upon the relations between States is, therefore, to create a double standard of morality. There is one system of morals for the individual and another for the State so that men who, in private life, are humane, honest and trust-worthy, believe that, when they have dealings on the State's behalf with the representatives of other States, they are justified in behaving in ways of which as private individuals, they would be heartily ashamed.*[158]

Now just see that when the situation is such that:

(1) Human beings of the world are divided into different nationalities.

---

[155] Aldous Huxley, *Ends and Means*, p. 40
[156] Adam de Hegedus, *The State of the World*, p. 11
[157] Quoted by R. H. Murray in *The Individual and The State*, p. 216
[158] C. E. M. Joad, *Guide to the Philosophy of Morals and Politics*, pp. 729-730

(2) Every nation is concerned only about its own interests – not only concerned with protecting its present interests but also to accumulate as many interests as possible and

(3) there are no such limits and restrictions according to which transgressing in order to achieve one's objective could be considered immoral, then what will be the state of the world?

This reality is in fact the product of Machiavellian ideology which, at this time, dominates the West and (also in following the West) is spread throughout the world. That doctrine according to which Machiavelli advises the ruling class:

*'A prince being thus obliged to know well how to act as a beast must imitate the fox and the lion, for the lion cannot protect himself from traps and the fox cannot defend himself from wolves. One must, therefore, be a fox to recognize traps, and a lion to frighten wolves. Those that wish to be only lions do not understand this. Therefore, a prudent ruler ought not to keep faith when by so doing it would be against his interest and when the reasons which made him bind himself no longer exist.'*[159]

And his follower, Frederick II, who invariably acted on its principles in his dealing with other rulers, wrote in his *Political Testament* as follows:

*'The great matter is to conceal one's designs and to cover up one's character....Policy consists rather in profiting by favourable conjunctures than in preparing them in advance. This is why I counsel you not to make treaties depending on uncertain events, and to keep your hands free. For then you can make your decision according to time and place, and the conditions of your affairs, in a word, according as your interest requires of you.'*[160]

It is obvious that according to this concept of politics, if any thought of following an ethical principle arises in someone's mind, then he will not be considered fit to be in government. It was a belief of Lord Grey that:

*'I am a great lover of morality, public and private; but the intercourse of nations cannot be strictly regulated by that rule.'*[161]

This is why Walpole said:

*'No great country was ever saved by good men, because good men will not go to the lengths that may be necessary.'*[162]

---

[159] N. Machiavelli, *The Prince and the Discourses*, p. 64
[160] R.H. Murray, *The Individual and the State*, p. 209-212
[161] Quoted by L. S. Stebbing in *Ideals and illusions*, p. 13
[162] Quoted by L. S. Stebbing in *Ideals and Illusions*, p. 14

Cavour has summed this view in a nutshell:

*'If we did for ourselves what we do for our country, what rascals we should be.'*[163]

## 12.13 Outcome of the Discussion

If we wish to summarise what we have written in the previous pages, then it will be as follows:

(1) People have to live together.
(2) As a result of living together, there is a clash in mutual interests, and conflicts are born from this.
(3) The concept of a political system emerged for this purpose that there should be no clash in the interests of different people, and if there is a clash, then no conflicts emerge.
(4) None of the political systems which human intellect has devised so far have been successful in this objective.
(5) The last system among these systems is national democracy but this system is also proving to be failing badly, firstly, because there remains a mutual clash between different parties within a country and secondly, the emotions of hatred and rivalry among different countries and nations make the world into a continuous hell.

The question is, have Western intellectuals even thought about a solution to these difficulties? And if they have, then what is it, and what are the hurdles in following its path?

## 12.14 What Kind of System Western Thinkers Desire

We have seen that the fundamental error in the system of democracy is that 'sovereignty' is considered to be in the hands of the people and the decisions made by the majority of the representatives of the people are considered to be the final word. Discussing this issue, Professor Cobban says:

*'The traditional justification for the sovereignty of the people is that the government must be founded on either force or consent, and that since force cannot make right, rightful government must be based on consent. But this is neither logical nor is it true. The fact that a million people consent to an act which is wrong, does not make it any the less wrong. If words have any meaning, the rightfulness of any government's authority depends on its objects and on the way in which it is exercised. A will ought to*

---

[163] Cavour, *Foreign Affairs*, July 1952

*prevail only if it is a good will; but this is dependent not upon whose will it is but upon its content.*[164]

Rousseau states that 'general will' will always be right otherwise it cannot call itself general will. If this statement is correct, then there is no question even remaining of majority and minority. When general will can only call itself general will when it says the right thing, then why can it not be said thus, that whatever matter is right according to the moral standard, that is truth (even if not a single hand is raised in its support).

Professor Cobban has proposed 'moral values' as the standard for judging right and wrong, rather than the majority vote. In reality, when Locke presented the doctrine of democracy, he also viewed it as the practical implementation of an 'immutable law' which he interpreted as a 'natural law'. Hence, in this regard he said:

*'There is an immutable law governing the just relations between man and man, independently of any society or state to which they may belong. This natural law would serve like natural rights as a limitation on the absolute rule of governments, however constituted and whatever other ends they may pursue.'*[165]

### 12.14.1  Natural Law

Locke put his trust in natural law to guide aright. He argued that people followed the natural law, as long as they lived naturally, and were without culture and civilization. At this time, reason was their guide and not sentiment. Later on, they were guided by sentiment and ceased to live in accordance with the natural law. The revival and enforcement of the natural law was what society needed now. But when we ask how this natural law can be discovered, Locke refers us to the 'will of the majority'. Here he seems to be arguing in a circle.

### 12.14.2  Locke's Mistake

Have you observed how such an eminent thinker is going around in meaningless circles around a central point, like a piece of wood ensnared in a whirlpool. Alarmed at the mistakes of human decisions and the intrigues of vested interests, he cries out, 'No government has the right to carry on doing whatever it wishes, it must remain obedient to the eternal law of nature'. And when he is asked, where is this eternal law of nature to be found, he cannot conceive of anything else other

---

[164] Alfred Cobban, *The Crisis of Civilisation*, p.76
[165] Quoted by J. D. Mabbott, in *The State and the Citizen*, p. 76

than, 'This law will be found in the decisions of the majority'. This is like standing under a dripping roof gutter to take refuge from the rain.

However, we were saying that Western thinkers are now coming to realise this reality, that under the democratic system considering all decisions of the majority as being right in every circumstance, is wrong. For any decision to be right or wrong an external criterion is needed. According to Locke, this external criterion is the 'natural law'. Professor Cobban calls it the 'moral standard'.

### 12.14.3   Divine Law

The famous Italian patriot, Mazzini, however puts it in a more definite shape when he says that the principle of universal suffrage was a good thing, inasmuch as it provides a lawful method for a people for guarding against forces of destruction and continuing their own government. However, for a people who have no common beliefs, all that democracy can do is to safeguard the interests of the majority and keep the minority subdued. We can, he adds, be subject to God or to man, one man, or more than one. If there be no superior authority over man, what is there to save us from the subjugation of powerful individuals? Unless we have some sacred and immutable law which is not man-made, we can have no standard for discriminating between right and wrong. A government based on laws other that God's Will, he continues, produces the same result whether it is a despotic or a revolutionary one. Without God, whoever is in authority will be a despot. Unless a government conforms to God's law it has no right to govern. The purpose of government is to enforce God's Will: if a government fails in its purpose, then it is your right and duty to try for and bring about a change.[166]

In other words, it means that according to Mazzini, the criterion for right and wrong should be the Divine laws whose implementation is the duty of a government. It is obvious that these Divine laws can be availed from religion.

### 12.14.4   Divine Laws Cannot be Obtained from Christianity

But in the words of Professor Joad, the state of the religion (Christianity) which is prevalent in Europe, is such that:

*'Christianity places man's true life not in this world but in the next. While the next is wholly good this world is conceived to be, at least to some extent, evil; while the next life is eternal, life on earth is transitory. For man's life hereafter, this, his present existence, is to be regarded as a preparation and a training; and its excellence consists in the thoroughness and efficiency with which the training is carried out. Nothing on the*

---

[166] Quoted by Griffith, in *Interpreters of Man*, p. 46

*earth is wholly and absolutely good, and such goods as earthly life contains are good only as a means to greater goods which are promised hereafter.*[167]

The Spanish scholar Dr. Falta de Gracia writes:

*'The notion of justice is as entirely foreign to the spirit of Christianity as is that of intellectual honesty. It lies wholly outside the field of its ethical vision.'*[168]

Professor Whitehead writes:

*'As society is now constituted, a literal adherence to the moral precepts scattered throughout the Gospels would mean sudden death.'*[169]

Dorsey, the historian of civilisation, has asserted that today millions of people feel that Christianity is the religion of the defeated. They accept the religion but admit solemnly its defeatist spirit. Nothing is satisfactory in life, they argue. 'Desire for satisfaction is wrong and satisfaction of wrong desires is sin' is a slogan which makes a true and healthy life impossible. It destroys humanity.[170]

It is obvious that from this kind of religion those Divine laws could never be obtained which Mazzini had declared as the immutable criteria for right and wrong. There was no other way now for Europe to solve their problem except to knock at some other door.

## 12.15 Declaration of Human Rights

The same is the case with other religions, both in the East and the West. It is, in fact, futile to seek in religion the Divine laws for a standard of absolute right and wrong. Religion itself is man-made. In these circumstances, modern man, a frustrated, helpless, pitiable soul, had perforce to seek objective standards outside the field of religion. He turned for help to the UNO. The UNO appointed a Commission to state and define the fundamental rights of man. On the basis of the recommendations of the Commission, in 1948 the UNO published its famous Declaration of Human Rights. This document listed the basic fundamental human rights. The UNO asked its member states to guarantee them to all their subjects and to regard them as sacred and inviolable. The Declaration was hailed as the biggest achievement of the modern age. It was hoped that governments all over the world would, in future, desist from encroaching on these rights of man. This hope, unfortunately, has not been fulfilled. UNESCO, an organ of the UNO, had

---

[167] C. E. M. Joad, *Guide to the Philosophy of Morals and Politics*, p. 127
[168] Quoted by Robert Briffault, in *The Making of Humanity*, p. 333
[169] A. N. Whitehead, *Adventures of Ideas*, p. 18
[170] George A. Dorsey, *Civilisation*, p. 446

circulated a questionnaire on the draft of the proposed Declaration. The answers to the questionnaire have been published with an introduction by Jacques Maritain. His view is that, 'Rights, being human, should have some limits imposed on them, and be regarded as liable to amendment and change' (p. 15). John Lewis, the editor of the *Modern Quarterly*, London, is equally outspoken in his criticism of the Declaration. He writes that it is mere fiction that 'human rights' are absolute or inherent in human nature and came into being before man began living in an organised society (p. 51). Gerard, a professor in the University of Chicago, writes that the Declaration is an attempt to determine the proper relationship between man and society and that the 'rights' cannot be viewed as unalterable for all times (p. 20).

This means that man did not even have the satisfaction that he would continue to receive on a permanent basis whatever he had achieved after so much effort and struggle, and that there would be no kind of modification or change in it. For the protection of rights, Maritain has written that it is not a question of defining human rights, rather, in the problem of unity of agreement in their application in daily life, the first condition is to agree on the criteria for values. For the respect of human rights, it is necessary that the concept of human life should be common for all people. This is what is called the 'philosophy of life' (p.17). This same reality is expressed by Professor Joad in these words:

*'I suggested that the good life for the individual consists in the pursuit of certain absolute values. If I am right, if, that is to say, it is by the pursuit of values that a man develops his personality, we may add that the object of the State is to establish those conditions in which the individual can pursue absolute values and to encourage him in their pursuit. We are thus enabled to establish a principle of progress in society, which is also a standard of measurement whereby to assess the relative worths of different societies.'*[171]

## 12.16 In Search of the Permanent Values

In other words, the whole discussion has finally reached this conclusion, that the solution to this problem of human society can be nothing other than that the mutual matters of human beings be resolved according to the Permanent Values and that these values should serve as the criteria for right and wrong. This is that final destination at which man has arrived after thousands of years of his failed experiments. But even after having reached this destination, man stands perplexed and confounded, because he cannot know from where he can find these Permanent Values. Through their intellect they try to figure out some values but one is contradicted by another.

---

[171] C. E. M. Joad, *Guide to the Philosophy of Morals and Politics*, p. 806

Come! Let us now see what solution Islam offers for this extremely important and difficult problem of mankind. We have already stated that the whole structure of the Islamic system is raised on this foundation, that man is not only defined by his body, but other than his body, he has been bestowed with a self as well. Every human child is endowed with this human self at the time of its birth equally. This very thing is what makes man worthy of respect and dignity. Because of this, every human child deserves equal respect just due to the fact of being human. In this, there is no question of caste, race, parents, status of family etc. The revolutionary declaration of the Quran is:

*Verily, We have honoured every child of Adam...(17:70)*

This means We (Allah) have created all children of Adam (human beings) equally respectable. According to this, no man has superiority over another man from the point of view of being a human being and nor is any man inferior to another man. This is the first and fundamental principle of Islam.

The fundamental trait of a self is also that no self can become the tool for another self or serve as a means to fulfil another self's objectives.[172] From this it is obvious that:

(1) When every human being has been bestowed with a self equally and
(2) No self can be the tool of another self

Then no human being can either be the subject and slave of another man or subservient. The second fundamental concept of the Islamic System is that no human being has the right to enslave another human being. The Quran states:

*It is not right for man that Allah should give him the Book of law, power to judge and (even) messenger-hood, and he should say to his fellow beings to obey his orders rather than those of Allah. He should rather say: Be you faithful servants of Allah by virtue of your constant teaching of the Book and your constant study of it. (3:79)*

The question is that when, according to the Quran, no human being has been granted the right to rule over another human being, then is its purpose that no system of government be established in the world? That man should live a life of anarchy? Not at all. The Quran establishes human society according to laws and

---

[172] In defending slavery, Aristotle argued that some men are born slaves. They are therefore to be treated as chattels, i.e. used as tools as a craftsman uses his tools. The Quran, on the other hand, has categorically rejected such ideas, and in restoring to man his lost dignity has struck the death blow to all forms of slavery. This point is argued further in the chapter on Woman which will clarify how much the concept of slaves and concubines is against Islam.

procedures, and teaches how to live life according to these. It states that no man has the right to rule, only Allah has this right:

*...the command is for none but Allah...(12:40)*

Only Allah has the right to govern and He does not include anyone in his rule (18:26). But Allah is a transcendental reality – we can neither see Him nor hear His voice. So how can we have our matters adjudicated by Him? How can we espouse His rule? For this, He has directed that His rule will be established by following those laws which He has preserved through the revelation in the Quran:

*Say: 'Shall I seek for judge other than Allah? when He it is Who hath sent unto you the Book, explained in detail...(6:114)*

Since these laws are not formulated by a man or a group of men, their obedience is therefore not the obedience of man. Furthermore, because these laws are equally applicable to all men – no man, no matter how high his position, can remain outwith their jurisdiction. Hence, in an Islamic system there is no distinction whatsoever between a ruler and the ruled. What is commonly called the 'government' or 'State' is, in the Islamic System, nothing more than the machinery to implement the Divine laws.

Now let us proceed. We have seen that:

(1) Man is defined by his body and his self.
(2) In the human body, there are changes taking place every moment, therefore its requirements also keep changing. But the human self is unfamiliar with change. External changes do not affect it; it always remains changeless.

Since the Islamic system fulfils the needs of man as a whole, it is therefore a mixture of change and permanence i.e. it is a mixture of elements of permanence and capacity for change and modification. In the words of Iqbal:

*The ultimate spiritual basis of all life, as conceived by Islam, is eternal and reveals itself in variety and change. A society based on such a conception of reality, must reconcile in its life, the categories of permanence and change. It must possess eternal principles to regulate its collective life; for the eternal gives us a foothold in the world of perpetual change. But eternal principles, when they are understood to exclude all possibilities of change which, according to the Quran, is one of the greatest signs of Allah, tend to immobilize what is essentially mobile in its nature.*[173]

---

[173] M. Iqbal, *Reconstruction of Religious Thought in Islam*, p 140.

It is for this purpose that the Quran has given those principles which satisfy the unchanging requirements of the human self. These principles remain unchanged forever and are the ones which are called the Permanent Values:

*The Word of your Sustainer does find its fulfilment in truth and in justice: None can change His Words (the Permanent Values): for He is the one who hears and knows all. (6:115)*

The proclamation of your Sustainer has been completed with justice and truth. There is none to change his proclamations (Permanent Values and principles), because these principles are not the creation of some blind nature but are precisely defined by Him Who hears and knows all.

These immutable principles[174] (or Permanent Values) are those boundary lines which no-one has the authority to transgress. The Quran gives freedom to man of every era to devise sub-laws for himself according to the specific requirements of his time while remaining within the four walls of these principles. These sub-laws will keep varying with changing circumstances, while those principles within which these will be framed will always remain immutable. These sub-clauses will be settled through mutual consultation of the representatives of the Ummah (42:38). To this extent the Islamic System will be the mirror image of democracy.[175] The Quran does not argue with the machinery of consultation. It just gives this principle. According to this, any kind of machinery can be devised or adopted depending upon the prevailing circumstances of the time and that will be right.

We will discuss in further detail in a later chapter as to what type of immutable principles (or Permanent Values) these are. At this point it is important to clarify this much, that when an individual decides to live under this system, then he will know with certainty and without any doubt that whether people come and go, government forms or dissolves, no-one will be able to make any change or modification in these principles. Similarly, other nations of the world will also have complete surety and security that this nation will never overstep these principles. Today the state of the world is such that, if there is a presidential election in the USA, or the death of a head of state in Russia, the heart of the whole world starts palpitating because it is unknown what the policy of the new ruling party will be. This is because they do not hold such principles which are immutable. Even their

---

[174] The Quran has given some other laws in addition to these principles which are also immutable like these principles. These laws are mostly applicable to human family life and the Quran accords great importance to these.

[175] The Quran has given the value of *Taqwa* i.e. righteousness as the criterion (49:13) for deciding the selection process. The system must be such that righteous individuals can be selected to run it. (Ed)

constitution can be changed. But in the Islamic system, a change in government, or the death of a person in a position of the highest responsibility, cannot affect state policy in any way. This policy remains within the confines of these Permanent Values which are determined not by man but by Allah, and which no-one has the authority to change. In this system, the authority to formulate a constitution and legislation is not unlimited, it always remains within the boundary of these principles. That is why, in this system sovereignty only belongs to the Book of Allah which is the last, complete and immutable code of life for the whole of mankind.

## 12.17 Concept of Global Humanity

Now let us look at the second pillar of the political system i.e. nationalism, which has made the world into a hell. The fundamental concept presented by the Quran is that humanity is an indivisible unit and the division of it into different parts is the greatest of crimes. This concept of the Oneness of the Creator is the foundation stone of Quranic teaching and its system. It has announced to the whole world:

*Verily, the whole of mankind is one Ummah…(2:213)*

Remember, the whole of mankind is one Ummah, one nation, one universal brotherhood. The example of its creation and the beginning of life in it and its resurrection is like that of one person:

*And your creation or your resurrection is in no wise but as an individual self …(31:28)*

The great aim of the teaching which was continuously revealed from Allah was to maintain the unity of mankind. Those who oppose this teaching are charged by the Quran with the greatest crime of all:

*…and who sunder what Allah Has ordered to be joined …(2:27)*

That which Allah had ordained to be kept united, they shatter into pieces.

## 12.18 The Practical Programme of the Quran

The great beauty of the Quranic teaching is that it not only presents concepts and principles, it also puts forward a programme to shape these concepts practically. The beginning of the practical programme which it has given for the unity of mankind is referenced from the time of Abraham. The Quran tells us that the different nations of the world had built their own individual 'national houses'.

Similarly, different religions had established their own respective centres. Nowhere in the whole world was there such a 'House' which could be called the Centre of universal humanity. Therefore, for this purpose Abraham was asked to lay the foundation for such a Centre which could be declared as the 'House for Global Humanity'. In Surah *Al Imran* it is noted:

*The first House appointed for men was that at Bakkah: Full of blessing and of guidance for the whole of mankind. (3:96)*

It is a reality that the first 'House' which was made for the good of all of mankind (which was this very Ka'bah) was constructed in the abundant land of Makkah and was to serve as a lighthouse for the guidance of the whole of mankind. Its fundamental aim was:

*... Whoever enters it attains peace and security ...(3:97)*

Whosoever comes within its protection, is secured from all the dangers of the world. It is obvious that by 'House' is not meant a house made of mud and bricks. From this is meant such a universal System which is established for the welfare and development of mankind. The tangible centre of this system is the Ka'bah. In the same way that (for example) a flag, throne, capital city etc. are the symbols of a State, similarly the Ka'bah is a symbol of the central status of the Divine system. These things are declared by the Quran as *Sha'ayr* Allah (symbols of Allah). Hence, when it was said that the Ka'bah is declared as the 'House' for mankind, by this it was meant that Allah gave the concept of such a system which should encompass the whole of humanity. In another verse, it is stated:

*Remember We made the House a place of assembly for men and a place of safety...(2:125)*

This also makes it clear that by Ka'bah is meant the system which is shaped on the fundamental concept of the unity of mankind.

In these verses, the Quran has stated that whichever human being comes under the protection of this system, he will be at peace from every kind of danger. Though there is no doubt that being protected from dangers is not a small blessing by any means, it is nevertheless a negative aspect. The Quran goes a step further and states:

*Allah made the Ka'bah, the Sacred House, so that it becomes an asylum of security for men...(5:97)*

195

Allah made the Ka'bah as a House worthy of respect so that it can become the Centre for establishing humanity. This means that the next characteristic of this system will be that as a result of this, the whole of humanity will become capable of standing on its own feet. No human being in the world will be dependent on another human being for their needs. This is clarified further in Surah *Al Hajj* – the Centre of this system will have the status of an open city and every human being of the world will be able to be its citizen:

*...which We have made open to all men - equal is the dweller there and those from outside of the land...(22:25)*

After the construction of this Centre, Abraham was told:

*And proclaim the Hajj[176] among men...(22:27)*

You should make an announcement to the whole of mankind, that people should gather at this place so that their disputed matters are resolved through reason and logic (this is the very meaning of Hajj). And then it is stated:

*That they witness the benefits for themselves...(22:28)*

And that they see their good in front of them in concrete form. The nations of the world create their own centres for the protection of their national interests but the Centre of the Divine system is made for the good of the whole of mankind. There is an open invitation to gather in this Centre extended to all:

*...Hajj thereto is a duty men owe to Allah, those who can afford the journey; but if any do not accept this invitation, Allah stands not in need of any of His creatures.*
*(3:97)*

It is incumbent on the whole of mankind that whoever among them has the wherewithal to reach here, they should do Hajj of this House for Allah. It is an open invitation but for the one who does not accept this invitation, the loss will only be his, there will be no loss to Allah. Allah is free from all needs from his creation. It is also obvious from this that in inviting the whole of mankind there is no hidden self-interest of this system itself. This invitation is to the whole of mankind for the benefit of all for their protection and preservation, and to devise solutions and to formulate a programme for this purpose.

---

[176] Hajj is the universal gathering of the Islamic world and is held in the Centre of this nation, so that solutions to their collective problems are sought in the light of the Quran. In this way, this nation is able to see the benefits with their own eyes. *Lughat-ul-Quran*, Vol. 1, p. 303 (Ed)

## 12.19 For the Sake of Humanity

But there is one condition in this, and this is a fundamental condition i.e. that those who are participating in it should also not come with any idea of self-interest in their heart. They should come with the motive of good for the whole of mankind. The Quran has termed this great truth using the word *Lillah* (for the sake of Allah). In another verse it is stated, 'Fulfil these gatherings for Allah' (2:196). 'For Allah' means the completion of the programme which is prescribed by Allah in the Quran for the welfare and development of mankind. If in the hearts of all those who are participating there are interests of a nationalistic, tribal or some non-Divine programme, then this participation will no longer be *Lillah*. This will become *Shirk* (associating other systems with the Quran), not *Tauheed* (Oneness of Allah). This is why it is made clear in another verse that if there is to be participation in this Centre:

> *Being true in Eimaan to Allah, and never assigning partners to Him (His system): if anyone assigns partners to Allah, he is as if he had fallen from heaven and been snatched up by birds, or the wind had swooped (like a bird on its prey) and thrown him into a far-distant place. (22:31)*

In other words, removing all feelings of selfishness from your heart, and cutting yourself off from all directions, face straight towards Allah and gather here, and do not let not any other motive come near. On this basis, it is stated in Surah *Al Tauba*:

> *O you who believe! Truly the Mushrikeen[177] are impure[178]; so let them not, after this year of theirs, approach the Masjid-ul-Haram[179]...(9:28)*

And the announcement of this was also made (for the very first time) at the gathering of Hajj itself, so that mankind becomes informed about this decision:

> *And an announcement from Allah and His Messenger, to mankind on the day of the Great Hajj - that Allah and His Messenger dissolve obligations with the Mushrikeen...(9:3)*

---

[177] *Mushrikeen* – those who do *Shirk*, i.e. associate man-made laws with Allah's laws. (Ed)

[178] The word used for impure in the Quran is *Najs*, which means there is impurity which can be seen with the eyes, i.e. physical, and the other which can be felt with insight, like the impurity of the inner self. *Lughat-ul-Quran*, Vol 11, p. 563

[179] *Masjid* here means the Centre which is the symbol for establishing Allah's Laws on earth. The Ka'bah has been declared as *Masjid-ul-Haram* (28:27). It is the Centre which represents the system which symbolizes the unity of Allah. (It is not a place for mere ritualistic bowing). *Lughat-ul-Quran*, Vol 1, pp. 652-653

If, after this proclamation, a representative of any nation participates in this gathering with intentions of malevolence and harm to others, then not only will he be thrown out but he will also be severely punished for this:

*...and any whose purpose therein is evil or wrong-doing - them will We cause to taste of a most Grievous Penalty. (22:25)*

## 12.20 Global Community

Did you notice what the first characteristic of the Quranic system is? This system is established for the complete benefit of universal humanity, rising above and beyond the concept of divisions into groups based on nationalism, tribalism, race, language or religion etc. Hence, the Quran states about that *Jamaat* of Momineen (group of Believers) through whose hands this system is established:

*You are the best of Peoples, rising from mankind, enjoining what is right, forbidding what is wrong, and having Eimaan in Allah...(3:110)*

In Surah *Al Baqarah* it is firstly stated that the Ka'bah has been proposed as a Centre of your system and after this it is stated:

*Thus have We made of you an Ummah justly balanced, that you may be witnesses over mankind...(2:143)*

And in this way, We have made you an international Ummah i.e. such an Ummah which is equidistant for all of humanity so that you can be a witness on the conduct of all men and that your messenger (Centre of the system) is a witness on you. From this, this Ummah will attain the *Imamat*[180] of mankind (just like Abraham):

*...I will make you (Abraham) an Imam for mankind...(2:124)*

From these explanations, it is clear that the duty of the Muslim Ummah has been declared to be to shape such a system in which the Permanent Values defined by Allah can be implemented practically within human society, and in this way the caravan of humanity is directed, prosperous and joyous, to its intended objective. Hajj is a segment in the practical programme of this system, in which the Muslim Ummah invites all those nations who are willing to participate for this aim, that they should gather in the Centre of this System and provide practical evidence for the tasks of welfare and development for mankind. In this way, the Quran keeps broadening the paths of its universal system, so that the whole earth shines with the light of its Sustainer:

---

[180] *Imamat* - leadership, to serve as a model of righteousness in the light of the Quranic values. (Ed)

*And the Earth will shine with the Glory of its Sustainer...(39:69)*

## 12.21 Religious Freedom

Have you noticed how the Quran keeps referring to *An-Naas* (mankind) in this system from the beginning to the end. This is the first system in the world which is proposed for the universal good of mankind. The need for this system arose because:

*...Had not Allah checked one set of people by means of another, there would surely have been pulled down monasteries, churches, synagogues, and mosques, in which the name of Allah is commemorated in abundant measure. Allah will certainly aid those who aid His (cause); for verily Allah is full of Strength, Exalted in Might. (22:40)*

From the above discussion, this reality has become clear to us that the Quranic system is the system of universal humanity which takes us out of the narrow spheres of nationalism, tribalism and religion into the boundless environment of 'universalism'. This is why the giver of this programme, Allah, is called *Rabb-ul-Alameen* (Sustainer of the Worlds) (1:1); the messenger through whom this system was revealed is called *Rahmat-ul-Alameen* (Blessing for the Worlds) (21:107); and the Book of this system is called *Zikr-ul-Alameen* (Eminence for the Worlds) (6:91).

## 12.22 Justice (*Adl*) and Balance (*Ihsan*)

The structure of the Quranic system of government is erected on the immutable principle of justice and balance. The Quran has stated:

*Allah commands justice, the doing of good...(16:90)*

The meaning of *Adl* is to accord someone his full rights and *Ihsan* means to fulfil someone's need or compensate for a deficiency i.e. in this system no reduction will be made in someone's rights under any circumstance, but if such a situation arose that despite giving someone his right, there is still a need which remains unfulfilled, then meeting this need will be the duty of the Quranic system. The word *Adl* is very comprehensive – it does not merely mean 'justice through courts', its meaning covers all aspects of the sphere of life. In this regard, the Quran has detailed two principles, firstly:

*That no bearer of burdens can bear the burden of another. (53:38)*

In other words, it will not be the case that a crime is committed by one person and its punishment is suffered by another, that responsibility belongs to one person and is shouldered by another, the duty belongs to one person but it is carried out by another. This will not happen in this society. Nor that effort is made by one person and its reward is taken away by someone else. In this society, every individual will receive that for which he makes an effort and for which he takes action. And secondly:

*That man can have nothing but what he strives for. (53:39)*

In the case of *Adl*, there will be no differentiation of us and them, be they friend or foe - *Adl* will be done to all. In Surah *Al Ma'idah* it is stated:

*...let not the hatred of others to you make you swerve to wrong and depart from Adl (justice)...(5:8)*

So much so, that even if the decision of *Adl* goes against your own self even then you should do *Adl*:

*O you who believe! stand out firmly for justice, as witnesses to Allah, even as against yourselves, or your parents, or your kin, and whether it be (against) rich or poor: for Allah can best protect both. Follow not the lusts of your hearts (desires), lest you swerve, and if you distort justice or decline to do justice, verily Allah is well-acquainted with all that you do. (4:135)*

The duty to establish *Adl* on this system has the status of universality. In other words, this system is not only responsible within its own sphere for the operation and implementation of *Adl*, but its responsibility is also that wherever in the world there is injustice and exploitation, it should stand up with all its might and means to counter it. For this, even if it has to pick up the sword then it must. The Quran states that the sword was made for this very purpose i.e. to defend truth (*Haqq*) and justice (*Adl*). In Surah *Al Hadid* it is stated:

*We sent aforetime our messengers with Clear Signs and sent down with them the Book and the Balance (of Right and Wrong), that men may stand forth in justice; and We sent down Iron, in which is (material for) mighty war, as well as many benefits for mankind...(57:25)*

## 12.23 Permission for War

With regards to war, at another place it is stated that war will be unavoidable till the war ends:

*...Until the war lays down its burdens...(47:4)*

With regard to what has been written about war so far, it becomes evidently clear that in the Islamic system permission for war can be given for the followings aims:

(1) For the protection of the places of worship of every religion.
(2) For the establishment and protection of the system of *Adl* i.e. to eradicate evil and injustice from the world.
(3) To end war itself from the world.

With regard to 'religious freedom', this much further explanation is required that according to the Quran, no kind of compulsion whatsoever can be made in the matter of Deen. The Quran has stated:

*There is no compulsion in Deen...(2:256)*

This is a clear announcement of the Quran. In fact, the acceptance of some proclamation with the agreement of the heart is called Eimaan. Therefore, compulsion and Eimaan are two mutually contradictory things which cannot be together in one place. No-one can be forced inside Deen, nor can anyone be kept forcibly inside it. Whoever wishes can adopt Deen, and whenever he wishes he can leave it:

*...Let him who will Believe (have Eimaan), and let him who will, reject it...(18:29)*

By compulsion in Deen not only is it meant that an individual will not be made a Muslim at the point of a sword, the Quran calls it duress even if a matter is forcibly made acceptable by suspending someone's intellect and reasoning. This is the reason that it repeatedly clarifies that We have not given Rasul-ullah any miracle other than the Quran. Allah says to Rasul-ullah:

*...will you then compel mankind, against their will, to Believe (have Eimaan). (10:99)*

## 12.24 Ideological Differences

As has been noted previously, the fundamental characteristic of the Quranic system of government is that it views the whole of mankind as one community (universal brotherhood):

*Mankind was but one Ummah...(2:213)*

Therefore, it is against the division of mankind into different groupings (nations) on the basis of colour, race, language and nationalism. It states the whole world as one nation and all mankind as one unit, and declares only one criterion for the difference between them i.e. the difference in ideology. In other words, it views all those people in the world who accept the Permanent Values which are revealed through the revelation as being the objective of life, as part of one nation (no matter which part of the world they are living in and no matter what their race); and those people who adopt a different ideology, contrary to this one, as belonging to the other nation. In Quranic terminology, this is called the division of *Kufr* and Eimaan:

> *It is He Who has created you; and of you are some that are Unbelievers, and some that are Believers (in Eimaan)....(64:2)*

According to the Quran, there is no other criterion for nationality acceptable apart from this. But this division does not mean that it considers those people who do not accept this aim (i.e. who are not Momin) as 'untouchables' - not at all. It declares them holders of full human rights and fights for the protection of their rights with all means and force, regardless of whether these non-Muslims are living within the boundary of the Islamic State or outside it. As has been stated under the subject of system of *Rabubiyat*, the Quran declares the sustenance and development of non-Muslims to be the fundamental responsibility of the State and in return does not ask for any recompense. The Quran says to them:

> *We feed you for the sake of Allah alone. No reward do we desire from you nor thanks. (76:9)*

We provide means of sustenance for you because this is a duty upon us from Allah. We do not wish any return from you for this, not even that you should be grateful to us. The status of that which is called *Jizya*[181] is no more than this, that those non-Muslims (people of the book) in the time of Rasul-ullah who wished to remain as only citizens of the state, this was a symbol of their obedience to the system (9:29).

We have seen that the ultimate objective of the Quran is that there should be one system established in the whole world and its aim should be the implementation and preservation of the Permanent Values which were received through revelation for the prosperity and development of mankind. Till the time that such a system is not established in the whole world, and the world remains divided into nation states, the Islamic system will cooperate with other nations in all matters which are for the good of mankind:

> *...Help you one another in righteousness and virtue, but help you not one another in crime and malice...(5:2)*

---

[181] *Jizya* was a type of proportionate tax paid by those who were at war with the Islamic state and eventually submitted, in return for the provision of protection and sustenance by the Islamic system. They were not required to give their lives or possessions in the path of Allah (9:11). (Ed)

This is also obvious that when the Quranic system declares the whole of mankind as being one community and accepts all Momineen of the world as one nation, then the idea of religious sects and political parties cannot even be conceived of within a Quranic state. It declares sectarianism to be *Shirk* (30:31-32), and tells Rasul-ullah that he has nothing to do with such people who create sects:

*As for those who divide their Deen and break up into sects, you have no part in them in the least...(6:159)*

According to the Quran, mutual differences are a punishment from Allah:

*Be not like those who are divided amongst themselves and fall into disputations after receiving Clear Signs: For them is a dreadful penalty. (3:105)*

And remaining protected from this, His blessing:

*If your Sustainer had so willed, He could have made mankind one people: but they will not cease to dispute. Except those on whom your Sustainer has bestowed His Mercy (Rahmat[182])...(11:118-119)*

And as far as political parties are concerned, the Quran declares their existence to be a concoction of 'Pharaonic wisdom':

*Truly Pharaoh elated himself in the land and broke up its people into parties...(28:4)*

In this system, there will be one constitution for all and its principles will be immutable; and according to this constitution the whole of the Ummah will establish the System of *Adl* and *Rabubiyat* for which no illegitimate means or method will be adopted. Its objective will be to make the whole world into one universal community and by establishing peace among the whole of mankind, its ultimate goal will be to provide the means of sustenance for their realisable hidden potentials. And this is Deen – straight and true (98:5).

Today, man, plagued by nationalism, is in search of such a religion which can remove its burden from his chest. In this regard J. M. Murray writes in his book, *Adam and Eve*:

*'If religion is essential for our salvation...it must, first, be a religion which compels from the person an allegiance which completely overrides the claims of nationalism; and*

---

[182] *Rahmat* means all types of sustenance which are required for the nourishment of the body as well as for the development of the human self. This also includes the guidance of the Quran. *Lughat-ul-Quran*, pp. 548-550

*secondly it must be a religion which enlarges and strengthens man's capacity to act as an individual.*[183]

Western thinkers felt that the solution to this problem lay in the ideology of internationalism, therefore they first established the League of Nations and after its failure, the UNO was brought into existence. About this ideology and to what extent its practical steps can be a solution to this problem, Emrey Reves writes in his book, *The Anatomy of Peace*:

'*We have played long enough with the toy of internationalism. The problem we are facing is not a problem between nationalisms. It is a problem of a crisis in human society, caused by nationalism, and which consequently nationalism or internationalism can never solve. What is needed is universalism. A creed and a movement for creating a system of values which transcends the nation-state structure.*'[184]

Cast an eye once again on what has been written in respect of the Islamic system of politics in the previous pages and then see that the ideology or movement which Reves proposes as the solution for the problems of the modern era, where can it be found other than in Islam? F. Hertz elucidates this point further and writes:

'*It is now generally recognized that a mere machinery of international organization cannot work if the right spirit is lacking. But how can this spirit be created or strengthened. The proclamation of general principles obviously is not enough. Neither is it sufficient to lay down that nations must be educated toward that spirit, if a practicable plan and an adequate number of qualified educators are not available. The habit of treating such questions in an unrealistic and perfunctory way is bound to lead to failure, disillusionment and cynicism. Education towards world citizenship, moreover is not merely a matter for the schools. It is connected with all the great issues of political and economic life and could be solved if the political nations of the world would adopt detailed plans based on identical principles.*'[185]

This means that, according to him, there is no solution to these problems other than that one type of economic and social order be established in the world. This is that solution which the Quran proposed fourteen hundred years ago when the world did not even have any idea of the concept of global humanity.

---

[183] J. M. Murray, *Adam and Eve*, p. 66
[184] Emery Reves, *The Anatomy of Peace*, p. 164
[185] F. Hertz, *Nationality in History and politics*, p. 413

# 13  FATE OF NATIONS (IMMUTABLE LAWS OF THE RISE AND FALL OF NATIONS)

We have seen the concept of Allah which the Quran has given, according to which He has initiated those laws upon which the great system of the universe is wholeheartedly in pursuit. He has established similar laws for the human world. In the human world, there is the life of the individual – these laws are applicable to both an individual's physical life and the development of his self. But far more important than this, is the life of nations. Though a nation is merely the name given to a collection of individuals, its psychology is unique and specific. The Quran has also given those laws according to which the rise and fall and the death and life of nations are decided. It says that if any nation lives its life according to the laws prescribed by Allah, i.e. shapes such a system and society which is based on the foundation of the Divine laws as defined by Allah, then this nation achieves great prosperity and success. And if it goes against these laws then it is ruined and destroyed. This is called the collective Law of Requital, and it is absolute and immutable in the same way that the Law of Requital is for individuals.

According to the Quran, history is a record of the functioning of this collective Law of Requital. In other words, it informs us that a certain nation established a certain system based on a certain ideology of life and its fate was like this, while another nation spent its life according to another ideology, and its outcome was like that.

## 13.1  Significance of History

In modern terminology, this is called 'Science of History' or 'Philosophy of History'. The presentation of history as a science or philosophy was done for the first time by the Quran. This is the reason why it gives great significance to history. So much significance that it presents history as evidence for the verification of its claims i.e. when it says that We have declared that the nation which spends its life in this manner will be ruined and destroyed, then for the evidence in support of this claim it asks you to look at the history of mankind, and observe for yourself whether, whatever nation in whatever land and in whatever era adopted this path, its end was ruin and destruction or not.

For the verification of the Quranic claims (or the Divine laws) this is such a criterion which is openly accessible to the whole world. This is the reason that the Quran has expressly directed its followers to carry out a detailed study of history. Two advantages will result from this. Firstly, evidence for the truth of the Quranic claims will become manifest to them, and secondly, they will keep checking to see that no step of theirs is being lifted in the wrong direction.

## 13.2  The Quran and History

Hence, Allah has stated that We have made available two things in the Quran for your guidance:

*We have already sent down to you verses making things clear, an illustration from (the story of) people who passed away before you...(24:34)*

In other words, on the one hand those clear laws according to which decisions about the life and death of nations are made, and on the other hand the circumstances and condition of previous nations (history) from which the truth about these laws can be affirmed. If you study the Quran, the circumstances and outcomes of previous nations are given with such clarity and detail that it appears as if is a Book of history, but it is not a Book of history. Its style is that, first of all, it explains those laws which determine the rise and fall of nations, and after this, by presenting the circumstances of these past nations, it directs us to look and see how these laws produced their defined immutable consequences, and then immediately draws our attention to the fact that if you too follow this kind of path, your end will be the same also. About the opponents of the Quranic system of truth and righteousness it declares:

*Do they not travel through the earth and see what was the end of those before them? They were more numerous than these and superior in strength and in the traces (they have left) in the land: Yet all that they accomplished was of no profit to them. (40:82)*

What, have these people not travelled through the earth, that they could have seen with their own eyes what the end was of those nations which had gone before them and had adopted a wrong path like them?

## 13.3  Fate of Nations

The rubble of the ruins of their cities and dwellings are perpetually crying out to us about the tales of their glorious past - those nations were far greater in number than them (the ones who are now opposing this system), and far greater in power as well. The flags of their power and glory were fluttering firmly in the land, but when the time came for their destruction due to the results of their wrong path, then neither the greatness of their numbers was of any aid to them, nor could their wealth and power save them from this. This destruction did not reach them all of a sudden; Allah had earlier sent His messengers to them so that they could warn them that the path on which you are treading is leading you towards the destruction of hell:

*For when their messengers came to them with Clear Signs, they exulted in such
knowledge (and skill) as they had; but that very (Wrath) at which they were wont to
scoff hemmed them in. (40:83)*

But when the messengers of Allah came to them with such clear reasonings, they
refused to accept their message and announced that we are satisfied with the path
that we are taking, this is providing us with all the pleasures of life, you are saying
that destruction is awaiting us for no reason. But, ultimately, they were encircled
by the destruction which they used to mock:

*But when they saw Our Punishment, they said: 'We believe in Allah - the one Allah -
and we reject the partners we used to join with Him'. ('40:84)*

When they saw the destruction facing them, at that moment they began to avow
that we have Eimaan in one Allah and we reject the powers which we used to
associate with Him. When the results of following the wrong path manifest and
confront you, then at that time refraining from these is of no benefit:

*But their professing Eimaan when they (actually) saw Our Punishment was not going
to profit them. . .(40:85)*

And this was not a new or strange thing which was only applicable to them – it is
the immutable Law of Allah according to which decisions about the death and life
of all past nations are made:

*. . .(Such has been) Allah's Way of dealing with His Servants (from the most ancient
times). . .(40:85)*

And this is that point at which those who reject truth and righteousness remain
in loss.

## 13.4  The Grip of the Law of Requital

In another verse, it is stated:

*How many were the populations We utterly destroyed because of their iniquities,
setting up in their places other peoples? (21:11)*

The state of this nation about to be destroyed was such that they were given a
thousand warnings about their wrong path, but they listened to not even one.
When they saw Our punishment approaching in a visible form, they attempted to
flee from it:

*Yet, when they felt Our Punishment (coming), behold, they (tried to) flee from it.*
*(21:12)*

But the Law of Requital called out after them:

*Flee not, but return to the good things of this life which were given you, and to your*
*homes in order that you may be called to account. (21:13)*

Do not flee, where can you escape to by running away? Go back towards your palaces and those luxuries which used to provide you with such comforts, return so that you may be questioned from where did you obtain so much treasure and wealth? Who were those exploited human beings whose illegitimately obtained blood became the source for the decorative colouring and beautification of your palaces and lifestyle:

*They said: 'Ah! woe to us! We were indeed wrong-doers!' (21:14)*

At this they cried that we certainly used to do a lot of evil and tyranny and all this material wealth is the consequence of that very evil and tyranny:

*And that cry of theirs ceased not, till We made them as a field that is mown, as ashes*
*silent and quenched. (21:15)*

In verse (21:12) quoted above, it is stated that 'when they saw Our punishment manifest clearly in front of them, when they realized the truth of this' – this means that though the destructive consequences of a wrong social and economic order begin right from the very first day, these effects are extremely imperceptible, and can only be seen by those eyes which are not covered with the veils of vested interests. These consequences keep multiplying deep within, till one day they become apparent in a visible form.

## 13.5 The Real Cause for Destruction

'Becoming apparent in a visible form' means that their destruction happens by those means and causes which can be seen in a comprehensible form. But these causes are just an instrument in destroying their wrong system; the real cause is their wrong path of life. Historians (for whom history is merely the record of events and incidents) declare these visible causes as the reason for their destruction. But the Quran, which presents history as a science or philosophy, does not accord the least importance to these events and incidents (i.e. apparent causes) – it points to the underlying cause of the disease instead of the symptoms of the disease and states that this was the real cause and reason for their destruction.

## 13.6  *Sunnat-Ullah* (Divine Practice)

You have also seen that the Quran terms this law according to which decisions regarding the life and death of nations are made, as *Sunnat-Ullah*. The literal meaning of this term is the 'practice of Allah' and from this is meant that Law of Requital which is operating consistently from the beginning, and is immutable. All the laws of Nature are *Sunnat-Ullah* in which there is never any change or modification. In Surah *Al Ahzab* it is stated:

*...It was the practice (approved) of Allah amongst those of old that have passed away. And the command of Allah is a decree determined. (33:38)*

What is Allah's practice? This is His decision which has taken the form of an immutable law. In the same Surah, a little later it is stated:

*(Such was) the practice (approved) of Allah among those who lived aforetime: No change will you find in the practice of Allah. (33:62)*

Similarly, in Surah *Fatir* in relation to previous nations, their destruction, and its underlying causes, it is stated:

*...Now are they but looking for the way the ancients were dealt with? But no change will you find in Allah's way (of dealing): No turning off will you find in Allah's way (of dealing). (35:43)*

So they should know that the same law of Allah will be applicable to them as well, because you will not find any change in this law of Allah, nor will there be any possibility once the law is implemented that someone can turn its direction to face another direction.

## 13.7  Philosophy of History of Hegel[186] and Marx[187]

In our times, Hegel (and following after him, Marx) has presented history as a philosophy. But what is their philosophy of history? Hegel stated that one idea is born and grows, and when it reaches maturity, decline commences in it and then another concept emerges counter to it. It also meets the same fate and another concept emerges from this, which is the opposite to it. The whole of history is a tale of these mutually conflicting concepts. Marx also said the same with this proviso that this is not a war of ideas but of economic systems. One economic

---

[186] Georg Wilhelm Friedrich Hegel was a German philosopher of the 19th century.
[187] Karl Marx was a German philosopher, economist, sociologist, and journalist of the 19th century.

system emerges, grows, then another system emerges counter to it which ends the first system and replaces it. After a period of time, its end is also the same. When Hegel was asked, what is the power with which this continuous struggle of this regular process is being driven, he said it is Zeitgeist[188]. And when the same question was put to Marx, he replied that the basis of it is historical necessity.

According to this philosophy of history, there is neither a purpose in front of the universe nor an objective to a destination; nor any concept which is in itself virtue or evil; nor is there in any concept or system the ability to progress further and to be self-sustaining. Nor behind this great functioning universe is there any such power which is making this magnificent system operate according to some purpose – there are some blind forces which are in action mechanically; and helpless and hapless man is being crushed for no rhyme or reason within these meaningless conflicts and endeavours.

## 13.8  Quranic Philosophy of History

But the philosophy of history put forward by the Quran is completely different from this. It says there is a persistent struggle continuing in the universe between *Haqq* (Truth) and *Batil* (Evil). *Haqq* is absolute, established and immutable and its outcome is constructive and progressive. Contrary to this, *Batil* is like a weathercock changing direction all the time and its outcome is decline and destruction. In this struggle between *Haqq* and *Batil* it is *Haqq* which ultimately succeeds because overcoming *Batil* is inherent in its nature:

*Nay, We hurl the Truth against falsehood...(21:18)*

*Haqq* smashes the skull of *Batil*, when We strike *Batil* with *Haqq*, and the consequence of this sustained striking is that it flees out from the arena:

*...and it knocks out its brain, and behold, falsehood does perish! Ah! woe be to you for the (false) things you ascribe (to Us). (21:18)*

The consequence of whatever you people state against this doctrine is nothing other than destruction and ruin.

---

[188] Zeitgeist - the defining spirit or mood of a particular period of history as shown by the ideas and beliefs of the time. (Wikipedia).

## 13.9  The Universe[189] is Created in Truth

Now the question is, for what purpose does this struggle between *Haqq* and *Batil* and the ultimate victory of *Haqq* and defeat of *Batil* occur? And what force is acting behind this? The Quran states that Allah has created this universe with a purpose and not in vain. In Surah *Al Dukhan* it is stated:

*We created not the heavens, the earth, and all between them, merely in (idle) sport. We created them not except for just ends: but most of them do not understand.* (44:38-39)

But most people have no knowledge of this and think that the universe has simply come into existence and is operating without any aim. This belief is wrong. All the forces of the universe are operating in action for the purpose that every deed produces its precise effect:

*Allah created the heavens and the earth for just ends, and in order that each self may find the recompense of what it has earned, and none of them be wronged.* (45:22)

*Yea, to Allah belongs all that is in the heavens and on earth: so that He rewards those who do evil, according to their deeds, and He rewards those who do good, with what is best.* (53:31)

Since the universe is created in *Haqq*, therefore every doctrine, every deed and every system of life which is in accordance with *Haqq* (Permanent Values) will live and progress forward, and that which goes against this and is harmful to the development of humanity, will become destroyed. At this point, it is possible to say that this is contrary to our daily observation and experience. We see that the fields of the oppressors bloom, whereas the existence of those people who wish to live according to justice and honesty becomes constrained.

## 13.10 Scales for Determining the Life of Nations

There is no doubt that this is indeed our daily experience but observation of a doctrine or system of life or the state of the nation holding this ideology cannot be done in one day. For this, centuries are required. This is why the Quran has stated that every single day of the laws of the universe is equivalent to thousands and thousands of years of your calculation and reckoning. In Surah *Al Hajj*, it is noted:

---

[189] The Quranic concept of the universe will be covered in the next chapter.

*Yet they ask you to hasten on the Punishment! But Allah will not fail in His promise. Verily a Day in the sight of your Sustainer is like a thousand years of your reckoning. (22:47)*

Nations are neither made in one day, nor are finished in one day. Their scales of life and death are different from the scales at the level of individuals. Therefore, if the destructive result of a nation's wrong social system does not show up quickly, it should not be concluded from this that the consequences of their wrong actions are not even being formed. In the balance of the universe, every miniscule portion of their deeds is being weighed:

*Then shall anyone who has done an atom's weight of good, see it! And anyone who has done an atom's weight of evil, shall see it. (99:7-8)*

## 13.11 Balancing of Deeds is Ongoing

Here, no deed can remain without its result being manifested, but as with individuals, the principle of the health and disease of nations (and life and death) is that while the balance of good deeds remains heavy, the nation stays alive and progresses forward – but when the balance is tilted more towards evil deeds, then the decline of the nation commences:

*Then, he whose balance of good deeds will be found heavy, will be in a life of good pleasure and satisfaction. But he whose balance of good deeds will be light, will have his home in a (bottomless) pit. (101:6-9)*

This is because good deeds continuously remove the ill effects of wrong deeds:

*…For those things that are good remove those that are evil…(11:114)*

Contrary to this, if the balance of evil deeds keeps weighing heavier (tilting further down), then the nation gradually moves towards the annihilation of hell in such an unwitting way that they do not even realize that they are steadily slipping towards destruction. In the words of the Quran:

*…By degrees shall We punish them from directions they perceive not. (68:44)*

If this nation rectifies its wrong path before its destruction, and in its place adopts the right path of life, then it saves itself from ruin, but if it does not do this and reaches the destruction of hell, then there is no opportunity left for it to recover:

*But there is a ban on any population which We have destroyed: that they shall not return. (21:95)*

And it is destroyed in such a way that in the words of the Quran:

*And neither heaven nor earth shed a tear over them: nor were they given a respite.*
*(44:29)*

## 13.12 The Meaning of *Ajal* (Appointed Term)

In the same way that diseases of the physical life of individuals are different, the evils of the social and economic systems of nations are also different. Then, in the same way that for every disease and the time interval to death resulting from it varies - e.g. the patient suffering from tuberculosis dies after years of suffering, whereas meningitis does not grant respite for even a few days - respite from the wrongs of the social and economic systems and the consequent annihilation due to these is also of different durations. In Quranic terminology, the final limit of this time of respite is called *Ajal*. In Surah *Yunus* it is stated:

*...To every people is a term appointed: when their term is reached, not an hour can they cause delay, nor (an hour) can they advance. (10:49) See also (23:43)*

There is an *Ajal* for every nation; before that time there is respite to mend their ways, but when the final time arrives then there cannot be a delay of even a second. This is because (like physical diseases) there is an absolute law established for collective life and death and all this takes place according to this law. This is the reason that where it is stated that there is an *Ajal* for every nation or system (10:49), in another verse this is clarified by stating that for every *Ajal* there is an established law (13:38). The rise and fall of nations happens in accordance to this very law:

*Allah does blot out or confirms what He Will (as per His law): with Him is the Mother of the Book (the basis of all laws). (13:39)*

And all this happens as per this Will of Allah, according to which these laws have been established for the death and life of individuals and nations.

## 13.13 Death and Life Based on Laws

From the above discussion this fact becomes evident that, according to the Quran, the life and death of nations does not occur purely as a result of chance or mere accident, nor is it due to the mere trickery of 'some blind force of nature' either - all this occurs through procedures and laws. The Quran states:

*...That Allah might accomplish a matter already enacted (as a result of deeds); that those who perished would perish upon a clear Sign (which had been given), and those who lived might live after a clear Sign (had been given)...(8:42)*

So that the one who is killed, is killed due to a reason, and the one who lives, lives due to a reason also – here, life is not received as a charity nor does death and destruction occur through deceit. This is because:

*...It was not Allah who wronged them, it was they who wronged themselves. (29:40)*

Allah does not do wrong to any nation; it is the nation that does wrong to itself and as a result is destroyed.

## 13.14 Allah Does Not Wrong Anyone

Allah does not receive pleasure by being cruel to others, so that He should watch others' pain and torment by subjecting them to the punishment of hell. The Quran states:

*What can Allah gain by your punishment, if you are grateful and you have Eimaan? Nay, it is Allah that Appreciates and Knows all things. (4:147)*

If you adhere to Allah's established principles and respect the time span of life, what will Allah gain from subjecting you to Hell? To the nation that thinks 'Allah has humiliated us for no apparent crime or fault' (89:16), the Quran emphatically declares:

*Nay, nay! But you honour not the orphans. Nor do you encourage one another to feed the poor. And you devour inheritance, all with greed. And you love wealth with inordinate love. (89:17-20)*

Your state was such that you did not respect any such individual who was left stranded alone in your society, nor did you encourage each other that it was necessary to arrange means of subsistence for the one whose business had failed. Contrary to this, your state was such that you would gather together all the inheritance received from your forefathers and devour it all yourselves and you loved wealth to such a degree that you desired that the possessions and subsistence of others should also come within your grasp. You had put in place such a system whose crucial consequence was your own humiliation and ruin. This is the reason why you were disgraced – Allah did not humiliate you like this without any reason. Allah never does this. During the time that a nation continues to adhere to a system promoting good, it will remain protected from destruction:

*Nor would your Sustainer be the One to destroy communities for a single wrongdoing if its members were likely to mend. (11:117)*

Destruction only visits those who give up the right path and adopt the wrong path:

*...But can any be destroyed except those who transgress? (46:35)*

## 13.15 What is Meant by 'Destruction of Nations'?

The question is, what is meant by the destruction of nations? By this it is not meant that every individual of this nation is guillotined one by one and thus all sign of them is erased from the page of life. There is no doubt that in the initial stages of the life of humanity it sometimes happened that a complete nation was destroyed physically and in this way all signs of it disappeared. But the Quran states that by the death of nations is meant that this nation loses its power, supremacy and government and its place is taken by another nation. This is called the Law of Succession and Substitution of Nations. For example, in Surah *Muhammad* it is stated:

*Behold, you are those invited to spend (of your substance) in the cause of Allah: but among you are some that are miserly. But any who are miserly are so at the expense of their own selves. But Allah is free of all wants, and it is you that are needy. If you turn back (from the Path), he will substitute in your stead another people: then they would not be like you! (47:38)*

Look, your state is such that when you are told to give your surplus wealth for the welfare and development of mankind, then among you are those people who do not wish to do this. They wish to accumulate all the wealth and keep it reserved for their own benefit. So, you should remember that the individual who hoards wealth like this and wishes to keep others deprived of nourishment and development is, in reality, depriving his own self of nourishment and development. When Allah told you to spend this wealth for the nourishment and development of others, this instruction was for your own good and welfare. Allah is not in need of your wealth, He is not dependent on you - you are dependent on Him. In any case, you should understand this well, that if you turn your back on the righteous system of life (in which the duty of society is the nourishment and development of the whole of mankind) then Allah will bring another nation in your place and they will not be like you.

Here the Quran has only stated this much that the nation which will take your place will not be like you. In another verse, it is stated that this will be a better nation than you:

*...that We can certainly substitute for them better (men) than they...(70:40-41)*

It is obvious from this that the nation taking the place of another nation is in any case better than the one departing. One of the forms of mutual confrontation between nations is on a physical level. From this aspect, the nation which has more material power achieves supremacy i.e. none among them has a righteous system - their doctrine is 'the law of the jungle'. Therefore, their competition is at an animal level. Regarding this, the Quran has stated:

*And thus do We make the wrongdoers turn to each other because of what they earn.*
*(6:129)*

In this way, We make one group of wrongdoers rulers over another group of wrongdoers. Or civil war starts within a nation itself. About this the Quran states:

*Say, 'He has power to send calamities on you, from above and below, or to cover you with confusion in party strife, giving you a taste of mutual vengeance – each from the other. See how We explain the signs by various symbols; that they may understand.*
*(6:65)*

In other words, it sometimes even happens that tyrants impose themselves on a nation and become a source of misery and the people become downtrodden by them. The reaction to this is that from below the people rise up and institute a rebellion against these rulers. And sometimes it also happens that the leaders and the people join together and create different parties and these parties compete and fight against each other. The consequence of all this competition and confrontation is ruin and destruction. But the point that the Quran draws out for our attention is this, that a nation may not be lacking in power and wealth, may be numerous in numbers, may have supremacy and sovereignty, but because its system is based on the wrong foundations, it becomes ruined and destroyed. For example, in Surah *Al Rum* it is stated:

*Do they not travel through the earth, and see what was the end of those before them? They were superior to them in strength: they tilled the soil and populated it in greater numbers than these have done: there came to them their messengers with clear signs. (Which they rejected, to their own destruction): it was not Allah who wronged them, but they wronged their own selves. (30:9)*

## 13.16 Confrontation Between Wrong and Right Systems

But their system was wrong, therefore Our messengers came to them but they did not pay attention to their guidance and were destroyed. So, Allah did not wrong them, they wronged themselves. In another verse, the Quran states that it is not that these people were savages and ignorant – they possessed intellect and reasoning, but despite this they did not understand how fragile were the foundations on which their social system was erected.

## 13.17 Destruction Despite Knowledge and Vision

Hence, the Quran states about the *Aad* and *Thamud* (previous nations):

> *...the Aad and Thamud, (peoples): clearly will appear to you from (the traces) of their buildings (their fate): the Evil One made their deeds alluring to them, and kept them back from the Path, though they were gifted with intelligence and vision.*
> *(29:38)*

Their destruction is visible from the ruins of their dwellings. Their vested interests made their wrong system appear very attractive and appealing in their eyes and in this way prevented them from following the righteous path, although they were seeing all this with their own eyes. In another verse, it is stated:

> *And We had firmly established them in a (prosperity and) power which We have not given to you and We had endowed them with (faculties of) hearing, seeing, heart and intellect: but of no profit to them were their (faculties of) hearing, sight, and heart and intellect, when they went on rejecting the Signs of Allah: and they were (completely) encircled by that which they used to mock at! (46:26)*

But since they denied the Divine laws and were running their system on their self-made laws, therefore their intellect and reasoning was of no use to them and the destruction which they used to ridicule overwhelmed them. This is that point which the Quran brings out very clearly i.e. a nation has a great abundance of wealth, there is no deficiency of sustenance and they have everything - power, prosperity, supremacy and status; along with this there is no deficiency of worldly knowledge, but their desires based on vested interests are so intense that they make their ears deaf and eyes blind and they cannot even see what is the end of the path they are treading. The correct Divine system is even presented before them but they oppose it intensely (as it goes against their immediate gains). The consequence of this is nothing but destruction and ruin because their system is based on wrong foundations.

## 13.18 Decline of the Roman Empire

In the course of a discussion of the decline and fall of the Roman Empire, Briffault has made some thought provoking observations, which we will do well to ponder over:

'No system of human organization that is false in its very principle, in its very foundation, can save itself by any amount of cleverness and efficiency in the means by which that falsehood is carried out and maintained by any amount of superficial adjustment and tinkering. It is doomed root and branch as long as the root remains what it is.'[190]

He goes on to say:

'Humanity does not necessarily stand upon a higher plane of being when riding above the clouds, nor does a hundred miles an hour constitute progress; man is not intellectually transformed by being able to weigh the stars and disport his mind over wider spheres of knowledge. There is a deeper aspect of human affairs. There is something which stands nearer to the essence of human worth than any form of material or intellectual power, than the control of nature or the development of the mind's insight. Power, civilization, culture count for naught, if they are associated with moral evil. The real standard by which the worth of the human world is to be computed is a moral standard. It is in an ethical sense that the word 'good' bears its essential meaning, when applied to things human; and no process of human evolution can be counted real which is not above all an evolution in 'goodness'.'[191]

A society based on false principles inevitably disintegrates. We quote again from Briffault:

'What really happens is that the phase of society, the order of things in which disregard of right is habitual and accepted, inevitably deteriorates and perishes. However much the individual may temporarily benefit by inequity, the social organization of which he is a part and the very class which enjoys the fruits of that inequity, suffer inevitable deterioration through its operation. They are unadapted to the facts of their environment. The wages of sin is death by the inevitable operation of natural selection.'[192]

This was an analysis of the causes and effects of the ruin of an ancient civilization.

## 13.19 The Fate of the Western Civilisation

Western thinkers are themselves clamouring loudly about the outcome and end of Western civilization whose glitter and sparkle makes the eyes of even great visionaries shine, as is evident from their frequently published books and articles

---

[190] R. Briffault, *The Making of Humanity*, p. 159
[191] Ibid, p. 259
[192] Ibid, p. 262

on this subject. We quote from Rene Guenon who writes in his book, *The Crisis of the Modern World*:

*'Modern civilization has gone downwards step by step until it has ended by sinking to the lowest elements in man and aiming at little more than the satisfaction of the needs inherent in the material side of his nature, an aim which is, in any case, illusory as it constantly creates more artificial needs than it can satisfy.'* [193]

He goes on to say:

*'Not only have they limited their intellectual ambition to inventing and constructing machines, but they have ended by becoming in actual fact, machines themselves. The inventions whose number is at present growing at an ever increasing rate, are all the more dangerous in that they bring into play forces whose real nature is quite unknown to the men who utilize them.'* [194]

Guenon ventures to predict the ultimate result of these activities:

*'Those who unchain the brute forces of matter will perish, crushed by these same forces, of which they will no longer be masters.'* [195]

Einstein's remarks on this point deserve careful attention:

*'By painful experience we have learnt that rational thinking does not suffice to solve the problems of our social life. Penetrating research and keen scientific work have often had tragic implications for mankind, producing on the one hand, inventions which liberated man from exhausting physical labour, making his life easier and richer, but on the other hand, introducing a grave restlessness into his life, making him slave to his technological environment, and most catastrophic of all – creating the means for his own mass destruction. This indeed is a tragedy of overwhelming poignancy.'* [196]

He warns us against entrusting our destiny to intellect:

*'We should take care not to make the intellect our God: it has of course powerful muscles, but no personality. It cannot lead , it can only serve, and it is not fastidious in its choice of a leader. This characteristic is reflected in the qualities of its priests – the intellectuals. The intellect has a sharp eye for method and tools but is blind to end and values.'* [197]

---

[193] Rene Guenon, *The Crisis of the Modern World*, p. 26
[194] Ibid, p. 259
[195] Ibid, P. 262
[196] Albert Einstein, *Out of Later Years*, p. 152
[197] Ibid, p. 260

This is the state of society through the hands of civilisation. The condition of the individual is even worse than this. The result is that in the words of Jung, 'along the great high-roads of the world, everything seems desolate and out worn'.[198]

This is that man about whom Iqbal had long ago said:

*He explores the inter-stellar spaces, but has left the world of the mind unexplored.*
*He has captured the power locked up in the sun's rays, but his own life remains enveloped in darkness.[199]*

In 'the dark night of life' the light of dawn shines through the rays of the Permanent Values which are received through revelation and which are now preserved within the folds of the Quran. These darknesses cannot be lifted till the system of Deen is established based on these values.

## 13.20 Internal Change

At this juncture this important question arises, what is that thing due to the absence of which nations, despite possessing abundant wealth and glory, power and prosperity, intellect and wisdom, knowledge and vision, still go and tumble into the devastation of hell? This question is very important, but the more that the vision and intellect pay attention to the answer which the Quran has provided, the more elated man becomes. The Quran asks us to remember:

*Because Allah will never change the grace which He has bestowed on a people until they change what is in their (own) self: and verily Allah is He Who hears and knows (all things). (8:53)*

This happens because Allah never snatches away the blessings which He has provided to a nation, till such a time as that nation does not change its self (psychological world). Remember! Allah hears and sees everything.

In this short verse, the Quran has detailed the philosophy of the rise and fall of nations, which cannot even be condensed into many heavy volumes of books. It says that the external world is actually a reflection of the internal world of man. Until there is a change in his internal world, there will never be a change in his external world. Then whatever type of change occurs in his internal world, a similar type of change will occur in his external world. His internal world is changed by that thing that the Quran calls 'Eimaan' in its terminology i.e. the correct angle of

---

[198] C. G. Jung, *Modern Man in Search of Soul*, p. 251
[199] M. Iqbal, *Darb-e-Kalim*

view. Through the righteous aim of life and firm conviction in the Permanent Values which are given by revelation, the internal forces of man are focused on one point, and through this such astounding results are crystallized which cannot be otherwise even imagined. This is that 'thing' regarding the absence of which Bertrand Russell laments and writes:

*'In the world in which we find ourselves, the possibilities of good are almost limitless and the possibilities of evil no less so. Our present predicament is due, more than anything else, to the fact that we have learnt to understand and control to a terrifying extent, the forces of nature outside us, but not those that are embodied in ourselves.* [200]

Dr. Jung, who has been mentioned earlier, set himself the task of diagnosing the disease from which modern man suffers. He reached the conclusion that while modern man's body is satisfied, his soul is not. He is out of tune with the universe. He yearns after unification with the universe but finds that a widening gulf separates him from the heart of reality. Somewhere he took a wrong turning, and in the midst of luxury, is a prey to acute discontent. [201]

All these investigations of modern historians and researchers are the interpretations and explanations of the Quranic verse which we have noted earlier (8:53). See also (13:11). The Quran clarifies the secret of the rise and fall of nations through the change within their selfs and a change in the self comes through conviction in the values of the revelation.

## 13.21 Hierarchy is First to Become Corrupt

The Quran also tells us that the beginning of the crimes of nations starts from the top echelons and spreading from there affects the lower levels. The Quran states:

*Thus have We placed leaders in every town, its wicked men, to plot (and burrow) therein: but they only plot against their own selfs, and they perceive it not. (6:123)*

These great criminals continually invent such types of tricks so that the knots of their wrongly established system are not loosened – these 'criminal leaders' are those who indulge in a life of luxury and hedonism at the expense of the hard work of others:

*...But the wrong-doers pursued the enjoyment of the good things of life which were given them, and persisted in crimes. (11:116)*

---

[200] Bertrand Russell, *Authority and the Individual*, p. 125
[201] C. G. Jung, *Modern Man in Search of Soul*, p. 264

These people remain in pursuit of their self-interests and profligacies, and in this way, evil and tyranny and exploitation becomes the norm. These are the very people who become leaders of the caravan of the nation, but then take this caravan and deliver it into the abode of destruction. The Quran states:

*Have you not turned your vision to those who have changed the favour of Allah into Kufr (exploitation) and caused their people to descend to the House of Perdition? Hell - which they will endure - an evil abode to stay in! (14:28-29)*

But, after condemning the leaders as criminals, the Quran does not exempt the public from its responsibility – it declares it an equal partner in crime. This is because its aim is not that the public, with heads down like sheep, should simply tread according to the call of the shepherd. It declares it to be the responsibility of the public to recognise fake from true, and to only tread that path which is one of safety and security for them.

## 13.22 Dialogue in Hell Between Leaders and Followers

The Quran has referred to this truth in a very appealing manner – it has stated that leaders and their followers will both be gathered in hell and will reproach and accuse each other. The followers will say to their leaders that you have destroyed us, if you had not been there we would most certainly have followed the right path:

*The Unbelievers say: 'We shall neither believe in this scripture nor in (any) that (came) before it.' Could you but see when the wrong-doers will be made to stand before their Sustainer, throwing back the word (of blame) on one another! Those who had been despised will say to the arrogant ones: 'Had it not been for you, we should certainly have been Believers!' (34:31)*

In reply to this, the leaders will say, the fault is all yours and you accuse us unjustly. The right path was in front of you, if you had wished to follow it who could have stopped you from doing this? We have never said to you that you should leave the right path of life and follow behind us. You yourself are criminal yet hurl accusations on our heads:

*The arrogant ones will say to those who had been despised: 'Was it we who kept you back from Guidance after it reached you? Nay, rather, it was you who transgressed.' (34:32)*

In reply to this, the people will say that it is certainly correct that you did not say it with your tongues that we should become perpetrators of crimes, but you were busy day and night in such intrigues and trickeries from which escape was not within the remit of simple people, in this way you obliged us indirectly that, leaving the Divine laws, we should come out and tread on your suggested paths:

*Those who had been despised will say to the arrogant ones: 'Nay! it was a plot (of yours) by day and by night: Behold! You (constantly) ordered us to be ungrateful to Allah and to attribute equals to Him!' They will declare (their) repentance when they see the Penalty: We shall put yokes on the necks of the Unbelievers: It would only be a requital for their (ill) Deeds. (34:33)*

In another verse, it states that these followers will request Allah to give double punishment to these big leaders of ours who have destroyed us along with themselves – one part as a result of their own crimes, and one part for those crimes which they had done by us:

*And they would say: 'Our Sustainer! We obeyed our chiefs and our great ones, and they misled us as to the (right) Path. Our Sustainer! Give them double Penalty and curse them with a very great Curse!' (33:67-68)*

In these and a few other similar verses, this reality has been made clear from these types of examples of dialogue between leaders and followers, that in the destruction of nations both the public and the leaders are equal participants. Leaders, because they make the public instruments for their own vested interests, and the public because they become agreeable to be tools for the sake of the greed of these evil leaders. The power of leaders is indeed via the public.

## 13.24 Leader Nations and Follower Nations

Then, just as the different classes of a nation by becoming influenced by each other become different links in the chains of destruction and ruin, in the same way one nation by imitating another nation falls into the hell of destruction. The Quran states:

*He will say: 'Enter you in the company of the peoples who passed away before you - men and jinns - into the Fire.' Every time a new people enters, it curses its sister-people (that went before), until they follow each other, all into the Fire. Says the last about the first: 'Our Sustainer! it is these that misled us: so give them a double penalty in the Fire.' He will say: 'Doubled for all': but this you do not understand. (7:38)*

In reply, they will be told that there is double punishment for each one among you, because if previous nations deserve double punishment because they misguided others, then the nations who followed in their path also deserve double punishment because why did they shut their eyes and imitate them? According to the Quran, not making use of intellect and reasoning (as already covered in a previous chapter) and blindly following others is such a path which throws both individuals and nations straight into the pit of hell. Therefore, according to the Quran, it is essential for every nation that it should make use of its intellect and reasoning and that it should follow the path prescribed by the Divine laws. In this way, it will come onto the path of prosperity and success. But if it stops making use of its reasoning and wisdom, then this crime alone of theirs will be sufficient for their destruction. The Quran does not even give permission to follow the righteous path without the use of one's intellect and reasoning:

*Those who, when they are reminded with the Signs of their Sustainer, droop not down at them as if they were deaf or blind (25:73)*

Even if the following of another nation is merely because it has acquired greater power and strength in the world. As we have seen before, even a wrong system attains temporary power, sovereignty and wealth (for a short duration) but its end is still ruin and destruction:

*And how many populations We destroyed, which exulted in their life (of ease and plenty)! now those habitations of theirs, after them, are deserted, - All but a (miserable) few! and We are their heirs! (28:58)*

This was because their system was based on wrong foundations. Look and see, these are their ruins which after them were scantily occupied and We alone became their inheritors:

*How many populations have We destroyed, which were given to wrong-doing? They tumbled down on their roofs. And how many wells are lying idle and neglected, and castles lofty and well-built? (22:45)*

And only tales of them remained:

*Say: 'Go you through the earth and see what has been the end of those who were criminals.' (27:69)*

Say to them that you should tour through different lands and ask the stones of their ruins, 'what is the end of nations given to wrongdoing?' In this way the Quran presents the tales and states of past nations, and through the study of historical evidence points to this fact, as to what the end result of a wrong system of life is. But along with this it also states that only those nations who make use of their intellect and reasoning can learn lessons from these historical evidences. In Surah *Al Hajj* it is stated:

*Do they not travel through the land, so that their hearts (and minds) may thus learn wisdom and their ears may thus learn to hear? Truly it is not their eyes that are blind, but their hearts which are in their breasts. (22:46)*

This is because it is not the eyes of men which are on their faces which are blind, but it is their hearts which are in their chests which are blind.

From the above discussion, this reality becomes apparent that according to the Quran, the decision regarding the rise and fall and life and death of a nation happens according to the system which the nation adopts for itself. The character and foundation of such a system, and its constituents and features which become the assurance for the rise and maintenance of nations, has been discussed at length in the previous chapters. But the basic principle which the Quran has given in this connection is of such importance that it is necessary to reiterate it and this principle is:

*...while that which is for the good of mankind remains on the earth...(13:17)*

Only that ideology, that principle of life, that social system can survive in the world which is for the good of the whole of mankind. In other words, on the one hand it should be beneficial and profitable and on the other hand its profitability should not be limited to a particular group, particular party or to a particular country or nation, but instead it should be beneficial for the whole of humanity.

This is that universal principle on whose foundations the Quran establishes its system of life, and this principle alone can provide a true guarantee to the life of nations.

We have said in the previous pages that even if a nation harnesses the forces of nature, is advanced in power and wealth, dominates a large part of the world, also possesses vast knowledge and technology and has no lack of wisdom and intellect, if its system is based on wrong foundations then, despite all these resources and means, it can achieve neither peace nor stability. As long as this system endures, people remain fearful and perturbed and together with this, due to its inherent fundamental crimes and corruptions, this system automatically progresses towards decline and decay. How the civilisation of today is living evidence of this claim of the Quran, we will examine in the next chapter.

# 14 MAN AND THE EXTERNAL UNIVERSE

Whether it is an individual or nations (especially nations), one essential element in the decision about their life and death is also that what is their viewpoint or attitude towards the external universe? This is that question which has always kept man perplexed – the Quran has assigned great importance to it and presented its correct explanation in extremely clear, precise and sparkling words.

When human consciousness first opened its eyes, it found itself in a strange world. Above its head a great, flaming, overpowering sphere; mountains in all four directions; shoreless oceans all around and their fearsome stormy waves; rivers with dread-laden floods in their laps; miles and miles of frightening forests containing dangerous beasts and serpents; sometimes thundering from clouds; sometimes the heart-shattering crack of lightning; sometimes awful dust storms; sometimes frightening hurricanes; sometimes the scorching life-threatening attack of volcanic lava; sometimes the horde of destruction from earthquakes, diseases and epidemics - and the helpless progeny of Adam surrounded by these, without the aid of companions and without resources.

## 14.1 The First Reaction of Man

You can understand that, under these circumstances, what could his reaction to the outer universe be other than to kneel down prostrate before every horror, imploringly. Wherever a danger appears, he bows his head to it. In this way, different forces of nature became his 'god' and he became their worshipper. The moon, sun, stars, lightening, rain, dust storm, fire, river, serpent, lion, even epidemic diseases - all were accorded the concept of gods and goddesses. And in their presence, offerings, entreaties, resorting to praise and flattery to gratify them, and techniques to seek their appeasement began to be adopted to seek their pleasure. This was the first reaction of man (in that environment) regarding the external universe. Gradually, this reaction adopted the form of a religion and we know that when a belief or concept takes on the face of religion, then no matter how much the circumstances may alter, no modification occurs in it. Hence, most of the religions of the world are manifestations of the first reaction of man towards the universe.

This world was one of superstitions. On the other hand, if you come to the world of knowledge and vision, there, unfortunately, humanity was confronted by another tragedy which resulted in a loss greater than the ignorance of superstition. As far as historical parchments are able to guide us, the first home of knowledge and wisdom is thought to be Greece, in which Socrates is given the status of the father of all wise men. The doctrine of Socrates was that only the human self was worthy of study, not the outer universe.

## 14.2 Platonic Doctrine

Plato, who was the disciple of Socrates, but is a leader of a different ideology in his own right, went even further than this. He said that this perceptual world (external universe) does not in reality have its own existence. The real world is a world of ideas, which is located somewhere beyond the universe and this perceptual world is its reflection. The intellectual conclusion which can be derived from this doctrine is obvious i.e. when this perceptual world does not have its own existence, and rather is a deception and mirage (in fact, actually a dream state), then whatever knowledge is acquired about it through the human senses will have no reality either. Real knowledge will be that which man - by keeping eyes shut, ears closed off and lips sealed - will achieve after this by remaining absorbed within his own inner world. Only this knowledge will be trustworthy and certain. Perceptual knowledge will never be trustworthy.

This was the Platonic doctrine about the universe and perceptual knowledge, on the basis of which the edifice of Greek mysticism was raised.

## 14.3 Doctrine of Mysticism

This mysticism, having come out of Greece, influenced the whole world. On reaching India, it took the shape of *Vedant*. Hence, according to this philosophy, *Prakarti* (the material world) is *Maya* (deception). The universe is a dream of *Brahma* (God), the day his eye opens this dream will vanish. The great functioning universe is *Laila* of *Eishwar* (a sport of God) – in which nothing is present in its true colours but is a simile of reality. This is the philosophy which, in the hands of Persian mystics, became the 'favourite wine' of saints and spread euphoria even to the Christian monasteries. It was the outcome of this philosophy that the universe was declared false and the world was conceived as a detestable thing, fleeing from which was considered to be the hidden secret of human salvation.

This was the reaction of the human mind regarding the universe in the era when the Quran was revealed i.e. the world of religions was bowing in front of the universal forces by making them gods; and the world of intellect and the universe of mystics, by declaring the universe false, were discovering from this the secret of spiritual ascendency through this aversion. There is no doubt that before the advent of the Quran, certain such signs can be found in which the rightful position of the universe also becomes evident. This was the consequence of teachings based on the revelation which passed through various *Anbiya* from time to time. But since at the time of the advent of the Quran the teachings of the revelation were not available anywhere in their original and true form, the status of human intellect therefore was in general as noted above.

## 14.4 Quranic Doctrine

The Quran arrived and it first of all challenged the world of religion – it detailed metaphorically the story of the mutual relationship of the universe and Adam in the second Surah. Be aware that the story of Adam is not the tale of a particular individual – Adam is man himself and his story is the narrative of man himself. It declared that the status of man is that all the forces of nature (which the Quran refers to by calling them *Malaika*[202]) are bowed down before Adam:

> …*We said to the angels, 'Bow down to Adam'; and they bowed down…(2:34)*

With this one (revolutionary) declaration, the Quran made the worshipped the worshipper, and the worshipper the worshipped. It proclaimed to man:

> *And He has made subject to you the sun and the moon, both diligently pursuing their courses; and the Night and the Day has He (also) made subject to you. (14:33)*

It also stated:

> …*it is He Who has made the ships subject to you, that they may sail through the sea by His Command; and the rivers (also) has He made subject to you. (14:32)*

He has given into your control the oceans and rivers, and in short:

> *And he has subjected to you, as from Him, all that is in the heavens and on earth; behold, in that are Signs indeed for those who reflect. (45:13)*

These are all tied up within the chains of the prescribed laws of Allah - your task is to acquire knowledge of these natural laws and through this bring all these forces into your use.

Have you seen how the Quran, by unveiling the status of Adam, transformed the map of the universe and of the human world also! Through this truth revealing teaching, all invented idols, gods, goddesses, jinn, ghosts and witches of the human mind stood bowed before him in his service. And man, who once rubbed his forehead prostrated before stones, how he became the master and served by even the lightning from the skies!

---

[202] *Malaika* – usually translated as angels in English.

## 14.5 Defeat of Platonic Mysticism

On the other side, the Quran confronted the world of mysticism, and with one thunderous announcement blasted Platonic mysticism into smithereens, and dispersed these into the air. It declared:

*Not without purpose did We create heaven and earth and all between! That were the conjectural thought of Unbelievers! (38:27)*

We have not created the universe and the heaven and the earth and whatever is between them in falsehood - this is speculation and conjecture on the part of those people who deny truth:

*...But woe to the Unbelievers (those who do not accept truth) - their efforts become ashes (Hell). (38:27)*

The efforts and deeds of those who falsify the universe, thus rejecting the established truth, become a heap of ash. And ultimately their share consists of nothing but regrets and disappointments, destruction and annihilation.

Have you noted how, by declaring the wrong viewpoint about the universe as being *Kufr* (and contrary to this giving the right viewpoint the status of Eimaan), how much importance the Quran has given to this question! The person who declares the universe as false is not a Momin according to the Quran, but is a *Kafir*. Allah did not create the universe as false:

*Allah created the heavens and the earth in truth (reality): verily in that is a Sign for those who have Eimaan. (29:44)*

Its existence is not a deception or a trick. This exists in reality, and has been created for a specific purpose. To those who assert the universe as being sport, the Quran states:

*We created not the heavens, the earth, and all between them, merely in (idle) sport. We created them not except for just ends: but most of them do not understand. (44:38-39)*

This thought, that the universe has been created only as a sport and a pastime, is the speculation of those people who are ignorant of knowledge and truth.

## 14.6 Definition of Knowledge

After producing such an earth shattering revolution in the opinion about the universe, it was necessary that a change be created within the human viewpoint about sense perception. Hence, in this respect the Quran has stated:

*And pursue not that of which you have no knowledge; for every act of hearing, or of seeing or of intellect will be enquired into. (17:36)*

Your hearing, observation and thinking – all of these will be questioned, 'What, did you verify through evidence that issue which you assumed to be correct?' This verse demands deep reflection. In it, knowledge is declared to be that about which evidence is provided by hearing, observation and intellect. Hearing and observation are human senses whose task is to provide information about the external universe to the mind and then the mind should process this information. In this definition of knowledge, both perceptual knowledge and conceptual knowledge are included. You can evaluate how much importance 'hearing, observation and the mind' have according to the Quran from the fact that it has stated in clear words that those people who do not make use of this are living life not at a human level but are living at an animal level and are meant for hell.

## 14.7 Those Not Making Use of Hearing and Observation Belong to Hell

In Surah *Al A'raf* the Quran states:

*Many are the Jinns and men We have made for Hell: They have hearts wherewith they understand not, eyes wherewith they see not, and ears wherewith they hear not. They are like cattle - nay more misguided: for they are heedless (of warning). (7:179)*

Their state is such that they have hearts in their chests but do not make use of them to comprehend. They have eyes but do not make use of them to see. They have ears but do not make use of them to hear. They are not humans but are animals and yet even more lost than them, because these people remain in a state of ignorance about the realities of the universe.

## 14.8 Those who Reflect and Ponder over the Universe

Contrary to these people, the Quran refers to another category of people about whom it states:

*Behold! in the creation of the heavens and the earth, and the alternation of Night and Day, there are indeed Signs for men of understanding. (3:190)*

The state of such men of understanding is that:

*Men who keep the laws of Allah (in mind), standing, sitting, and lying down on their sides, and contemplate the (wonders of) creation in the heavens and the earth, (With the thought): 'Our Sustainer! not for naught Have You created (all) this (based on evidence)! Glory to You! Give us protection from the penalty of the Fire. (3:191)*

Our Sustainer, You have not created this great system of the universe in falsehood – it was totally impossible from You, that Your creative programme could be without purpose - such a thought cannot even be conceived about You. This is solely our inadequate knowledge and deficiency in research (investigation), due to which we remain ignorant about the advantageous side of many things of the universe, and thus continually burn and suffer from their poisonous effects. Our yearning is that You bestow on us such an ability that we are able to protect ourselves from the destructive effects of the things of the universe due to our inadequate knowledge. This is because those nations which do not research and investigate the forces of nature and so remain ignorant of their beneficial effects, they spend a life of ignominy and humiliation in the world:

*'Our Sustainer! any whom You do admit to the Fire, Truly You cover them with shame, and never will wrong-doers Find any helpers!' (3:192)*

And such nations find no friend or helper in the world.

## 14.9 These are the Momin and *Mutaqee* (Righteous Ones)

At this point the Quran has declared those people who, after research and investigation into the things of the universe unveil the secrets of nature, as men possessing 'intellect and vision'. In another verse, the Quran declares them as being Momineen:

*Verily in the heavens and the earth, are Signs for those who have Eimaan (Momineen). (45:3)*

These are those people who maintain firm conviction in Allah and His laws:

*And in the creation of yourselves and the fact that (other) animals are scattered (through the earth), are Signs for those of assured conviction. (45:4)*

These are the people who have vision and understanding:

*And in the alternation of Night and Day, and the fact that Allah sends down*
*Sustenance from the sky, and revives therewith the earth after its death, and in the*
*change of the winds - are Signs for those who are wise. (45:5)*

After placing so much emphasis on contemplation and reasoning about the
universe, the Quran states:

*Such are the Signs of Allah, which We rehearse to you in truth; then in what*
*exposition will they believe after (rejecting) Allah and His Signs? (45:6)*

## 14.10 Eimaan Can Only be Acquired Through This

These are those signs of Allah which Allah presents before you in truth. Ask these
people who even after this do not accept Eimaan in truth, in what else will they
have Eimaan? Have you observed what a great truth the Quran has proclaimed at
this point? It states that there are two aspects of having Eimaan in Allah. Firstly,
after contemplating and reasoning on the things of nature to reach this conclusion
that the system of the universe is being managed by a Knowledgeable and All-
knowing Being according to His established, immutable and constructive laws.
Secondly, consider and reflect on the Quranic teaching which proclaimed the
harnessing of control of the universe for man in that era when the whole world
had either made the forces of nature into idols or, considering them to be illusory
and worthy of hatred, were running far from them. In such circumstances, raising
this type of revolutionary voice is not the work of a human intellect – the source
of such a 'voice' could surely only be that All-knowing and Hearing Allah Who is
cognizant of the rightful status of both man and the universe. Therefore, if an
individual after studying nature and after pondering and reasoning about the
Quran still does not have Eimaan in Allah, then no such thing remains through
which he can have Eimaan in Allah.

Eimaan is that concept of life which forms the basis and aim of human life. After
this comes *Taqwa*[203] which can be understood as being that pattern and manner
according to which a Momin lives his life. We have seen earlier how important it
is for the Momineen to use their intellect and reasoning about the signs and facts
of the external universe. In another verse, the Quran states that this intellect and
reasoning is just as important for the *Mutaqee*[204]:

*Verily, in the alternation of the Night and the Day, and in all that Allah hath created,*
*in the heavens and the earth, are signs for those who are righteous. (10:6)*

---

[203] *Taqwa* – normally translated as righteousness. See verse (2:177). (Ed)
[204] Those who follow *Taqwa*. (Ed)

Surely in the alternation of day and night and whatever Allah has created in the heavens and the earth, there are signs for the righteous nation.

## 14.11 Living Creation in the Heavens

We have seen above that the Quran has placed emphasis on paying attention to and reflecting on 'the heavens and the earth'. One field of reflection on the heavens (galaxies) is that which is called astronomy, but the Quran goes even further than this. It states that there is life not only on earth but in the galaxies as well and it is important to reflect on this. In Surah *Al Shura* it is stated:

> And among His Signs is the creation of the heavens and the earth, and the living creatures that He has scattered through them: and He has power to gather them together when He wills. (42:29)

Note that the first pointer to the existence of living creations in the heavenly bodies was done by the Quran itself.

## 14.12 Definition of *Ulema* (Scholars)

We have seen earlier what the definition of knowledge is according to the Quran i.e. knowledge is that for which evidence is provided by the human senses and support for it should be provided by the human mind. Now let us see who are the scholars according to the Quran. The word *Ulema* has appeared twice in the Quran, in one place in Surah *Al Shu'ara* it is stated:

> Is it not a Sign to them that the Ulema of the Children of Israel knew it as true? (26:197)

In the second place in Surah *Fatir*, *Ulema* is mentioned among the servants of Allah. It is stated:

> See you not that Allah sends down rain from the heavens? With it We then bring out produce of various colours. And in the mountains are tracts white and red, of various shades of colour, and black intense in hue. And so amongst men and crawling creatures and cattle, are they of various colours. Those truly fear Allah, among His Servants, who have knowledge (Ulema): for Allah is Exalted in Might, all Protecting. (35:27-28)

Have you observed how many matters are being cited in these verses? Different aspects of the universe, various departments of the field of nature, different subjects of science including physics, botany, zoology, geology, meteorology and all matters of the human world come into it. After mentioning all these subjects and categories, the Quran states that the reality is that from among His people, the *Ulema* are indeed the ones whose hearts are overwhelmed by His greatness and stature, because they witness with their own eyes the truth of how Allah is the Master of such great powers. And how, by protecting it from every type of disintegration, Allah is taking this incredible system of the universe towards its intended purpose.

Have you seen for which type of people the Quran uses the word *Ulema*? For those people who, in modern terminology, are known as scientists and international philosophers.

## 14.13 Signs Within the Human Self and in the Universe

The Quran has also stated that, just as only those people who reflect on creation and the constituents of the universe can understand the greatness and supremacy of Allah, similarly the people who achieve conviction in the Quran as being the established truth are only those who reflect and use their reasoning about the external universe and the human world. It states:

*Soon will We show them our Signs in the (furthest) regions (of the earth), and in their own self, until it becomes manifest to them that this is the Truth. Is it not enough that your Sustainer does witness all things? (41:53)*

This means that as the undiscovered facts wrapped within the convolutions of time keep manifesting through the process of research and investigation, these will become proofs, one by one, of the declarations made by the Quran. The Quran is the Book of that Allah from Whose eyes no secret remains veiled. Everything in the universe lies uncovered before Him and this fact is sufficient proof in itself that whatever Allah will state about the realities of the universe will definitely be true:

*Say: 'The (Quran) is sent down by Him who knows the mystery that is in the heavens and the earth'...(25:6)*

Hence, those people who pay attention and reflect on these signs within their inner self and in the external world see the Divine light being unveiled in these. Regarding those nations which pass by these signs of Allah with eyes closed, it can be understood as if they do not feel they can see 'God' being unveiled in this way:

*Ah indeed! Are they in doubt concerning the Meeting with their Sustainer? Ah indeed! It is He that does encompass all things! (41:54)*

Even though they do not have to go very far for this – for whatever thing they research in this way, the lights of the law of *Rabubiyat* will become visible like reflections in water because Allah's law encompasses everything and is not tied to one thing only.

## 14.14 Conquest of Nature Alone is not Eimaan

We saw earlier that the Quran has stated that there are signs of Allah everywhere in the universe for the Momineen and *Mutaqeen*. From this it should not be assumed that Eimaan and *Taqwa* means attention, reason, research and investigation into the things of the universe and that those nations which harness nature are Momin and *Mutaqee*. Momin and *Mutaqee* are those who, after conquering nature, use these forces of nature according to the Divine laws (the Quran) for the *Rabubyiat* of mankind and in this way, provide the means for their self-development. To be a Momin, both of these conditions are necessary i.e. harnessing of nature and obedience of the Divine laws which are preserved within the Quran.

## 14.15 Conditions to Become a Momin

If a nation is deficient in even one of these two conditions then it cannot call itself Momin and *Mutaqee*. The Quran declares:

> *...If any do fail to judge by what Allah has revealed, they are Unbelievers. (5:44)*

The nations which manage to subjugate the forces of nature but do not make decisions on the matters of life according to the Book of Allah are *Kafir* also. Due to harnessing of the forces of nature, they achieve the benefits of the material world, but since they do not utilise these forces according to the Divine laws, they also therefore become ultimately destroyed and ruined, just like those who do not bring these forces under their control in the first place. These are the very nations about whom the Quran declares:

> *...But of no profit to them were their hearing, sight, heart and intellect, when they went on rejecting the signs of Allah; and they were (completely) encircled by that which they used to mock at! (46:26)*

## 14.16 Summary of the Discussion

Therefore, according to the Quran, the state is as follows:

(1) Those nations which, using their hearing, observation and intellect, harness the forces of nature and then use these forces according to the

Divine Laws (the Quran), they are Momin and *Mutaqee* – their life in this world is prosperous and bright and their life in the hereafter is also pleasant and evergreen.

(2) Those nations which, despite conquering the forces of nature, do not follow the Permanent Values of the Quran, they only reach the status of humanity but do not reach the level of a Momin and *Mutaqee*. They achieve power and glamour in the life of this world but their future is dark – the future in this world and the future in the life of the hereafter also.

(3) And those nations which from the beginning do not even harness the forces of nature, never mind becoming Momin and *Mutaqee*, they cannot even reach the status of humanity. For them there is humiliation and deprivation in this world and destruction and ruin in the hereafter also. In the words of the Quran:

*Their abode is in the Fire, because of what (the evil) they earned. (10:8)*

This is because:

*But the one who is blind in this world, will be blind in the Hereafter...(17:72)*

# 15 THE PERMANENT VALUES

In the previous chapters the reality that the structure of Deen revolves around the Permanent Values has become apparent; or it can be said that Deen provides us with those Permanent Values by which if life were lived, this life also becomes a life of paradise (*Jannat*) and the life of the hereafter is assured of success and prosperity. In this chapter, these values are being introduced briefly. 'Briefly', because to detail them the complete Quran would need to be presented.

## 15.1 The Human Self

Among the Permanent Values, the highest value is the human self itself, therefore this discussion commences with its introduction. As noted in Chapter 1, the Quran refers to the human self by calling it *Nafs* and declares it to be Divine Energy. Though details have already been given in this connection in Chapters 1 and 2, it would not be inappropriate if we reiterated some points here so that with this recap the matter becomes clearer and may find a place in the heart. When the Quran, after mentioning the different stages of man's creation (which is related to his body and physical form and which is shared in common with other animals), states: '...and breathed into him something of His energy...' (32:9), from this it means this very human self for which this link in the stages of the evolutionary process (man) becomes separated and differentiated from its previous stages (completely advanced from the animal life). The Quran states:

*...then We created out of it another creature...(23:14)*

'Then We made it into a completely new creation' is meant by this. The purpose of human life is the nourishment and development of the human self, the procedure for which is taught by Deen:

*Truly he succeeds that purifies it. And he fails that corrupts it. (91:9-10)*

Man's every deed (act) affects the human self. Righteous deeds are those from which strength is produced within the self, and evil deeds are those due to which weakness and deterioration ensue in it. By strengthening of the self man can achieve immortality:

*Nor will they there taste Death, except the first Death...(44:56)*

In this life of paradise, they will not face another death apart from the first death which affects the body.

The term 'Divine Energy' requires some further clarification. There is manifestation of energy everywhere in the universe, but this energy manifests itself through physical cause and effect, or physical laws. This is referred to as energy of matter. Animal bodies also manifest this energy, even the human body. But in the case of man there is another form of energy also which manifests itself in the form of his freedom to choose and intent. This energy is far more powerful than material energy because material energy is subservient to it. In order to differentiate this energy from material energy, Allah has related it as 'from Himself'. And by calling it *Rooh-ha'na* (My energy) has termed it thus, and this is what is known as the human self. For this we have used the term 'Divine Energy'. It should be made clear that the human self is not part of the Divine Self[205]. This energy is bestowed by Allah, and to differentiate it from energy of matter[206] it is called Divine Energy.

The human self is the highest Permanent Value. The remainder of the values become the means for its development and when strength is developed in it, then these values keep sprouting and rising automatically from it like the rays of the sun.

It should be made clear that this does not mean that the human body has no worth or value – according to the Quran, human bodies (i.e. human physical life and its means of sustenance) have their own values which need to be protected, but these values are relative, not permanent. When there is a clash between the interests of physical life and the human self, then for the protection of the interests of the human self, physical life and its interests should be sacrificed. Details on these aspects will be discussed later.

Therefore, the first and fundamental value is the human self.

## 15.2 Respect for Humanity

Since the human self is received by every human child equally, as a consequence every man becomes worthy of respect and dignity purely due to being human:

*…We have honoured the children of Adam…(17:70)*

Therefore, respect for a human being is a Permanent Value which cannot be sacrificed under any condition for any interest or aim. As a result of this, all discriminations of caste, creed, race, colour, gender etc are eliminated. Drawing the attention of the whole of mankind, the Quran states:

---

[205] The self is an indivisible unity. *Islam: A Challenge to Religion, by G. A. Parwez*, p. 93
[206] Otherwise energy of matter is also bestowed by Allah and has come into existence according to the laws established by Him.

*...Who created you from a single life-cell...(4:1)*

Hence, from the viewpoint of birth even man and woman have no preference over one another. Therefore, the next part of the verse quoted above is:

*...He divided this life-cell into two, and from these men and women in great numbers dispersed in the world...(4:1)*

Dividing this life-cell into two parts He made a pair (i.e. ovum and spermatozoon), and from these scattered a great number of men and women throughout the world; though men have been endowed with some particular traits which women do not have, and some particular traits are in women which are not in men and in this way one gender is given preference over the other, men over women and women over men (4:32). Further details on these matters will be covered in the last chapter.

Therefore, the second Permanent Value is 'respect of a human being'.

## 15.3  Status According to Deed

From the viewpoint of birth all human beings deserve equal respect but after this the level of their status will be defined according to their deeds (works). The Quran states:

*And to all are assigned degrees according to the deeds...(46:19)*

Everyone will have their status established according to their deeds (works) – whoever follows the Divine Laws most closely, he will be the most honoured:

*O mankind! We created you from a male and a female, and made you into tribes and families[207] so that you may know each other. Verily, the most honoured of you in the sight of Allah is the most righteous of you...(49:13)*

The third Permanent Value is that the criterion for honour and elevation is personal character, not worldly assets and possessions.

## 15.4  Justice

To consider all human beings as equal in relation to birth; to provide equal opportunities to everyone for his self-development; to assign status and position

---

[207] You made these tribes and families for yourselves.

according to their effort and deed; to give remuneration according to the work; to not devour the rights and dues of anyone and to make decisions on all matters according to that law which is applicable to all equally, is called justice. About this, the Quran states:

*Surely, Allah commands justice…(16:90)*

This is a Permanent Value whose hold should never be let go from your hand at any time and under any circumstance, even to the extent that it is essential to do justice to those people who act with enmity towards us. The Quran directs us:

*…and let not the hatred of others towards you make you swerve to wrong and depart from justice…(5:8)*

(As has been said above, *Taqwa* – carrying out duties – is the criterion for being honoured). From this you have also seen what it is that is called a Permanent Value. Ordinarily it will be said, how can justice be applied to the nation which is bent upon enmity? But since justice is a Permanent Value, someone's friendship or enmity can never influence it. Just as the child of an opponent will be considered worthy of respect and dignity due to being a human being, in the same way justice will also be done to an enemy. Hence, the fourth Permanent Value is justice.

## 15.5 Consequence of Committing a Crime

The deliberate flouting of a law is called a crime. Because the system of justice breaks down as a result of this, the prevention of this attitude and these kinds of occurrences is important. This prevention is called the punishment of a crime or *Qisas*. *Qisas* means to pursue a criminal and to give him the recompense of his deed. In *Qisas* is hidden the secret of life for mankind:

*In Qisas there is life for you, O men of understanding so that you become Mutaqee. (2:179)*

But this *Qisas* is not an individual matter, it is the responsibility of the government e.g. in relation to the crime of murder, the Quran states:

*…And if anyone is slain wrongfully, We have given his heir authority (to demand Qisas) but let him not exceed bounds in the matter of taking life, for he is helped by the law. (17:33)*

In today's terminology, we can say that in these crimes the government itself becomes the prosecutor or plaintiff. But punishment should always be proportional to the crime and should never be to take revenge. The Quran states:

*But those who have earned evil will have a reward of like evil...(10:27)*

If the criminal repents of his deed and the possibility of reformation is visible in him, then he should be forgiven. In Surah *Al Shura* it is stated:

*The recompense for an injury is an injury equal thereto (in degree), but if a person forgives and makes reconciliation, his reward is due from Allah (system)...(42:40)*

Justice also demands that the punishment for a crime should be received by the criminal – it should not be the case that a crime is committed by one person, whereas the punishment for it is given to another:

*...Every self draws the meed of its own acts on none but itself...(6:164)*

Therefore, the Law of Requital and the demands of justice are one Permanent Value.

## 15.6  Responsibility of One Will Not be Borne by Another

It is also a requirement of justice that every person takes responsibility for himself. It should not be that responsibility belongs to one person and another person is going around fulfilling it. The Quran states:

*...No bearer of burdens can bear the burden of another...(6:164)*

This principle is so comprehensive that it can be applied to every branch of life.

## 15.7  Injustice (Doing Evil)

When justice is such a great value, then it is obvious how flawed evil (which is the opposite of justice) will be. In this regard, not only has the Quran stated that you should not do injustice to anyone, but also that none should have the audacity to do injustice to you or anyone else:

*...Deal not unjustly and you shall not be dealt with unjustly. (2:279)*

This is a Permanent Value or an immutable principle of life i.e. neither to do evil to someone, nor to allow evil to take place. Or in other words, develop so much power within yourself (in this way creating a system), that an unjust and tyrannical individual dare not have the audacity to raise his hand not only against you but even against the weak and feeble - for this, if there is a need to even go to war (i.e.

if there is no other option to stop this tyranny of the tyrant except by war) then the Quran permits this:

*To those against whom War is made, permission is granted to fight, because they are wronged – and verily Allah is most Powerful for their aid. (22:39)*

Not doing wrong yourself and stopping injustice is a Permanent Value.

## 15.8 *Ihsan* (Restoring Balance)

You employ a labourer for some work and you pay him according to the amount of work he performs the whole day. This is justice:

*…And give measure and weight with (full) justice…(6:152)*

You should maintain with justice the scales of measurement and weight and never digress from this and commit any excesses. But if you see that the labourer, despite working to his utmost, cannot earn enough to support his family, then it is also incumbent on you that you should compensate for this shortfall – this is called *Ihsan*. The meaning of *Ihsan* is to create balance and beauty which is indeed the other name for proportion. Therefore, restoring the balance of one whose balance is disturbed is called *Ihsan*. This is also a Permanent Value:

*Indeed, Allah commands justice, and the doing of Ihsan…(16:90)*

Justice demands recompense and retribution i.e. in it what is due to others is paid. But in *Ihsan* there is no question of retribution or payment, therefore the expectation of a return for *Ihsan* is contrary to this Permanent Value and is a non-Quranic concept. The Quran has stated:

*Is there any reward for Ihsan other than Ihsan? (55:60)*

This means that you corrected the disturbed balance of someone and this balance was restored (i.e. you made an effort to create beauty and beauty was created), now what more do you expect in return? If you did *Ihsan* to someone with this thought in mind, that in return for it you will receive a greater amount then this is not *Ihsan*. There is no need to do such an *Ihsan*:

*Nor expect, in giving, any increase (for yourself). (74:6)*

The Quran states that your point of view should be this:

*We feed you for the sake of Allah alone: No reward do we desire from you, nor thanks. (76:9)*

Keep this in mind, that after the establishment of the Quranic system, this *Ihsan* (restoring of balance) will be carried out by the system itself which is responsible for the *Rabubiyat* of all members of the society. But until this system is established, this duty will need to be carried out via individuals. Within the system itself, this duty is, in reality, also carried out by individuals but in a collective form and indirectly.

Therefore, meeting the deficiency of others is also a Permanent Value.

## 15.9  No-one Can be the Slave or Subject of Another

An essential consequence of the respect of humanity means that no human being should be the subject or slave of another human being. Everyone should be accorded equal freedom. The clear decision of the Quran on this issue is:

*It is not (possible) that a man, to whom is given the Book, and Wisdom and Nabuwwat (messenger-hood), should say to people: 'Be you my servants, rather than of Allah'...(3:79)*

In a society, no judiciary or executive has the right to use any individual of the society under their own will nor in the world of religion, leaving aside all others, has even a *Nabi* the right to make people his servants and subservient to him. The freedom of every person, and respect for this freedom, is a fundamental and Permanent Value which cannot be overturned under any circumstances.

## 15.10 Obedience of the Law

But it is obvious that no society or system can be established and survive unless some limits are imposed on the people. The Quran states that these limits will be prescribed through law. And the limits of the principles of these laws will be prescribed according to the revelation (from Allah). Therefore, the remaining part of the verse whose first part is quoted above from Surah *Al Imran*, states:

*...Be you followers of Him Who is truly the Cherisher of all: For you have taught the Book and you have studied it earnestly. (3:79)*

The complete verse will be translated as follows: 'that no man has been accorded the right that Allah gives him a code of laws, government and *Nabuwwat* and he should say to the people that, leaving Allah aside, you become my subjects and slaves. What he should say is this, that you should all become *Rabbani* (bearers of the system of *Rabubiyat* of Allah) according to that code of laws (which you have received from Allah) and which you teach each other and keep imprinting on your hearts'.

From this, two matters become clear: firstly, that no human being even if he is given the authority to formulate sub-clauses or to implement laws or even if he receives *Nabuwwat* from Allah has the right to ask another human being to obey his whim – he will only have the law obeyed. Secondly, that the principles associated with this law will not be devised by human beings themselves but will be prescribed from Allah. Therefore, obedience in reality will be of the Divine laws, not of the laws devised by men themselves:

> *Follow the revelation given unto you from your Sustainer, and follow not, as guardians or protectors, other than Him...(7:3)*

This law will be applicable equally to every individual of society, even individuals holding the highest rank will not be exempt from this, so much so that even the messenger himself, through whom the Divine laws are received by mankind, also proclaims this great truth that:

> *...I follow but that which is revealed to me by inspiration...(46:9)*

And similarly:

> *...I am the first of those who bow to His Will (Divine Laws). (6:163)*

This means that the messenger follows this law himself first of all and then asks others to follow it. In this way, no individual is the slave or subject of another individual. Decisions on disputed matters are resolved according to the Book of Allah which is applicable equally on all individuals. The Quran states:

> *...If any do fail to judge by the light of (what Allah has revealed), they are Unbelievers. (5:44)*

As for the government which is not established according to the Book of Allah – these very people are *Kafir*.

To obey the Divine laws and to ask others to follow them is a Permanent Value.

## 15.11 Consequence of Every Deed

Obedience of the law means that no deed of anyone should remain without an outcome – the good result of a good deed should become apparent and punishment for an evil deed should be received. (By 'good deed' is meant working according to the Divine laws and by 'evil deed' is meant going against this law). For this purpose, society establishes a system based on police and judiciary, but the arrangement of Allah who has established the Permanent Values is such that no deed of anyone, even if it remains hidden from the police, can remain unaccounted for under any circumstances. Allah has stated that this grand and amazing machinery of the universe is consistently working with this aim that every deed keeps producing its precise result. The Quran states:

*Allah created the heavens and the earth in Truth; in order that each self may get the recompense of its deeds and none is dealt with unjustly. (45:22)*

This is called Allah's 'Law of Requital', from whose grip (apart from visible acts) even the errors within the heart and the glances of the eyes cannot escape:

*(Allah) knows of (the tricks) that deceive with the eyes, and all that the hearts conceal. (40:19)*

This is because:

*Then shall anyone who has done an atom's weight of good, see it! And anyone who has done an atom's weight of evil, shall see it. (99:7-8)*

In this regard, never mind others, even Rasul-ullah is not exempted. In Surah *Yunus*, the messenger is told to proclaim:

*...I follow naught but what is revealed unto me: if I were to disobey my Sustainer, I should myself fear the penalty of a Great Day. (10:15)*

The grip of Allah's Law of Requital is very strict:

*Truly strong is the Grip (and Power) of your Sustainer. (85:12)*

According to this law, it never happens that the deeds of anyone go wasted:

*...Never will I (Allah) let the work of any of you go wasted, be he male or female...(3:195)*

The Quran makes it clear:

*If any do deeds of righteousness, be they male or female - and have Eimaan, they will enter Paradise, and not the least injustice will be done to them. (4:124)*

There is no reduction made in anyone's recompense, nor does it happen that someone is anointed without making any effort:

*That man can have nothing but what he strives for. (53:39)*

Therefore, establishing the precise result of every deed is a Permanent Value.

## 15.12 Human System of Justice

This justice (the result of every deed being precisely established) functions according to the universal system of Allah. As far as the judicial system which is devised by men is concerned, separate Permanent Values are given for this. For example:

(1) Never hide *Haqq* (truth) knowingly:

*...nor conceal the Truth when you know. (2:42)*

(2) Neither create confusion between *Haqq* and *Batil* (falsehood):

*And cover not Truth with falsehood...(2:42)*

(3) Evidence should never be concealed:

*...Conceal not evidence...(2:283)*

(4) True evidence should be given for the sake of truth, without any consideration for any kind of greed or favour, or hatred of or prejudice against someone for personal benefit or advantage:

*O you who believe! stand out firmly for justice, as witnesses to Allah, even as against yourselves, or your parents, or your kin, and whether it be (against) rich or poor: for Allah can best protect both. Follow not the lusts (of your hearts), lest you swerve, and if you distort justice or decline to do justice, verily Allah is well-acquainted with all that you do. (4:135)*

(5) Neither there can be any advocacy for criminals.

*...so be not (used) as an advocate by those who betray their trust. (4:105)*

*Contend not on behalf of such as betray their own self; for Allah loves not one given to perfidy and crime. (4:107)*

Neither can one be a supporter of criminals. Moses said to Allah:

*...never shall I be a help to those who are criminals. (28:17)*

Hence, establishing a system of justice in the world and providing full support for its functioning and sustainability are Permanent Values.

## 15.13 Managing According to the Law

It is the duty of every individual in society and of the Quranic society itself to direct everyone to live life according to the Divine law and to prevent violation of the law:

*You are the best of peoples, evolved for mankind, enjoining what is right, forbidding what is wrong...(3:110)*

Therefore, establishing such a society is a Permanent Value.

## 15.14 Lawlessness Should Not be Spread

Spreading lawlessness or rebelling against the Divine law (which is called *Fasaad* in Quranic terminology) is a very great crime. In Surah *Al Baqarah* it is stated:

*When he turns his back, His aim everywhere is to spread mischief through the earth...(2:205)*

He will first himself turn his back on the constitution and law and becoming a dictator will force people to obey him with the rod of his whim, and on seeing this the rest of the people will also begin to flout the law, the consequence of which will be that respect for the law will depart from people's hearts. For such people, very severe punishments have been revealed:

*The punishment of those who wage war against Allah and His Messenger, and strive with might and main for mischief through the land is: execution, or crucifixion, or the cutting off of hands and feet from opposite sides, or exile from the land: that is their disgrace in this world, and a heavy punishment is theirs in the Hereafter. (5:33)*

## 15.15 System Based on Mutual Consultation

A righteous system of government in the world has this duty that it should implement the Permanent Values within the society. But Permanent Values are usually in the form of fundamental principles or boundary lines. The practical sub-clauses of these principles have to be worked out by the system of the society itself according to the requirements of every era. The Quran has stated that this task should also not be assigned to one individual but should instead be accomplished through mutual consultation by the representatives of the nation:

*...who conduct their affairs by mutual Consultation...(42:38)*

So much so that Rasul-ullah himself is not exempted from this. He is also told this:

*...and consult them in affairs...(3:159)*

Therefore, in the system of a nation, mutual consultation is also a Permanent Value, but this consultation is not the Western democratic system in which every decision made by those who get fifty one votes becomes compulsory on those who receive forty nine votes. This consultation will be for the resolution of matters within the domain of sub-clauses while remaining within the boundaries of the Permanent Values.

## 15.16 Do Not Assign National Responsibilities to Incompetent People

In a righteous society, people who solve problems and fulfil commitments are in truth the custodians of the wealth and possessions of the nation. For this it is essential that this custodianship is only handed over to those who are capable of safeguarding it – this should not be put into the possession of incompetent people. The Quran states:

*Allah does command you to render back your Trusts to those to whom they are due; And when you judge between man and man, that you judge with justice: Verily how excellent is the teaching which He gives you! For Allah is He Who hears and sees all things. (4:58)*

This is also a Permanent Value.

## 15.17 Responsibility for Sustenance Rests on Society

One of the basic aims of establishing a society or national system is also in order that the provision of basic necessities of life for all its people should be its responsibility. This means that it is the responsibility of the society to ensure that the basic necessities of life continue to reach every individual:

*There is no moving creature on earth but its sustenance depends on Allah...(11:6)*

The aim of the Quran in stating this is that whichever nation comes into existence to implement the Divine laws, that nation takes all those responsibilities on itself which Allah has referred to Himself as His responsibilities. This nation gives a guarantee for this to all the people, declaring:

*...We provide sustenance (Rizq) for you and for them...(6:151)*

In the word *Rizq* are included all means of sustenance which are required for both physical development and for the development of human potentials. In Quranic terminology a comprehensive term *Zakat* is used for this, the literal meaning of which is 'nourishment'. The giving of *Zakat* means 'providing full means of nourishment to the whole of mankind', which is the first and fundamental responsibility of a Quranic society. The Quran states:

*They are those who, if We establish them in the land, establish the system of Salat and give Zakat...(22:41)*

Hence the responsibility of *Rizq* for all people is a Permanent Value for the system of a society which cannot be disregarded under any circumstances.

## 15.18 Resources and Means of *Rizq*

It is necessary for the system which takes such a great responsibility upon itself, that all the means of *Rizq* should be in its possession and under its jurisdiction. This is why, regarding the sources of production, the Quran has stated in clear words that these are created for the good of all of mankind:

*It is He Who has created for you all things that are on earth...(2:29)*

This means that it has been created so that all of you can draw benefit from this, not so that a few individuals or some particular group should grab it and sit on it. In another verse it is stated:

*It is We Who have placed you with authority on earth and provided you therein with means of sustenance... (7:10)*

It must remain freely and equally available for all those who are in need:

*...in accordance with the needs of those who seek sustenance. (41:10)*

In other words, these resources for nourishment have been created for the needs of the people, therefore its arrangement should be such that no individual becomes deprived of *Rizq*.

Hence, keeping the means of sustenance open for the use of the whole of mankind is also a Permanent Value.

## 15.19 What is Beyond Need

Not only is it the case that the means of sustenance and production cannot be made personal property but it is even the case that whatever one has that is beyond his legitimate needs, that too should be made available for the welfare and development of mankind, so that society can utilise it for this purpose according to need. The Quran states:

> ...they ask you how much they are to spend, Say: what is beyond your needs...(2:219)

Therefore this is also a Permanent Value. The state of those who believe in the Permanent Values is such that they will make available possessions and resources which are beyond their needs for the nourishment of others and will not desire any reward in return, not even a thank you. They will tell them:

> We feed you for the sake of Allah alone: No reward do we desire from you, nor thanks. (76:9)

## 15.20 *Rabubiyat* (Sustenance)

We do this because the nourishment of others (*Rabubiyat*) is a Permanent Value in which we have Eimaan and by doing this our own personality is strengthened. Hence the Quran states:

> ...those, Who spend their substance, Seeking to follow Allah's Laws, And to strengthen their self...(2:265)

## 15.21 Safeguarding Chastity

According to the Quran, protection of chastity is also a Permanent Value. The safeguarding of chastity means that sexual contact between man and woman should only be through the established procedure of *Nikah* (marriage). Other than this form, sexual contact is declared as fornication, going even near which has been forbidden:

> Nor come nigh to fornication; for it is a shameful deed and an evil opening the road (to other evils). (17:32)

Anyone who commits this act will be punished (24:2). *Nikah* is the name given to the contract of mutual agreement between an adult woman and an adult man. Becoming master of women through force without their agreement cannot be called *Nikah*. The Quran states:

> *...this is not halal (not permissible) that you become master of women forcefully...(4:19)*

The purpose of *Nikah* is not merely the satisfaction of sexual desire, its meaning is to establish a mutual relationship based on love and affection. The Quran states:

> *...He created for you mates from among yourselves, that you may dwell in tranquility with them and he has put love and mercy between your hearts. Verily in that are signs for those who reflect. (30:21)*

If this state no longer exists between a husband and wife then they can dissolve their *Nikah* (which is called *Talaq* i.e. divorce). The person for whom *Nikah* is not possible due to his current circumstances should control his self and protect his chastity. The Quran states:

> *Let those who find not the wherewithal for marriage keep themselves chaste, until Allah gives them means out of His grace...(24:33)*

As a consequence of sexual perversion, weakness occurs in the character traits of individuals. The Quran states:

> *...nor commit fornication - and any that does this meets punishment (decline). (25:68)*

If a nation makes fornication common in its society, then after a period of time (according to researchers after an interval of three generations i.e. approximately one hundred years), national decline and ruin sets in.

Therefore, the guarding of chastity is also a Permanent Value, whose hold can never be slackened.

## 15.22 Mankind is One Ummah (Universal Brotherhood)

It has been noted at the beginning that the birth of all mankind is from a 'single cell' (4:1), which means that from the viewpoint of origin, all human beings belong to one brotherhood and are branches of one tree. Hence, the purpose of life of mankind is to live as one universal brotherhood and as one nation. The Quran states:

*Mankind was but one nation, but differed (later)...(10:19)*

The way to make one Ummah from the division of mankind into nations and tribes is to have one code of laws for all of them (which is called One World Government in today's terminology). The Quran has presented itself as one common Code of Laws for the whole of humanity:

*O mankind! there has come to you a direction from your Sustainer...(10:57)*

Therefore, for the whole of mankind to live as one Ummah according to one code of life is also a Permanent Value.

## 15.23 What is Beneficial For Mankind

Confining the works of welfare and benevolence within the sphere of groups, parties and nations is against the fundamental concept of the Permanent Values. According to the Quran, only that deed has a long lasting benefit which is carried out for the good of the whole of mankind. The Quran has clearly declared:

*...While that which is for the good of mankind remains on the earth...(13:17)*

For this, the Quran suggests as a first step that all human beings (without differentiation of colour, race, nation or state) should cooperate in all such matters which are for the prosperity of mankind and should help in following the Permanent Values. And never assist each other in such matters which lead to weakness and ruin and become a cause for lawlessness among mankind. The Quran states:

*...Help you one another in righteousness and piety, But help you not one another in crime and rancour...(5:2)*

## 15.24 Criterion for Differentiation

But just as there is a clear difference between those individuals who follow the law and those among them who rebel and break the law, the Quran similarly differentiates and divides all men according to this criterion – that those human beings who accept the Permanent Values given by Allah and make obedience to them the aim of their life are individuals of one nation and those who reject these values and wish to follow their own self-created code, individuals of another nation. The former are called Momin (i.e. those who accept) and the latter, *Kafir* (i.e. those who reject). Thus this is the only division of human beings which comes into existence according to the criterion defined by the Permanent Values, other than this there is no other criterion for division and differentiation. In modern terminology, this is known as ideology. Therefore, according to the Quran, the criterion for nationality is ideology. The difference in colour, race, blood, language, and nation cannot be a cause for differentiation between human beings.

This criterion for division is in itself a Permanent Value. Hence in Surah *Al Taghabun* it is stated:

*It is He Who has created you, and of you are some that are Kafir, and some that are Momin...(64:2)*

## 15.25 There is No Compulsion in Deen

No-one can be made to accept the Permanent Values by force. Acceptance or rejection is the name given to the decision made by the human mind. A decision which is not made willingly and freely cannot even be called the decision of that individual. A decision is only that which is made according to one's own wish. Therefore, in the matter of Deen (the Code of Permanent Values) one cannot use coercion:

*Let there be no compulsion in Deen: Truth stands out clear from Error...(2:256)*

In another verse the Quran states:

*Say, 'The Truth is from your Sustainer': Let him who will, believe, and let him who will, reject...(18:29)*

Whoever accepts *Haqq* will benefit from its pleasant results and whoever rejects it and follows a different path will be confronted by its destructive effects. No kind of action will be taken against the ones who reject (*Kafir*) solely for this reason that why did they reject this path (i.e. leaving Islam, why have they adopted another religion). Not only is it the case that nothing will be done against them, they will be accorded personal liberty in religion, and the protection of agreements with them will be the responsibility of the Quranic system. In Surah *Al Hajj*, the Quran states:

*...Had not Allah checked one set of people by means of another, there would surely have been pulled down monasteries, churches, synagogues and mosques, in which the name of Allah is commemorated in abundant measure...(22:40)*

Therefore, responsibility for the protection of these places of worship (of non-Muslims) will belong to the Islamic State. Not only protection of their places of worship but also their life, property, honour, dignity, chastity - protection of every possession of life. Indeed, on the basis of equality, these people will have a right to all those rights and privileges which are received according to the Permanent Values due to being a human being.

It is clear in this regard that there can be no kind of compulsion on anyone (neither physical force nor mental persuasion) that they should accept Islam or accept another religion. But when an individual, having accepted Islam willingly of his own accord becomes a member of the Muslim society, then it will be incumbent on him that he should obey the Islamic laws. It cannot be that after becoming a citizen of the Islamic society (or in modern terminology the Islamic State) he can then be left to his own free will to obey whichever law he wishes and break whichever law he wishes by saying that 'there is no compulsion in Deen'. Compulsion is not applicable to which religion he accepts but when, through his own free volition, he becomes a member of the Islamic Society then he voluntarily makes the laws and rules of this society compulsory on himself also. If he does not wish to remain within the domain of these laws and regulations then he has permission to leave the sphere of Islam and adopt another religion.

## 15.26 Divine Attributes

In the previous pages there has been a brief introduction to the main values among the Permanent Values stated in the Quran. In this regard, if you study the Quran on these lines then ever new realities will be exposed to you. In reality, the origin of these Permanent Values is the Divine Self Himself. If we look more closely at the Divine attributes which the Quran has explained so beautifully, leaving aside a few[208] among them, the rest which are commonly called ethical attributes are all Permanent Values. The Quran has named these by using a comprehensive term *Al-asma-ul-Husna* (the Balanced attributes). Keeping these Divine attributes in front as a model, the requirement of life and the purpose of Deen is to continually manifest the human potentials within oneself. As strength continues to develop with the human self, these attributes (i.e. the Permanent Values) will keep manifesting. A Momin human being is one who manifests these attributes naturally through his self, exactly like a crystal which reflects the rays of light outwards without any effort and automatically. These are those individuals through whom the Quranic society is shaped.

Just think that if in the human world such a society is established in which respect for the Permanent Values surges from the depths of the heart and these are not let go under any circumstances, then how this world will transform into *Jannat*. In this *Jannat*, every person will have the security of this assurance that nothing will be done to him outwith the Permanent Values. The other meanings of Momin are

---

[208] Some of the Divine attributes such as 'He is the First and the Last' belong exclusively to Allah.

the one who is at peace himself and gives a guarantee of peace to others. In the human world, real peace can only be established through the hands of the *Jamaat* of Momineen.

# 16   RELATIVE VALUES

So far, we have written about those values which have a permanent status. Let us once again examine an example previously quoted in which we saw wealth is also a value but when a clash occurs between wealth and life, then wealth can be sacrificed for the sake of life (in fact it becomes necessary to do so). Similarly, when there is a clash between life and dignity then to protect dignity it becomes necessary to sacrifice life. This means that wealth and life are relative values whereas dignity is a Permanent Value. Apart from Permanent Values the Quran has also mentioned relative values.

## 16.1   Love for Spouse and Progeny

For example, in Surah *Al Imran* the Quran has stated:

*Fair in the eyes of men is the love of things they covet: Women and sons; Heaped-up hoards of gold and silver; horses branded...(3:14)*

This means that though these things have an inherent value, instances can occur when these material possessions and offspring can themselves become a cause for the disintegration of man. The Quran states:

*And know you that your possessions and your progeny are but a trial...(8:28)*

This happens when material possessions and children are on one side and the values which are higher than them are on the other side. At this juncture, if a man sacrifices some higher value for the protection of his material possessions or offspring, then these things (wealth, offspring, wife etc.) become the cause for his destruction and become his enemy. The Quran states:

*...Truly, among your wives and your children are (some) that are enemies to yourselves...(64:14)*

This is the reason that in the verse of Surah *Al Imran* in which wife, children and wealth have been declared as a reason for attraction, it is also stated:

*...Such are the possessions of this world's life; but in nearness to Allah is the best of the goals. (3:14)*

These are the chattels for the physical life of man. If at some point a clash occurs between this and the real life of man which is the life of the self, then it should be understood at that juncture that the importance and value of the human self is far greater:

*Say: Shall I give you glad tidings of things far better than those…(3:15)*

The individual who does not have Eimaan in this reality gives priority to the love of wealth over these higher values:

*And violent is he in his love of wealth. (100:8)*

## 16.2 Love of Wealth

But the one who has Eimaan in the higher values, despite having love for wealth gives it for the welfare of mankind:

*…to spend of your substance, out of love for Him, for your kin, for orphans, for the needy, for the wayfarer, for those who ask…(2:177)*

In Surah *Al Tauba*, where the contrast between lower values and higher values has been laid bare, it is stated:

*Say: If it be that your fathers, your sons, your brothers, your mates, or your kindred; the wealth that you have gained; the commerce in which you fear a decline: or the dwellings in which you delight - are dearer to you than Allah, or His Messenger, or the striving in His cause - then wait until Allah brings about His decision: and Allah guides not the rebellious. (9:24)*

In view of the importance of material possessions the Quran has proposed punishment for a thief (5:38). It has also been forbidden to devour one another's possessions through cheating (4:29). And getting work done through bribes has also been strictly forbidden (2:188). In other words, not only is there permission to earn wealth through legitimate means and to take care of it but there is instruction to do so. But on the other hand, when a need arises for this same wealth to be used for the protection of a Permanent Value, then it has been directed to give away all that wealth which is beyond one's need (2:219).

## 16.3 Value of Life

According to the Quran, human life is of far higher value than wealth. Its importance and value can be judged from this when the Quran states:

*…if any one slew a person - unless it be for murder or for spreading mischief in the land - it would be as if he slew the whole of mankind; and if any one saved a life, it would be as if he saved the life of the whole of mankind…(5:32)*

But if an individual murders an innocent man or turns the peace of a good society into mayhem, then his punishment is proposed as being the death penalty. Hence in the verse quoted above these words are also included i.e. 'unless it be for murder or for spreading mischief in the land'. In another verse, this is called the taking of life *Bil-Haqq* (in truth):

*Nor take life - which Allah has made sacred - except for just cause…(17:33)*

*Haqq* means to give the death penalty to a murderer or the one who causes tumult and terror in society in consequence of his crime. In view of the importance of the value of life, it has been strictly declared that no such step should be taken as a result of which a human being is killed:

*…and make not your own hands contribute to (your) destruction…(2:195)*

In the same way that this order is applicable collectively it is also applicable individually. Therefore, the protection of your own life is extremely important. In another verse, it is stated:

*…Nor kill (or destroy) yourselves…(4:29)*

Whereas this means 'do not kill your own people', it also means 'do not kill your own self'. The charge that the Quran has levied against the Jews for their crime also includes that they used to kill their own people and turn them out of their homes (2:85). From these explanations, it becomes clear what the importance is of human life according to the Quran. But when it becomes necessary to lay down one's life to defend the Permanent Values then those who step forward willingly and happily, offering their life held out in the palms of their hands and sacrifice their lives happily, they are declared to be the holders of the highest of ranks. So much so, that it has been stated regarding this 'not to call them dead':

*And say not of those who are slain in the way of Allah: 'They are dead.' Nay, they are living, though you perceive (it) not. (2:154)*

They are alive but you cannot comprehend this at the present level of your consciousness. It is obvious from this that despite being so precious, life is still a relative value. If a clash occurs between this and the protection of a Permanent Value, then giving your life for the protection of a Permanent Value is part of human eminence. This is what is meant by 'laying down of life for dignity'.

## 16.4 Protection of Crops and Cattle

The Quran has declared that individual (nation or system) who destroys crops and cattle, as the worst of criminals:

> *When he turns his back, his aim everywhere is to spread mischief through the earth and destroy crops and cattle. But Allah loves not mischief...(2:205)*

But when a nation is bent upon tyranny and destruction and there is no alternative except war to stop them in their path of destroying humanity, permission is given in this situation to go to war against them:

> *To those against whom war is made, permission is given to fight because they have been wronged – and verily, Allah is Most powerful for their aid. (22:39)*

It is evident that in war (despite thousands of precautions) there will necessarily be destruction of crops and cattle – so halting of tyranny is such an obligation for which the sacrifice of something of lower value is permitted. About war itself, the Quran has declared it to be legitimate up to the time that:

> *...until the war lays down its burdens...(47:4)*

In other words, permission for war has been given to end the existence of war from the world.

## 16.5 Fulfilling Commitments

The Quran has given the fulfilling of agreements great importance. It states that the characteristic of Momineen is:

> *...to fulfil the contracts which you have made...(2:177)*

This means that an agreement or contract is such a value which must be respected. But if there is fear of an agreement being broken, then this agreement can be returned to the nation with whom it has been made:

> *If you fear treachery from any group, throw back their covenant to them, on equal terms...(8:58)*

It should be made clear that the Quran has not given permission to break an agreement unilaterally. What has been said here is that if there is fear of a nation breaking an agreement, then say to them that after this an agreement between you and us will not remain. In this way, when both of you come to the same level after the dissolution of an agreement, then you can take a further step. If we look at it from this viewpoint, then respect for an agreement does not remain a relative value but becomes a Permanent Value. This is because the Quran has not given permission for the breaking of an agreement under any circumstances. In the case of treachery by the nation with whom an agreement is made, permission is given to revoke the agreement. After this, if any step is taken against this nation then it will not be a step against the agreement but instead will be a step against a nation with whom you have no agreement. It is evident that at the time of making an agreement with another nation, it will be made clear under what circumstances this agreement can be considered to be void. Other than flouting agreements, the Quran also strongly forbids the use of agreements as a tool to carry out deception. In Surah *Al Nahl* it is stated:

*...nor take your oaths to practice deception between yourselves, lest one party should be more numerous than another...(16:92)*

And then it is stated:

*And take not your oaths to practice deception between yourselves with the result that someone's foot may slip after it was firmly planted, and you may have to taste the evil consequences of having hindered (men) from the path of Allah...(16:94)*

From this it is evident that strict admonition has been given regarding the fulfilling of commitments. If we look at it from this respect, then the honouring of agreements is a Permanent Value but because in the event of the opposing party flouting an agreement there is consequently permission to dissolve the agreement, we have therefore included this under the section on relative values. This difference can be understood as follows. For example, doing justice is a Permanent Value. It is not conditional on this, that as long as the opposing party does justice, you too do justice, and when it abandons justice, then you resort to injustice. Whether the opposite side does justice or not you simply cannot lift your hand away from justice. But in the case of fulfilling an agreement, this is conditional on the opposite side remaining committed to the agreement. If they do not remain committed, then you too cannot be forced to remain committed to it. It is only due to this much difference that it is noted under the relative values, otherwise it too is a Permanent Value.

These are brief summaries of a few relative values which under normal circumstances it is essential to respect but which can be sacrificed for the protection of a higher value than these. By paying further attention to the Quran this list of relative values can be increased.

The Quran has clearly differentiated the mutual link between the Permanent Values and the relative values, and that in the case of any clash between them the latter should be sacrificed for the sake of the former. This concept has been illustrated very comprehensively through the following verse of Surah *Al Tauba* which has already been quoted and which we feel it is necessary to repeat again at the end:

> *Say: If it be that your fathers, your sons, your brothers, your mates, or your kindred; the wealth that you have gained; the commerce in which you fear a decline: or the dwellings in which you delight - are dearer to you than Allah, or His Messenger, or the striving in His cause; then wait until Allah brings about His decision: and Allah guides not the rebellious. (9:24)*

The correct path of life is that everything should be kept in its correct position, and whenever there is a clash between a lower and a higher value then the lower value should be sacrificed for the sake of the higher value.

It is this system of life which is called Islam. In other words, these are those Permanent Values which are declared to have the status of fundamental human rights in political language.

# 17 WOMAN

In the world, no animal has done to his partner what man has done to his companion in life. Among animals, other than this physical trait which has been specified by nature for the female, there is no difference or superiority in male and female. But the gulf of mutual difference between man and woman is so wide and deep that it appears as if they belong to two different species. This mutual difference of theirs is not created by nature but is created by man himself and its foundation has been laid by the hands of man himself. According to the programme of nature, amongst all animals the birth of a human child and its period of upbringing (which starts from conception) is the longest of all. During this period, for a time woman is nearly unable to carry out the normal business of life and during the rest of the time so busy that she has little time for normal duties and occupations. Man is free and unhindered from all these duties and engagements. Therefore, according to the principle of division of labour he earns sustenance and is responsible for meeting the needs of woman (4:34).

## 17.1 Is Woman Lesser Than Man?

Nature defined this programme for the reproduction and training of human progeny but man took unfair advantage of this constraint and feature of woman, and as happens with every indigent, he made her his subject and slave. In order to make the chains of slavery stronger, it is necessary that this belief is imbedded into the heart of the subject that he is inferior to the ruler and master and that nature has indeed created him solely for this purpose of obedience and compliance. To achieve this purpose, 'religion' (i.e. the self-devised religion of men) is a very effective instrument. Hence in this domain also, man thrust forward the agenda of religion and he began to make this belief widespread that the status of woman is grossly inferior compared to man. She is the source of all troubles and the originator of sins. She has faulty intellect and she should always remain obedient to man. Therefore, if you pick up the Bible and look, you will find these beliefs to be common in it according to which God created man (Adam) with His own hands. And when he (Adam) began to be continuously sad due to loneliness, woman (Eve) was created from his rib, in order to provide him with company for his pleasure. In other words, the sole aim was the creation of man, and woman was merely created as a toy to entertain man. Satan misguided woman and because of this Adam had to leave paradise. As punishment therefore for this crime of woman, God made the decision that she should give birth to children through the pains of labour and her children should enter this world laden with the burden of sins and live with trials and tribulations.

## 17.2 Christianity and Woman

In the Christian church, this issue remained under discussion for a while as to whether woman even has a soul or not. As far as woman's 'nature' is concerned, it was said regarding this that since she is created from the rib of Adam, she is therefore crooked like the rib. If we wish to straighten it, it will break but will not straighten. These beliefs about woman are not specifically confined to Christianity, nearly every religion of the world has given woman a similar position. She is created for man, therefore she has to bide by the will of man. In a society, she holds no status in her own right, so much so that even her introduction is not done through her own self – she is introduced as the daughter of Zaid, the wife of Bakr or the mother of Omer. She can neither be the owner of any property, nor has she any authority in the income of man. She cannot receive anything from the inheritance or wealth of her father, husband, or son as a right – if she is given anything then it will be in the form of charity. *Kanyadan* is an established part of Hindu society. According to this religion she cannot select her own husband – her father can hand her over to anyone he wishes, in fact this is even necessary that she should be married off before she reaches adulthood. This marriage will be a permanent tie which can never be broken, even after the death of her husband this woman will remain his wife. She will either need to burn to death on her husband's funeral pyre or spend her whole life as a widow.[209]

These beliefs about woman have continued throughout the centuries and are prevalent in nearly every part of the world (or it can be said that they were prevalent until recent times). The consequence of this was that woman herself began to realise that she has no position of her own in the world. She is only created for man. The purpose of her life is to satisfy the sexual desires of man and to become the means of producing his progeny.

## 17.3 European Woman

How deeply this belief about her own self has reached the heart of woman can be seen from the fact that the Western woman considers herself to be completely free. Her belief is that she does not lag behind man in any field, and she is not subservient to man. She rebels against every belief which contains any iota of the suggestion that she is inferior to man. But despite this, her extreme endeavour is that somehow or other she should become an object of attraction in the eyes of men. All her material for adornment and beautification, her efforts to promote her beauty and various techniques to exhibit her figure, her manner of speech, her way

---

[209] Hindus have changed these age-old beliefs and traditions but they have done this after abandoning their religion. According to their religion the position of a woman remains the same as noted above. In Christian countries also the changes which have come about in this respect happened after giving up religion.

of walking, the design and embellishment of her apparel, behind her every movement and appearance this motive is functioning that she should become as attractive as possible in the eyes of man. You can see that despite rebelling against man and being (apparently) free, this belief is still ingrained in the depths of her heart that she is created for man. In fact, in this respect woman of the age of ignorance was smarter than the daughter of modern civilization, even if she became the means of satisfying the desires of man, at least she was free from the trouble of earning a living. Now she earns herself and spends the majority of her earnings to become the toy of man. She makes full effort that somehow or other she remains trapped as prey in the eyes of man, and despite this keeps herself under this illusion that she is free from the grip of man. All this is the unconscious influence of that doctrine and belief which is rooted in the heart and veins of woman for thousands of years.

## 17.4 Revolutionary Proclamation of the Quran

The Quran arrived and it declared as false all these beliefs and doctrines about woman which man had spread for centuries. It was a very great revolutionary proclamation in the history of man. It stated that it was false that Allah created man and then woman was created from the rib of man. It has already been noted that according to the Quran this concept is wrong that the beginning of mankind happened as follows, that Allah somehow created a man (or a couple) and then from them the process of reproduction of mankind proceeded. The Quran states that life, traversing through its various evolutionary stages, reached up to the state of a human being. Its beginning was from a life-cell, there was no differentiation of male of female in this, then it became divided into two new parts - one part a spermatozoon possessing male traits and the other an ovum possessing female traits. By the coming together of these two the process of reproduction proceeded forward through birth. The birth of a human child (girl or boy) also takes place through this process, so it is wrong to say that man was made first and woman emerged from his rib. The Quran states:

*...Who created you from a single life-cell and from it created, of like nature, its mate (for man a woman and for woman a man) and from them twain, has spread abroad a multitude of men and women...(4:1)*

After this the Quran also contradicted the belief that woman was the cause of the error of Adam in Paradise. It stated that man and woman both have equal potential within them to follow the right path or to leave it. They can both commit errors (2:36). Therefore, it is wrong to think that woman is responsible for the sins of the world and man is completely innocent.

## 17.5  Meaning of *Zauj* (Pair)

Then the Quran stated that for the programme of reproduction it was proposed that this process moves forward with the mutual cooperation of man and woman, neither man alone can support this, nor woman alone. The things which come together in this way to fulfil a certain purpose are called *Zauj* (complementary) of one another. In this respect man and woman are *Zauj* of one another. Between the two some traits are given to man while woman is deprived of these, and some are given to woman which man is not in possession of. Therefore, each one surpasses the other.

*Allah has so created you that one excels the other (in certain respects)...(4:34)*

Pay attention to this that the Quran has not said that man has been given superiority over woman or that woman has preference over man – because of certain traits man surpasses woman, and due to other traits woman surpasses man, and the programme of nature is fulfilled through the companionship of both. These different traits of man and woman are only biological. As far as human potentials are concerned, both possess these equally. For thousands of years man kept woman deprived of those opportunities and means through which her human potentials could have been developed and then this *Fatwa* was proclaimed that woman is simply the possessor of faulty intellect. This is wrong – provide them with equal opportunities and then see how both progress side by side in the cavalcade of life.

## 17.6  Equal Potentials

The Quran has proclaimed:

*For Muslim men and women – for believing men and women, for devout men and women, for true men and women, for men and women who are patient and constant, for men and women who humble themselves, for men and women who give in charity, for men and women who fast (practice self-restraint), for men and women who guard their chastity, and for men and women who engage much in Allah's remembrance (following His Laws) – for them has Allah prepared protection and great reward.*
*(33:35)*

If men have the potentiality to develop their personality by harmonizing themselves with the laws of Allah, then women also have a similar potentiality; if men can be members of a movement that aims at world peace according to the inviolable laws of Allah, then women also can participate in it by becoming its members; if men can restrain their capabilities so as to develop them within the laws of Allah, so can women; if men can vindicate the truth of their conviction through its practical implementation in life, so can women vindicate it; if men can remain steadfast on the path they have chosen, so can women; if men have an inexhaustible capacity to be more and more in harmony with the laws of Allah once they are set on this path, so have women this inexhaustible capacity; if men can sacrifice lower values for higher values, so can women; if men can exercise control and do not violate the limitations set on them, so can women; if men can keep their sexual urge within the desired limits, so can women; if men can understand the laws of Allah and focus their activities in life on them, so can women. Now, if both men and women have equal capacities and potentialities, their results should also be the same for both of them. Hence, both will enjoy protection and security and all other such benefits and joy that will come out of their deeds.[210]

In another verse, the Quran has also stated another trait of Momin women as being those who travel (66:5), similar to men who travel (9:112).

Reflect on these explanations of the Quran, and then see concerning which part of life is it that it has stated that men have the potential for it but woman does not – man can do such and such but woman cannot do it, man can become all this but woman cannot. This is why the Quran has declared that the righteous deeds of both men and women will be worthy of equal recompense:

*If any do deeds of righteousness – be they male or female – and have Eimaan, they will enter paradise and not the least injustice will be done to them. (4:124)*

So much so that the Quran has also stated that whatever man will earn it will be his share, whatever a woman earns it will be her share:

*…To men is allotted what they earn, and to women what they earn…(4:32)*

## 17.7  Affairs of State and Woman

It is generally said that women cannot participate in the affairs of a state. But this belief is also based on ignorance of the Quranic teaching. The Quran has declared that the basic duty of the Islamic State is to 'promote good and forbid evil':

*Those who, if We establish them in the land, establish Salat and give Zakat, enjoin the right and forbid wrong…(22:41)*

About this duty it is stated:

---

[210] See the book titled *'Islam: A challenge to religion'* by the author, p. 339.

*The Believers, men and women, are protectors one of another: they enjoin what is just, and forbid what is evil...(9:71)*

From this it is clear that women are equal partners in the performance of duties in state affairs. In addition to these explanations, it is important to bear in mind one fundamental principle, that the basic teaching of the Quran is that there can be no differentiation between one human being and another by birth. The whole edifice of its teaching is raised on this very foundation. This is the reason why it does not differentiate between a *Brahmin* and a *Shudar* (classes in the Hindu religion) in relation to birth. It does not differentiate between a child who is born in a hut and one born in a palace. Keeping this principle in mind, see that if in some individual's house a boy is born and a girl is born, in this respect there is no magic trick of the boy because of which he became a boy and neither is there some crime of the girl's that she is born a girl. Now if we consider this principle as being true that a girl is inferior to a boy (or a woman to a man), this means that due to the criterion of birth we consider one set of human beings as being superior and another set as being inferior. And this differentiation between them is such that the inferior group (i.e. women) can never eradicate it though she may try a million times. Now consider how as a result of this wrong belief that man attains superiority over woman due to just being a man, the most eminent teaching of Islam is left torn from the very root of its foundations. This belief is of our own creation - the teaching of the Quran remains pure from this.

## 17.8  Importance of Family Life

An animal child is only in need of physical nourishment from the mother (or from the mother and father), it is not in need of any training. After physical nourishment, it becomes that which it was created to become – the offspring of a goat is a goat, the offspring of a lion is a lion. But, in order for a human child to become a human being, other than physical nourishment, training is also required. This training can take place in the environment of a home. This is that necessity for which the Quran gives great importance to family life. When examined closely, this reality becomes patently obvious that, what we term a society, is actually the expanded form of a 'home'. In the morning, homes expand and become a society and at night the society shrinks and becomes confined to the homes. In the Arabic language, the word 'Ummah' is used for a nation. The Quran has also used the word Ummah for the type of nation which it desires to shape (*Jamaat* of Momineen). The word Ummah is derived from 'Umm' which means 'mother'. This means that the growth of the Ummah takes place in the lap of the mother. This is the reason it wishes to make the home as a model for this society which it terms as an earthly paradise for the mankind.

## 17.9 Harmony in Intellect and Understanding

The fundamental condition to make a home a paradise is to have complete harmony of intellect and understanding, ideas and beliefs between husband and wife. The Quran states in clear words that to marry while holding conflicting beliefs about life is to make the home a hell. In contrast, the home becomes a paradise when there are compatible beliefs and outlook. It states:

*Do not marry unbelieving women, until they have Eimaan: A slave woman who has Eimaan is better than an unbelieving woman, even though she allure you. Nor marry Unbelievers until they have Eimaan: a man slave who has Eimaan is better than an Unbeliever, even though he allure you. Unbelievers do (but) beckon you to the Fire. But Allah beckons by His Grace to paradise and protection, and makes His Signs clear to mankind: that they may receive admonition. (2:221)*

For this it is necessary that a woman and a man should have full freedom and the right to select their partner. This is why the Quran tells men to marry women of their choice (4:3) and about women it states that men should not become their masters forcefully (4:19). Under these terms the question of marriage between a minor boy or a minor girl does not even arise. Hence, according to the Quran, *Nikah* is the name given to the mutual agreement, with full willingness according to their personal choice, between an adult man and an adult woman, that having become companions of each other, they will live a life in peace and love, in mutual harmony and with one outlook (30:21). And in this way, they will produce in society that kind of delightful environment in which future generations will be brought up possessing a balanced personality and will become the embodiment of the eminence of humanity.

## 17.10 Division of Labour

Because, as has already been stated earlier, in the unit of a home according to the principle of the division of work, the major share of a woman's time is devoted to the care and training of children, the fundamental responsibility for earning a means of subsistence falls therefore on man. Regarding this, the Quran states:

*Men are responsible for the maintenance of women (in the home)...(4:34)*

It should be made clear that this does not mean that a woman cannot even earn any subsistence. As has been noted earlier, the Quran has stated in clear words that a woman is the owner of whatever she earns (4:32). The reason why men are declared to be responsible for providing for the needs of life of women is that since in the management of home affairs the larger part of a woman's time is spent in the care and bringing up of the children and man is free from this, it is therefore fundamentally the responsibility of men to earn subsistence. As far as the responsibilities and rights of a husband and wife are concerned, the Quran has given both equal status. In this regard, it has specified such a principle which in its brevity and succinctness is unparalleled. It states:

*...And women shall have rights similar to the rights against them, According to what is equitable...(2:228)*

According to procedure and law, women have similar levels of responsibilities proportionate to their rights. And as for the mutual relationships between a husband and wife, for this too the Quran has specified a similar concise and succinct principle:

*...They are raiment for you and you are raiment for them...(2:187)*

You are for each other like the apparel you wear, which has such an intimate and direct relation to the body that no other thing can come between them.

## 17.11 Divorce (*Tallaq*)

The Quran has called *Nikah* the mutual agreement which takes place as a result of the heartfelt agreement between the two parties (4:21). It emphasises that a proper appraisal should be carried out prior to this agreement and it should be assured in every way possible that this agreement will last for the duration of life with success and harmony. After this it gives such instructions according to which this agreement becomes ever stronger in the marital life of husband and wife. But despite this, the Quran does not hide from the realities of life. It accepts that despite this amount of care and emphasis, such a situation can occur where differences arise between the parties. In such an eventuality, it makes it the responsibility of society that it should try its utmost to erase their mutual differences. For this it suggests that a consulting board should be constituted, comprising of representatives of both parties, which will make every effort possible to try and resolve their differences (4:35). But if their efforts are fruitless and they reach the conclusion that no possibility remains of reconciliation between this husband and wife, then this agreement of *Nikah* of theirs should be dissolved. This is called *Tallaq*[211] [212].

---

[211] As in this book only the principles of Deen are discussed, detailed discussion has not been included about the sub-clauses. Further details on marital life can be found in my book, '*Letters to Tahira*'.

[212] The Quran has stated that only in one thing is man's right different i.e. in the case of a divorce, a woman has to wait for a stated period (which is called *Iddat*) before entering a second marriage, whereas a man has no need to wait. See verse (2:228).

## 17.12 Polygamy

Because the Quran declares the harmony of thought and outlook between husband and wife and the sweetness of love and peace in their relations as a basic condition, therefore the question of a second wife in the presence of a wife does not even arise in this. The general principle of Islam is monogamy. But in this regard, it does not ignore certain exceptional circumstances. It says that due to certain adverse situations (for example, as a result of war), such emergency circumstances can arise in which the numbers of widows (and the orphan children with them) and adult women become so great that, according to the principle of monogamy, there is no possibility of their getting married. In such a situation, it is obvious that sexual promiscuity can spread within society. The Quran states that in order to take control over such emergency circumstances, there can be an exception in the principle of monogamy. It states:

*And if you fear that you shall not be able to deal justly with the orphans, then marry women of your choice, Two, or three or four (as the situation demands), But if you fear that you shall not be able to deal justly (with them), then marry only one...(4:3)*

Bear in mind that those Muslim women who become widows or become of marriageable age and for whose marital life there are no Muslim men available, become an important problem for society. This is because a Muslim woman can never marry a non-Muslim man, she has to marry within Muslims and because of the principle of monogamy this is not possible. Due to this abnormal circumstance, the Quran has put forward this solution. But the basic condition for this is that justice be done to these new arrivals and their orphan children, and if this is not possible, then there is no permission for even this solution (4:3). The basic requirement for justice will be that there should be willingness for this from the first wife (and if someone has no first wife then between the women that he wishes to marry). If they are not willing for this, then justice will be impossible. The home will become hell.

This is the one time only and the sole verse in the Quran regarding having more than one wife. Consequently, apart from these circumstances there is no permission for more than one wife under any other condition or for any other reason.

## 17.13 One Important Reality

In relation to polygamy it is necessary to keep one important reality in mind. Within our homes there are present grown up sisters, daughters and other such female relatives with whom *Nikah* is not permitted. We interact day and night with these adult girls and women but not even the remotest idea of any sexual urge arises in the hearts of these men and women. In this environment life passes in complete security and chastity. Within this sphere adult girls and unmarried women have complete trust in these boys and men that there is no kind of danger from them. Why is this? Because this is that sphere in which *Nikah* is not permitted with each other. Now it is obvious that the degree of sexual security and peace prevailing within a society will be according to the extent to which this sphere is widespread, and women will feel an equivalent degree of peace and trust from men.

When monogamy has been accepted as a principle, then when one man marries some woman, then after this, in the presence of his wife, this man's *Nikah* becomes declared as illegitimate for every other woman in the world. Now see from this how wide that sphere has become within which the environment of sexual peace and security becomes the norm, and in which women have complete trust and freedom from fear of men.[213] (Be aware that we are discussing that society in which fornication is declared as haram). In this society (after the marriage of a man) neither can a woman look at this man with the thought that he should marry me, nor can the man cast an eye on another woman with the thought that he should marry her. Furthermore, see also how contented a life this man's wife will spend - she knows that in her presence her husband can never even have a passing thought about any other woman that he will marry her nor can he develop an illicit relationship with anyone.

But if in a society there is complete freedom regarding polygamy, then as a result this whole environment of peace and tranquility will become a hell of fearful heartbeats and trepidation and an inferno of doubts and suspicions. The wife of this man will be in a constant state of apprehension that who knows when he will bring along another wife. Whichever woman wishes, she can begin to attempt to attract this man to herself so that he can make her his wife. Man can look at every other woman with desire because to bring this woman into his *Nikah* is neither a crime nor a sin – have you contemplated how with this difference what the map of a society will change into and become?

By forbidding *Zina* and by establishing monogamy as a principle, the Quran has uprooted all those evils from society due to which woman remains apprehensive of every man. And from this created a paradise like environment of peace and tranquility. But along with this, recognizing the need for polygamy in special circumstances, also protected society from those devastations in which the West is so gravely immersed.

---

[213] It should be made clear that we are talking about that society in which *Zina* (fornication) is declared to be haram (forbidden).

## 17.14 Slaves and Concubines

At the time of the revelation of the Quran, slavery prevailed in nearly every nation of the world. We have seen that the fundamental teaching of the Quran is based on respect and equality of humanity. It declares this to be a Permanent Value which cannot be transgressed in any circumstance. It is obvious that in these circumstances how could it have declared this curse which was burning and destroying humanity, like slavery, to be legitimate and permissible. In this era, prisoners of war were made slaves and their women, concubines. The Quran gave the command regarding prisoners of war that they will in any case be released:

> ...thereafter (is the time for these prisoners of war) either (letting them go as) generosity or (through) ransom...(47:4)

While they remain with you as prisoners, they will be treated humanely because the *Jamaat* of Momineen can never do anything in any circumstance which is contrary to the Permanent Value of respect for humanity. In this way, the Quran closed the door on slavery.[214]

But in the society of the Arabs in those days slaves and concubines were plentiful. If the Quran had given the command to turn them out immediately, the structure of the society would have become chaotic. This is why it gave such orders and commands, due to which all the slaves and concubines could become gradually either free or assimilated as members of Muslim households. Wherever in the Quran 'or whom their right hands possess'[215] (23:6) is mentioned, this refers to those slaves and concubines who were present in the society at that time. Therefore, after they have become free or have become absorbed within the society, according to the Quran there is then no question even arising of slaves or concubines. This concept is against the fundamental teaching of the Quran.

## 17.15 The Purpose of Sex[216]

Regarding the mutual relations between man and woman, the greatest revolutionary concept that the Quran presents is about sex. There is no doubt that man says that the sexual relationship between husband and wife is for the sake of producing progeny, but it is an undeniable truth that due to this relation the foremost aim is satisfaction of sexual pleasure. Man has viewed and made woman a means to the satisfaction of his sexual desire and from marriage the objective is

---

[214]The door for future slavery was thus closed by the Quran forever. Whatever happened in subsequent history was the responsibility of the Muslims and not of the Quran.

[215] The words 'whom your right hands possess' occurring in the Quran are in the past tense and refer to those who had already been enslaved.

[216] This section is taken from the book titled '*Islam: A challenge to religion*', Chapter XVIII, *Woman*.

understood to be the gain of legal and social legitimisation of this sexual desire. We do not need to go into the details here of the degree to which devastations have been produced in the history of mankind due to this concept, that the objective of sexual relations is to satisfy personal desire. It is the consequence of this, that like wealth and land woman has also become a problem for man, and will continue to remain so till man establishes a correct concept about sex. The Quran has presented the correct view about sex.

If you look at animals, the purpose of sex is reproduction. It is not the satisfaction of sexual pleasure. As with other matters, nature has retained control of this in its own hands. Sexual desire only arises in animals when, according to the established programme of nature, the time for mating and conception occurs. Once this aim is achieved, this emotion falls silent in both the male and the female. They have neither control over this that whenever they wish they can make it come alive again of their own accord, nor control over this that after its arousal, they do not fulfil it.

As with animals, in humans too the means for reproduction is sexual mating. This means that sexual relations are associated with the physical life of man. But as we have already seen, the difference between man and other animals is this, that animals have been created constrained by nature, while man possesses free will and intention. A man and a dog both know that poison can be a reason for their demise. A dog will never eat poison of its own accord because it has never been given the ability to choose to eat what it wishes and to refrain from that which it wishes. But man can eat poison of his own accord and commit suicide. Man has been given a similar choice in the matter of sexual mating.

Man being a holder of free will and intent is a reason for him to receive a thousand benefits. But on the other hand, this very freedom to choose of his is also the reason for his destruction and ruin. The limitation of a dog, in that he cannot choose to eat poison, protects it from death but because of this he also remains deprived of the countless benefits of poison. If man utilises poison according to the law of nature, he can reap many benefits from it but if he uses it contrary to the law of nature, poison becomes the reason for his demise. In other words, the correct use of human choice and intent is a source of mercy in his favour, and its incorrect use a cause for death.

## 17.16 Birth Control

Regarding the issue of sexual mating, by creating animals to be devoid of free choice and to be constrained, nature has retained control over their reproduction. They are obliged to give birth to their young according to the programme of nature. They can neither cause a reduction in this, nor an increase. In the period that nature has fixed for them, they can neither desist from mating (period of conception) nor can they mate at times other than this period. But nature has given man freedom in this domain also, that he can, according to his own choice, exercise control over his reproductive faculty himself. In other words, he can produce as many children as he wishes but should not feel any obligation to have any more than this.

Though choice was given to him for this purpose, he considered sexual mating to be a means to obtain hedonistic pleasure for himself. Then, my goodness, what destructions were caused in that process. He made sex into such a problem for himself that he cannot comprehend any solution for it. No better example can be presented to correctly evaluate what kinds of difficulties the wrong use of human choice and intent creates for man than this. Firstly, through his erroneous vision and through the hands of his emotive desires, he created a problem for himself out of such a simple programme of nature and then in search of a solution to this problem, he created such tangled convolutions that, like the prince in a fairy tale, he remained lost forever in this maze. So much so, that Freud and his co-thinkers have even said that sex is that focal point around which the whole world of man revolves; and that the mutual attraction of mother and child and even the relation of (this is the creation of his own mind) 'God' and man is dependent on the result of these sexual urges.

## 17.17 Sexual Urge is Not a Physical Need

In this connection, the belief was created that the sexual urge is a physical need like food and water, whose satisfaction is essential. If this need is suppressed, then a thousand ills (and psychological diseases) are born as a result, and the greater the extent to which opportunity is given for it to play freely, the greater the degree to which the knots of human consciousness are untangled, even though this fact is very clear that the sexual urge is not physical like hunger and thirst. For example, if you are sitting engrossed in some work, then when the body needs water, the feeling of thirst will arise. Initially this feeling will be slight but if you do not quench your thirst, then it will increase in intensity and gradually will become so great that you will find it difficult to continue to work. If still you do not drink water, you will become ill and eventually your demise will occur. This is called 'physical need'. Contrary to this, the state of the sexual urge is that it never emerges until you cause it to arise by your own thinking. It has to be triggered to emerge through thoughts and it can become cold through thoughts. And it is also not correct that if this need is not satisfied that man becomes ill and eventually his death occurs. How many people are there who have not satisfied this need all their life and despite this there has been no harmful effect on their health. Never mind a harmful effect occurring, their health becomes even better. Its harmful effect results when you, through your thoughts, cause these urges to repeatedly arise. If your thoughts do not go in this direction, then there is a pleasant effect on human health and thought process as a result. In its support, the evidences of eminent physicians and experts in psychology and sexuality are available – and the greatest evidence is man's own experience. Whoever wishes can try it, the condition being to not allow your thoughts to approach in this direction.

## 17.18 This is a Psychological Urge

Therefore, the sexual urge is not a physical necessity, this is a psychological urge which man gives rise to himself. If he causes it to arise according to his own programme for the production of his progeny, then its consequence is beneficial both for him and for mankind. And if he causes it to arise purely for his hedonistic pleasure and provides the means for its fulfilment, both individual and collective ruins result from this. And man never considers how great a price he is paying for such a temporary pleasure. The purpose of food is to provide nourishment for the body; its taste is a secondary issue. The individual who eats purely for the sake of taste and thus keeps ruining his health, what can you call him other than insane. Similarly, the purpose of sexual relations is for reproduction, pleasure is a secondary issue. The person who approaches sexual relations only for the sake of pleasure, and in this way, having created thousands of complications for himself and for mankind and making society a hell, what doubt can there be in his insanity either! But what can be the solution to the fact that man, having adopted the wrong approach for thousands of years, upholds this madness to be a wonderful wisdom – and is also reaping its consequence.

The Quran has presented the solution to this most difficult (and self-created) problem of man in just a few words, when it states:

> *Your wives are as a tilth unto you, so approach your tilth when or how you will...(2:223)*

Here the example of a field has made the matter absolutely clear. The farmer only sows his field when he intends to grow a crop. He does not plough the field or sow seeds merely for the sake of pleasure. Therefore, the purpose of sexual mating of a husband and wife is to produce children, not to seek pleasure. Sexual mating should only be at a time when the aim is to produce children, and offspring should be produced according to your own programme. As for the sexual urge being unlike a physical need, the Quran has also made this clear. In the matter of things to eat and drink it has made some things haram, but along with that it has also stated that if such a situation arises that nothing else is available to eat and your condition becomes unbearable, then at that stage it is permitted for you to eat haram things according to your need (2:173). Contrary to this, regarding the matter of sexual urge it is stated:

*Let those who find not the wherewithal for marriage keep themselves chaste, until Allah gives them means...(24:33)*

This means the Quran has recognised the unbearable condition in the case of food and drink but has not accepted it in the case of the sexual urge. This is because, as stated earlier, the sexual urge is not a physical necessity; it is merely a psychological urge, the emergence of which is dependent on the thoughts of man himself. And regarding the matter which is a choice of man himself, what question is there of this being unbearable? This is the reason that the Quran has declared fornication to be haram and has not given permission for it under any circumstances.

## 17.19 Fornication is Haram

According to the Quran, this is a grave crime for which the punishment is severe. In Western society, if an adult couple (unmarried) establishes sexual relations with mutual agreement without *Nikah*, it is not considered to be a crime. But the Quran declares this also to be a crime, because the leading motive for fornication is this seeking of pleasure, not the birth of children. In the West, if the girl becomes pregnant in this situation and that couple get married after this, then this child becomes legitimate in the eyes of the law, because (according to them) in such a situation the purpose of the relationship no longer remains as the seeking of pleasure alone, the birth of children also comes into this. In other words, according to them also there is a difference in merely having sexual relations for the sake of pleasure and in the relationship which results in children. The Quran calls this fornication also, because the purpose in this was in reality the seeking of pleasure. This was merely an accident due to which pregnancy occurred. According to the Quran, the meaning of *Nikah* is such a contract according to which a couple make an agreement to spend a life together of mutual companionship. In this companionship, the nourishment of such offspring also enters into it, who as a result of righteous training, become eligible for the eminence of humanity. Such a relationship in which the seminal fluid is merely 'poured away', is declared to be against the purpose of *Nikah* by the Quran:

*...Provided you seek them in marriage with gifts from your possessions - desiring chastity not lust...(4:24)*

## 17.20 Family Planning

The world is presently facing a problem on such a scale which, as a result of its importance, is not in any way less dangerous than the 'atomic bomb'. The problem is that the population of the world is increasing so rapidly that the fear is that, after a period of time, the productivity of the earth will not be sufficient to feed it. The various governments of the world are also doing a lot to increase production but the assessment is that the rate of increase in production will not be able to keep pace with the growth in population. In order to counter this danger, it has been thought that this unchecked increase in population should be halted. For this purpose, contraceptive medicines and instruments are being invented and adult women and men are being enticed to use them. But these measures so far are not successful – firstly, these are not effective in all situations and secondly, there is a great deal of expense associated with them. Then the medical community has not reached any definite conclusions regarding the longterm effects and consequences of these because of which there is a lot being said both in their favour and against them – all this is happening and alongside it, the population is continually increasing. This question has created a tricky issue for the intellectuals and thinkers of the world.

But have you noticed what the fundamental reason for this problem is - this belief about sexual relations that its purpose is to seek pleasure. Both those who offer contraceptive measures and those who take them, desire that sexual pleasure should be acquired through sexual relations but that children should not be born. Until man brings about a change in this erroneous belief of his, a satisfactory solution to this problem will never be found i.e. this change that sexual relations should indeed only take place when the objective is to produce children. If this ideology is adopted, then not only will a satisfactory solution be found to the problem of overpopulation but many other issues about 'woman' will also be resolved.

Since this wrong belief about sexual relations is ongoing for centuries, it looks apparently difficult to bring about a change in it. But it is not impossible – what ideology is there in which change cannot be wrought through correct education and training? Even in this day and age, in every nation and tribe, you will find some sort of restriction imposed on sexual relations which is being followed unconsciously. For example, there cannot be a marital relationship between brother and sister, or that it is not right for a husband and wife to have sexual relations during menstruation. These constraints are being followed unconsciously because these are included in the education and training of children. Similarly, if this doctrine is also included in education and training that sexual relations are only for procreation, then after a few generations this boundary will also be followed unconsciously. This is particularly so because, as already noted, the sexual urge only emerges through thoughts. Therefore, to bring about change or improvement in any ideology related to sex, it is necessary to bring about change and improvement in thinking.

## 17.21 Need for Correct Education

In order to produce this kind of change through education and training, it is also essential that such an environment is created in society due to which the thoughts of the youth are not automatically drawn towards sex. The result of the prevailing wrong belief about sex is that the whole environment remains constantly loaded with such germs which serve as great provocations in arousing sexual urges - in women, the motive for self objectification, and for every type of new method and technique, and all kinds of opportunities and functions, blatant sexual literature and cinema films, provocative love songs – and above everything, this concept about life itself that human life is merely a physical life, there is no level above the animal level, and nor are there any such Permanent Values the protection of which is the reason for human eminence. The collective impact of all these different elements is that the youth do not even retain control over their thoughts, and when there is no control over thoughts, then what control can there be over sex?

## 17.22 Quranic Concepts

The Quran proposes such a comprehensive programme, by acting according to which, the right change takes place in the beliefs, concepts, thinking and perception of man, and the environment of the society remains pure and clean from these germs which become the reason for leading to wrong motives under the influence of emotions. For example:

(1) It presents a fundamental concept about life that it is not at an animal level, it is higher than this at a human level, and its development occurs by protecting those Permanent Values which have been bestowed through revelation. The protection of chastity is also a Permanent Value.

(2) It removes from the heart of woman the wrong assumption that she has been created for man, and that her only purpose in life is to somehow or other remain attractive in the eyes of man. It tells her that she has a separate, individual and unique status, and that the ultimate aim of her life is the same as that of a man. As far as being a human being, there is no difference between a man and a woman. The only difference between them is in physical traits, which are necessary for a woman in relation to the procreation of the human race. A woman can develop her human potentials in the same way as a man can, and after carrying out those duties which nature has specified for her, she can work alongside man in every field of life. When this incorrect belief is dispelled from her thinking that her purpose in life is to remain attractive in the eyes of man, then the lowly emotion of displaying her beauty will also leave her heart, and by the departure of this emotion hundreds of knots will be freed. The Quran does not wish to confine woman within the four walls of the home. It reforms

this wrong concept which becomes the motive in her for displaying beauty. Rather than becoming the toy of man, it teaches her to become his companion in the journey of life.

## 17.23 Adornment and Beautification

It should be made clear that the Quran does not declare adornment and beautification, ornamentation and decoration, as being haram. Contrary to this it clearly proclaims:

*Say: Who has forbidden the beautiful gifts of Allah which He has produced for His servants, and the things, clean and pure, which He has provided for sustenance...(7:32)*

The finer arts automatically come within the domain of 'adornment and beautification' because they are the means by which to demonstrate and manifest the beauty of the universe. The Quran forbids woman from self objectification on those occasions where she may become the instrument for provoking thoughts of sexual urge among men (24:30-31, 33:33).

(3) The Quran removes this wrong belief from the heart of man that the aim of the sexual relation is to satisfy lust. It tells him that its aim is only for procreation, therefore other than for the production of offspring, the sexual relation is against the will of nature. And in order to have children, the legitimate form of sexual relations is via organized marriage.

(4) It suggests such a programme of education and training for children through which their human potentials are developed, the higher purpose of human life remains plainly in front of them, and they do not fall to the lower level of an animal existence.

(5) It does not allow the environment to be contaminated with such germs which lead to the creation of sexual perversion.

(6) The Quran declares the protection of chastity to be a Permanent Value, and its transgression a crime, for which there is a severe punishment.

Western thinkers and researchers are themselves reaching this conclusion after their own investigation and research, that the safeguarding of chastity is extremely important for human evolution. In this connection, we consider it sufficient to note here briefly the summary of the research by Dr. J. D. Unwin[217] of Cambridge University. He studied the sexual practices of eighty primitive tribes living in various parts of the world and after this he studied sixteen societies of civilized

---

[217] The author has quoted from the book titled *'Sex and Culture'* written by J. D. Unwin. For further details see the book titled *'Islam: A challenge to religion'* Chapter 18, pp. 352-353.

nations. He published the outcome of this research with great care in his book, 'Sex and Culture'. He writes in the preface of this book:

*'Briefly stated, my final conclusion is that the cultural behaviour of any human society depends, first, on the inherent nature of the human organism, and, secondly, on the state of energy into which, as the result of its sexual regulations, the society has arrived.*[218]

The conclusions he reaches after studying the social culture of eighty tribes are as follows:

1. That group was on the lowest level of culture in which sexual intercourse without marriage was openly permitted;
2. The tribe in which there were some restrictions on sexual relations without marriage were on the middle level; and
3. At the highest level were only those tribes which insisted on pre-marital chastity.[219]

Summing up the results of his investigation, he says:

*'I submit, therefore, that the limitation of the sexual opportunity must be regarded as the cause of the cultural advance.*[220]

Again:

*'No society can display social energy unless a new generation inherits a social system under which sexual opportunity is reduced to a minimum. If such a system be preserved, richer and yet richer tradition will be created, refined by human entropy.*[221]

Unwin's concluding remarks deserve careful consideration:

*'If a vigorous society wishes to display its productive energy for a long time, and even for ever, it must re-create itself, I think, first by placing the sexes on a level of complete legal equality, and then by altering its economic and social organisation in such a way as to render both possible and tolerable for sexual opportunity to remain at a minimum for an extended period, and even for ever. In such a case the face of the society will be set in the Direction of the Cultural Process; its inherited tradition would be continually enriched, it would achieve a higher culture than has yet been attained; by the action of*

---

[218] J. D. Unwin, *Sex and Culture*, p. xiv.
[219] Ibid, pp. 300-325
[220] Ibid, p. 317.
[221] Ibid, p. 414.

*human entropy its tradition would be augmented and refined in a manner which surpasses our present understanding.*[222]

The Quran, by giving woman rightful equal status, lays such limits on sexual relations due to which human society, journeying through evolutionary stages, keeps reaching ever higher levels (83:19).

---

[222] Ibid, p. 432.

Made in the USA
Columbia, SC
30 August 2017